Getting Exposure

Getting Exposure

THE ARTIST'S GUIDE TO EXHIBITING THE WORK

The Editors of *Art Calendar*

THE LYONS PRESS

Copyright © 1995, 1998 Barbara L. Dougherty Inc./TA Art Calendar
Edited by Carolyn Blakeslee, Drew Steis, and Barb Dougherty

Designed by Desktop Miracles, Inc., Dallas, Texas

Printed in United States of America

10 9 8 7 6 5 4 3 2 1

Library of Congress Cataloging-in-Publication Data

Getting exposure—the artist's guide to exhibiting the work / by the editors of Art Calendar.
    p.   cm.—(An Art Calendar guide)
    An updated collection of articles originally published in Art Calendar magazine, 1995.
    ISBN 1-55821-731-2
    1. Art—Exhibitions.   2. Sidewalk art exhibitions.   3. Art—Exhibition techniques.
4. Art—United States—Marketing.   I. Art Calendar (Upper Fairmount, Md.)   II. Series.
N4395.G48   1998
706'.8'8—dc21   98–12129
                                                                    CIP

Dedicated to artists and writers everywhere.
Special thanks to the folks who contributed
to this book.

Self-portrait, 1993, oil on canvas, 18"x26", Elvi Jo Dougherty, Upper Fairmount, Maryland

Table of Contents

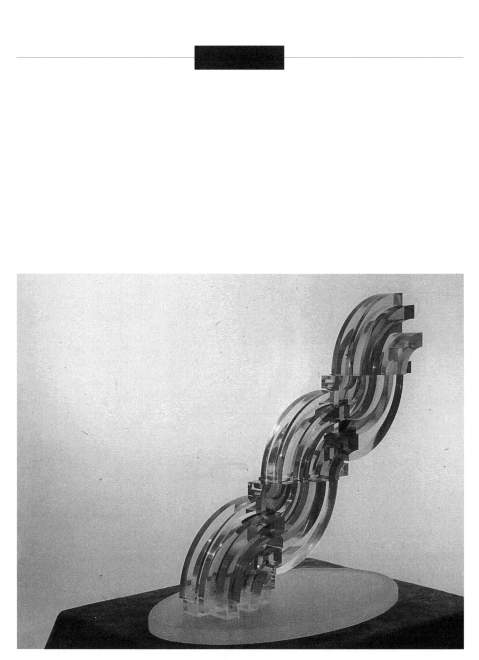

Where, 1997, cast acrylic, 38"x 34"x22", Norman J. Mercer, East Hampton, New York

Foreword

Exhibiting for artists is like publishing for college professors—it is all-important if your career is to prosper. But the opportunities for artists to exhibit are as varied as snowflakes and include everything from traditional galleries to vanity or other "for-pay" venues. So how does an artist who just wants to create art know a good opportunity from something that might not further his or her career? We at *Art Calendar* were asked this question so many times that we put together *Getting Exposure: The Artist's Guide to Exhibiting the Work*. It covers everything from showing your work in traditional spaces to booth shows and street fairs and festivals. We cover pricing, handling, shipping, display, and other considerations, and how to create your own special events such as conducting a successful studio sale.

Artists learn to translate what they see or imagine into two or three-dimensional images called art. That learning experience can either be formal training at an art school or on-the-job experience while actually creating art. The one thing artists are not taught is how to turn their art into a livelihood.

As art is not static, neither is the art of exhibiting. We are confident that this updated edition will be valuable to all artists who sincerely want to make a living from their art.

—Barb Dougherty
Publisher, *Art Calendar*

PART 1

Working
with Galleries

Flying Free #1, 1993, hand-dyed cotton fabric, pieced and quilted,
22" x 22", Caryl Bryer Fallert, Oswego, Illinois

CHAPTER 1

Working with Dealers

Successful Art Dealer/ Artist Relationships

Michelle T. Carter

Selling art is the bottom line for many self-supporting professional artists. Focusing on exhibition opportunities through an art dealer/artist relationship, rather than learning "How to Sell" techniques yourself, can indeed result in art sales. The teamwork of a balanced art dealer/artist relationship can result in exhibition opportunities reaching the proper audience of collectors and validating the creative efforts of the artist.

To avoid wasting the dealer's and the artist's time, a professional artist must know how to complete four tasks prior to attaining successful exhibition opportunities through an art dealer/artist relationship:

1. Evaluate the artwork for exhibition.
2. Understand the elements and steps of presenting your portfolio to the people who can help.
3. Understand how the art middlemen work.
4. Understand the ways an art dealer may be approached for representation.

Evaluating the Artwork

"What does the artist have to offer?" It is essential to understand the evaluation of artwork from a dealer's perspective. The art dealer's position in the art world is to educate the public regarding an artist's work. The dealer evaluates art with an "eye of interest" for his collectors.

Quality work, mature style, and identifiable technique are important factors supporting collector confidence in an artist. The artist's work should be consistent in form, color, line, and movement, showing confidence and proficiency in his medium. An artist can seek credible feedback and evaluation through participating in regional and national juried shows, workshops, and artists' organizations.

Part of the artist's evaluation process is understanding the correct venue for his artwork. Before approaching a dealer for representation, an artist must evaluate the subject matter, concept, and style of his art in relation to the art shown at the gallery.

The steps an artist takes in evaluating his artwork prior to seeking representation will greatly reduce the number of rejections.

The Elements of Art Presentation

Understanding the elements of art presentation is essential to the career advancement of the professional artist. The components of a presentation package—slides, the biography, artist statement, SASE, and a cover letter—will be the first link in the chain of events leading to dealer representation. The artist portfolio is the second link, with the presentation of the original art itself forging the art dealer/artist relationship.

The presentation package's components are educational tools used by the art dealer to introduce an artist to a collector. The artist supplies the dealer with the tools.

A biography lists the following information: birthplace and date, education, teaching experience, solo and group exhibitions, collections, awards, and galleries and art dealers representing the artist's work.

An artist statement explains why the artist creates art, the influences on his art, the medium he works in, his process, and the art elements of his work. Art elements would discuss color, line, form, and movement.

Slides in presentation packets should be labeled with the following information: title of work, medium, size, name/address/phone number of the artist, the three-pronged copyright notice (the copyright symbol ©, the year of completion—"1994," not "'94"—and the artist's name), and indications of the front and top of the slide image. Three to ten slides are sufficient for a presentation package.

The presentation package requires a cover letter to introduce the artist, state the purpose of the contact, and clarify what the artist wants of the dealer.

Always include a self-addressed stamped envelope (SASE) in your presentation package and request that the package be returned if the dealer is not interested in your work. An artist should always call to verify that the presentation packet reached its destination. If the dealer has reviewed the packet, the artist can then request an appointment to present his complete art portfolio.

A portfolio ideally should be the size of a business briefcase with removable non-glare acetate sheets to hold photographs of the art. The photographs should be high-quality and should present the best examples of his art. The photographs should be arranged to make a statement about the art in terms of subject matter, medium/media, and style. The artwork in the portfolio can be current inventory and/or previously sold pieces; the main idea of the photos is to present a body of work to the dealer. A well-assembled portfolio will entice the art dealer to schedule an appointment to review the original artwork.

This final step in the presentation process is showing the original art to the dealer. It is always best to have the dealer visit the artist's studio; an artist has a better chance of representation when he presents a complete body of eight to ten original works to the dealer. When the dealer visits an artist's studio, the artist should avoid explaining each piece of art. Trust the art background of the dealer, and allow him/her to assess the art. Respond to his questions.

If the art dealer expresses genuine interest, ask the question, "How do you work?" An artist should listen carefully to the policies of the art dealer to determine if there is potential for a relationship there. The ideal relationship for the artist and the dealer supports the good faith of the collector.

The Art Middlemen

In the current art world there are many kinds of art middlemen who present the artist's work to the public. Their role in relation to the artist depends upon their position or job title. Here are a few typical positions and titles of art middlemen supporting artists' careers: art dealers, art consultants, art reps, art publishers, art managers, museum curators, and university art gallery directors and curators.

Upon determining a mutual trust and communication between the artist and dealer, the artist must then determine how the middleman works regarding business. Prior to establishing a business relationship, ask questions to avoid future misunderstandings.

An artist can avoid giving away a larger than necessary percentage from the sales of his art by remembering to ask that all-important question, "How do you work?" It is a mistake to assume that every art middleman takes a standard per-centage of the art sales.

Investigate what the art middleman does to support the artist's career. Does he advertise through direct mail, magazines, and/or newspapers? Does he have an exhibition schedule? Is he active in the business and art community? How long has he been in business? What are his business relationships with the other artists he represents? Does he buy art outright, or does he handle art only on consignment?

An artist should establish his own policy before the art is given to the middle-man for consignment. Clarify the following ten points regarding art representation:

1. Decide on the percentage of commission paid to the middleman for the sale of the art.

2. Establish an art inventory list specifying an agreed-upon retail price for the art.

3. Specify how much freedom the middleman has regarding altering the retail price. For example, discuss authorizing a 10 percent discount from the retail price if a collector purchases more than one piece of art.

4. Address the issue of insurance of the artwork in case of theft or damage.

5. Confirm the location site(s) where the artwork will be exhibited.

6. Request that the collectors' names be sent to you on a regular basis.

7. Discuss the geographic territory represented by the middleman. Avoid exclusive representation unless the middleman is offering national visibility and has a proven reputation, and then agree to it only for a limited time (no more than one year at first).

8. Request the disclaimer "Rights of reproduction remain with the artist" on all sales invoices.

9. Determine the payment policy regarding responsibility for payment on a monthly basis or within 14 days of the sale, and net terms offered by the middleman.

10. Establish a termination policy for the middleman business relation-ship regarding future sales generated after the relationship is finished, i.e., a 3-month period.

When a middleman buys art from an artist, the artist can still request the name of the collector and a clause regarding copyright. Remember, copyright remains with the artist unless specified otherwise in the sales transaction of the original art. And it is to both parties' advantage to list all collectors' addresses.

Approaching the Gallery

Knowing how the middlemen work, and having established confidence in the quality and presentation of your artwork, you can now approach an art dealer for representation. Gallery representation, the primary career goal of most professional artists, can free the artist to create. A good dealer or network of dealers can give the artist confidence about his work being before the "right" public's eye. A dealer can also assist an artist in achieving other goals, such as museum affiliation, publishing, and commissions.

Four methods of approaching an art dealer for representation are the cold call approach, the collector referral, the artist referral, and the "discovery."

In the cold call approach, the artist researches galleries through the local *Yellow Pages* and gallery guides. Another source is the local library's computer files.

Before approaching any art dealer for representation, the artist should investigate the gallery's represented artists by attending shows and/or receiving gallery mailings.

If the artist believes his art would contribute to and enhance the art dealer's stable of artists, he then contacts the gallery director and asks if he is reviewing work for representation. When the artist has established the interest of the art dealer, a presentation packet is sent. In two weeks the artist should call the gallery director to schedule an appointment for the dealer to see the artist's portfolio or studio.

The 1990s is the decade of the regional artist, so an artist will be most effective with the cold call method if he initially researches the galleries in his local community and then researches galleries in vacation areas nationwide.

The collector referral method: the collector acts as an advocate to the artist's career by referring the artist to an art dealer. Collectors enjoy supporting the advancement of an artist's career, and a referral from a collector will usually result in an appointment with the art dealer. An artist can cause the collector referral method to work simply by telling his collectors he is seeking representation, specifying in which geographic area(s) he is seeking a dealer.

In the artist referral method, an artist who is represented by a gallery refers another artist to his dealer. A referral from a represented artist will usually result in the art dealer reviewing the presentation packet sent to him by the referred artist. Many established artists are willing mentors and a tremendous source of support to unknown or emerging artists. Networking in professional artists' organizations and attending gallery shows will support the artist referral method of attaining gallery representation.

The "discovery" is usually achieved by an artist who is willing to enter juried exhibitions and show at artists' organizations and other alternative gallery spaces. The fluctuating economy and decreased discretionary income have caused numerous galleries to close their doors, and alternative exhibition methods have gained increasing importance as avenues for dealer discovery. Juried exhibitions, studio shows, outdoor fairs, artist cooperatives, art trade shows and expos, artists' organizations, college and university galleries, and artist-in-residence programs have all become important ways for the artist to directly reach both collectors and dealers.

This method can work for an artist who is willing to research listings and decide on which competitions to enter. Before entering a juried exhibition or an alternative gallery competition, send for the prospectus so you can research what kind of art is exhibited, the criteria for the show, the entry or space fees, and the profile of the judges or audience. Only by seeing full prospectuses can the artist make an informed decision on which competitions to enter.

Once an artist has been accepted into a juried exhibition or alternative gallery show, and prior to the exhibition date, the artist should send a letter of invitation to local art dealers. The purpose of the letter is to introduce yourself and your art to the prospective art dealer—many dealers attend these kinds of shows to review possible new talent in the art scene.

A final comment on the career goal of gallery representation: Be patient with the art dealer's selection process for representing new artists. Introducing a new artist to the dealer's collectors is a substantial investment of both time and money. Remember that communication, trust, and teamwork are key components to a healthy and mutually beneficial art dealer/artist business relationship.

A professional artist who understands how to evaluate his work, present it, and work with art world middlemen to achieve representation, will create exhibition opportunities resulting in art sales.

Seeking Gallery Representation for the First Time

Carolyn Blakeslee

The foundation of being a successful artist is respecting your own work. When you are producing consistent work that you really like, in a direction you are excited about, then you are ready to share it with the public.

Preparing for the Approach

Art dealers are people too; they like it when an applicant artist is genuinely interested in showing at that particular gallery—when an artist comes in with some knowledge about their philosophies and show approaches. Attending shows regularly will bring many benefits. You will see for yourself the quality of work represented, the quality of the galleries' presentations, the extent of the galleries' advertising, and the sort of press coverage they generate. You will meet important and interesting people.

Build a list of galleries with whom you are interested in exhibiting. Put these galleries on your personal mailing list and send them invitations to any shows in which you are participating. Add collectors, curators, and critics to your list too; these people will become familiar with your name and with your work. Add other artists you respect to your list as you meet them—you never know when a referral might result.

Your Portfolio

Make sure your slides are truly representative of your work. The color saturation should be perfect, slide images should be squarely composed with no interfering background, and the slide labels and accompanying slide identification sheet should be neatly typed. A professional slide photographer will be able to assist you. Without fail, project your slides yourself and view them before you send them out to anyone.

Treat yourself to a good portfolio. Since the dealer is a professional salesperson, presenting your work clearly and neatly will show that you speak his language. A good portfolio speaks volumes about your professionalism over and above the quality of your work. A good portfolio includes a current resumé, an artist's statement, press materials (even ads) showing that you can generate press, photographs of some of your artworks, and slides.

If you are calling the gallery for an appointment to show your portfolio, offer to bring a couple of actual pieces if they are portable enough. If you are sending slides and a resumé, always enclose a self-addressed stamped envelope (SASE). These considerations are appreciated, and SASEs make it more likely that you will get your slides back.

It is possible that you will be turned down several times before you contract with a gallery. No matter who you are, you will receive more rejections than positive responses. I call this the Numbers Game; on the average you will need to send out 100 presentation packets to get three positive responses. That's a lot of rejection, and although it can be painful, *do not give up;* if your work is solid and presented well there is a dealer for you. Most dealers are always looking for new work even though they are often booked up to 2 years in advance.

Business Arrangements

Galleries we questioned about their business arrangements answer fairly uniformly. What follows are some of the usual policies, but terms vary, of course, from gallery to gallery.

Most gallery directors prefer a written agreement between the gallery and the artist. Specific policies should be addressed at contract time. Many galleries say their agreements and terms vary from artist to artist—for example, sometimes exclusive area representation is arranged, other times it is not required. When asked whether an artist owes the gallery a commission from work sold from the artist's studio, many gallery directors answer, "It depends."

Before you approach a gallery, check with the grapevine and other sources about the gallery's reputation. Call the Chamber of Commerce, the Better Business Bureau, and the local art dealer's association to see if any complaints have been lodged. Ask a few artists what they think of the gallery. If you trust your instincts and back it up with solid research of this kind, and take care of contractual arrangements in a careful and objective way, your association with your dealer should be happy, mutually productive and profitable.

Commissions run about 50 percent, give or take. The cost of mounting an exhibition really is quite high. Starting with rent, staff salary, spackling and painting after each show, and moving on through printed matter, advertising and promotion, and receptions, the gallery business is not for the fainthearted. Overhead can run thousands of dollars per show. Sometimes when discounts are agreed upon the discount comes out of the commission, sometimes not. Sometimes the gallery pays for advertising, framing, receptions, mailings, etc.— and sometimes not.

If a gallery is taking a 50 percent commission, it should earn it. If a gallery is taking 50 percent *and* is requiring you to pay for invitations, the reception, and other expenses, you should probably think twice. No matter what, make sure terms are understood. If they are not mutually agreeable and clear, no one will be happy for long.

Work is almost always insured at a reputable gallery.

Usually the artist is responsible for some or all of the framing, and for transporting the work to the show. The gallery almost always foots the bill for a fairly nice opening reception for your show, and sometimes springs for return shipping.

Galleries send out news releases announcing shows, and invitations to their list. It behooves the artist to send out news releases too. Send out invitations to your list; the gallery will usually print a color postcard or some other kind of announcement and give a few hundred to you. The gallery pays for postage to their mailing list, and the artist is usually responsible for postage to his list.

Sometimes a catalog can assist in the selling of your work, but fancy catalogs are not usually produced for an emerging artist. If the gallery director is requiring you to print a catalog, be wary. Weigh all such expenses against your likelihood of profiting from the show or from the association as a whole.

Sometimes the gallery is willing to pay for some or all print advertising. Make sure the image and copy are mutually agreeable.

The Long Run

Ideally the relationship between artist and dealer will develop and grow. As together you establish the salability and reputation of your work, the gallery should bear more costs. Gallery staff will prove themselves to you as they make sales and pay you promptly. You will prove yourself to them as you produce artwork with integrity and behave professionally.

A good art dealer is concerned about short-run sales, yet will be interested in representing you for many years. He should be able to assist you in obtaining representation in galleries in other cities, in museum collections, and in corporate and public collections. You are in a business partnership together. He is not your boss, nor is he your employee. Respect your relationship with your dealers and your buyers, and love the contribution to the arts that only you can make.

Editor's note: Good business practice dictates having a business contract with each gallery you deal with.

Working with Galleries Next Year
Barbara Dougherty

I paint large landscapes of the agricultural lands that are vanishing. The subject of this article is the gallery I owned until last year, when I sold the gallery and moved back East. The gallery, which was a custom framing shop as well, did very well.

I am reminded of the song "Both Sides Now." Although I am an artist, as a gallery owner I experienced that other artists approached me more as an enemy than as a member of a similar community.

Each community has its own biases, and sometimes the biases are very strong. Artists generally feel used and abused by galleries and their directors, and gallery owners dislike the general attitude of artists.

As an agricultural artist, I watch two sides of the agricultural world operate out of similar and legitimate disputes. The farm worker does hard work for little pay, and the landowner's costs are too high to pay the interest on his loans, and he is tired of the needs of the workers. These two communities are far apart and uncooperative. From my perspective as an artist, I see the vanishing fields and economically devastated agribusinesses.

I see each community needing to embrace each other for survival and being unable to do so.

After being a gallery owner and speaking with other owners, I see this now in terms of the art business. Artists, like farm workers, do not see the symbiotic relationship they must have to survive with gallery owners and vice versa.

Possibly an artist has to depend on others for assistance in marketing. And there are no perfect marriages. As I work through my relationships with agents, publishing companies, and those wishing to exhibit my work, I am constantly annoyed that they seem to have so little understanding of the investment I have in my work. I have spent an enormous amount of time, energy, and money becoming a painter with my own style, a solid customer base, and decent credentials; each piece I present also represents an investment in art and framing materials. Yet my work has been consistently mishandled and damaged, royalty agreements have not been kept, and a host of other aggravations have occurred over agreements.

On the other hand, as a gallery owner I could write a novel about the arrogant attitudes of artists who approached me about representing their work. Artists came into the gallery at all times of the day and night. Very few had any respect for the fact that our basic operation depended on conducting successful transactions with customers—some artists exhibited resentment at being asked to wait while a client was being helped.

A gallery is an unusual marketing project in that the customer is buying something they don't need, or at least can find the ability to do without. Almost every art buyer takes a leap into a world in which they have little confidence— that is, their taste in art. That is true both when they buy the art and when they buy the framing. So, the gallery itself has to have appeal and yet offer comfort. The sales approach has to be direct yet not overwhelming. The gallery has to keep the art new and fresh to continually generate reasons to remind customers to come in. This is a large project that is expensive and requires great attention.

Given my experiences, I have created a set of guidelines for my future relationships with galleries:

- For me to sell my art, I desire the help of others right now. Their work is important—I understand and greatly value their work.
- In having my work represented by others, I cannot succumb to allowing commercial pressures to replace the inspirations and integrity I have achieved.
- In negotiations I will hold myself to listening and responding rather than reacting.
- It is my responsibility to carefully document negotiations.
- In addition to offering my artwork to those who will represent me, I will also offer my loyalty.

All right, what do these principles mean? No, not just that I am going to stick my head in a noose and see if I get hung. No, I believe that art needs a community to survive, and not just a community of artists pitted against art marketers. I believe we must usher in, and herald, a new age of careful negotiations, respect, and loyalty in order to see the fields we plant bear fruitful harvest. So as to my principles, I see the following commitments necessary in order to be consistent with my personal ideals:

- The Principle of Equality. In situations where my art is represented, I am willing to accept commission agreements of 50 percent of the sale to the gallery. I believe there is much to gain by considering the work of marketing to be equal to the work of creating.

- The Principle of Integrity. I must be very clear, especially at the beginning of a relationship, that I do not want my art to evolve out of statements like "My customers like your blue paintings best—please paint more of them." I don't want my inspiration to be the like or dislike of anyone else. So, I will provide those that represent me a clear statement of my inspiration: It comes from the colors and the feelings in the land I am continually drawn to paint—the vanishing agricultural lands.

- The Principle of Careful Responding. The analogy I use for this is an experience I had in a science lab in college. We had some single-celled amoebae under the lens of the microscope and applied a chemical to the slide, at which the creature would wiggle, squirm, and gyrate. To the next slide containing the same type of amoebae we applied a different chemical—to which the amoebae responded by beginning the process of dividing. We were told that the animals in the first instance *reacted* to the chemical—they were alive to the changes in their environment. But the second experiment showed the creature *responding*—that is, the very nature of the animal changed. I use this description to try to understand my own attitudes in the environment of art marketing . There are times I feel elated, times I feel threatened. There might be reactions I will want to make, but unlike the amoebae I don't want those reactions to be the governors of my negotiations. I want to take my time, listen, and adjust to the implications of the negotiations both for myself and the agent, and *respond* in a way that will move to serve both our needs. I must know that when I do respond it represents a change in my basic current situation.

- The Principle of Documentation. I must make sure to provide enough written information. Critical information includes my contact address and telephone numbers, statements that accurately represent my work, and statements regarding my inspiration. It is my responsibility to be sure that all negotiations are documented and contracted to the best of my ability. This is especially crucial in view of my knowledge that good documentation does not necessarily prevent future problems in negotiations. But the more that's written down, the more of a foundation and framework you have to work in, even if—or perhaps especially if—the situation sours.

• The Principle of Loyalty. There are times one makes the best negotiation possible at the moment and then a better opportunity comes along the next day. Sometimes it seems like a great sacrifice when such opportunities are turned down for the sake of loyalty—but the truth is, a greater human sacrifice is made when loyalty is taken lightly. The people I work with are my world; they may not always do the best for me or themselves, but as long as there are not other moral compromises I want to offer my best work and my utmost loyalty to each agreement I make.

CHAPTER 2

Interviews with Gallery People

Nancy Hoffman: Twenty Years in SoHo

Drew Steis

When Nancy Hoffman decided to open a gallery in New York City she first took a night-school course called "How to Start Your Own Small Business."

She already knew how to run a gallery. "I majored in art history and during my last two years in school I worked full-time for a museum as well as going to school full-time," she told us.

"I worked for Asia House, a small Oriental-art museum where I did everything from registrar functions, writing press releases, doing guided tours, editing our catalogues which were art books, helping on installations, keeping slide books and clipping books and maintaining our library, to assisting the director and assistant director. It was a general factotum job and they didn't know what to call it because they had never had anyone in the position before.

"What happened as a result of that job is that I received an overall extraordinary education in art. It wasn't like working for a large museum where you are in one department and become the departmental specialist—I did everything. And it was fantastic."

Ms. Hoffman was with Asia House for 4 years before moving to French and Company where she started as public relations director and ended up running the gallery.

Then in 1972 she took a course in business operations and later that year opened the Nancy Hoffman Gallery in a former sheet metal manufacturing shop.

"It had the potential to be a really beautiful, clear space. It was in SoHo, the galleries were just starting to come in and there were two or three when I first found the space. This was where all the artists lived and it was a very stimulating area.

"The first year was very exciting. There were only two of us here and we never knew who was going to walk in the front door. I worked until ten or eleven o'clock every night, I worked every weekend, I did not have a day off for five years, literally. And I took no pay, no salary but we broke even after the first year."

Her gallery, at 429 West Broadway, is still in the same location 20 years later, specializing in contemporary oil and watercolor paintings, sculpture, drawings, and prints. Having been seminal in the emergence of SoHo as the mecca for artists, Nancy Hoffman says the art scene since 1972 "has changed enormously.

"When the gallery opened, there were maybe five galleries in SoHo but certainly no more than ten and it was still a kind of rough-and-tumble neighborhood where you had to be cautious at night. But that all changed during the 1970s and 1980s and now there are over 150 galleries in SoHo. It has become a neighborhood that is well known nationally and internationally and is truly the center of the art world.

"Artists live here; the largest concentration of galleries anywhere is in SoHo, so it is a hum of art and activity. In addition to which, the designers have moved in along with some chic restaurants and it has become the real place to be. Saturdays have become sort of a great parade in SoHo. "It is still a changing neighborhood in the most positive sense. In the beginning, the more elite people had access to art, the media wasn't as large and wide-reaching. People in certain lower financial brackets didn't realize that art was available to them on a reasonable basis. Now with all the media and all the advertising and all the blockbuster shows, people on many, many levels have access to works of art. That has brought a lot of people into the art world if not for buying certainly for viewing and for beginning their education in art."

Her philosophy of doing business has weathered the ups and downs of the art world.

"In the 1980s with the financial boom came a big boom in the art world. Prices simply went out of control and those prices had no basis in reality. But we never became subject to that. We never let the gallery swing with the fashionable tides or trends. We have never been a 'fashion-oriented' kind of gallery.

"I made the decision long ago when I first started the gallery that the commitment to the artist, my personal commitment, had to be based not on whether the work would sell, whether it was fashionable or not or whether it

looked good in the space, but on the commitment of the artist, the unique statement of the artist, and my commitment to that work on an ongoing basis. I am
not interested in working with somebody on a one-shot show.

"So during the 1980s we were the fortunate recipients of the boom as well
because that brought a lot more people into the gallery and we did very well in
terms of sales. But we also had the good fortune not to base our total livelihood
on the Wall Street clientele.

"The 1980s brought a whole new group of people into the gallery and in
the 1990s that's changing again. Some people still have a lot of money but they
are not necessarily spending it. Galleries have closed their doors but others have
opened. It is not necessarily negative, it is an absolutely necessary shifting
process. The 1980s couldn't stay like that, it became insane. There was an auction a few years ago in November, I'll never forget it, anything that went for
under a million dollars was peanuts. And that is not the real world, that has
nothing to do with art. That has to do with money and speculation and nothing
that really relates to the arts. It was truly not healthy."

When Nancy Hoffman opened the gallery, she gathered her artists from
those she had known in New York and from trips to the West Coast. The first
year she represented twenty-five which "at a certain point in the 1970s we built
up to thirty-five.

"I realized that was crazy, that I couldn't run a gallery like that and that I
didn't want to have that supermarket quality. Then we had to go through a very
slow sort of honing process to get back down to twenty artists, which took
through the 1980s to do."

Among her first artists was Joseph Raffael, whom she still represents.
Other artists include Ilan Averbuch, Carolyne Brady, Howard Buchwald, Rupert
Deese, Don Eddy, Rafael Ferrer, Viola Frey, Juan Gonzalez, Michael Gregory,
Rohan Harris, Claire Khalil, Susan Norrie, John Okulick, Frank Owen, Peter Pla-
gens, Bill Richards, Alan Siegel, and Jim Sullivan.

Shows at the Nancy Hoffman Gallery are planned a year in advance. The
gallery does nine to ten shows a year and Nancy Hoffman believes in heavy advertising in national art magazines as well as in *The New York Times*. She also sends
an announcement card and a brochure in which a few of the paintings are reproduced. A formal opening is held at the gallery. Sales commission is negotiated
individually with each artist.

"There is no typical day. The days are always new and fresh and exciting." With a staff of six, Ms. Hoffman first handles correspondence. And then there are "lots of phone calls, people and groups coming into the gallery, some to view work for acquisition, some to view work for education. We have a once-a-week staff meeting to go over all of the activities." The gallery has 7,500 square feet of space and is closed Sunday and Monday.

But it is the artists who take up the majority of Nancy Hoffman's time. Unlike some big-city galleries, Nancy Hoffman is willing to look at new work from not-yet-recognized artists.

"First of all, when artists contact us we tell them that the gallery is full, that we represent twenty artists, that we are not taking any new artists but that we are always happy to look.

"And we *are* always happy to look because we always learn something by looking at slides. We learn what is going on in the art world. At some point there is an ebb and flow, there is a change in what goes on in the representation within the gallery. Sometimes the changeover is one or two a year and some years it is nothing. But when we add it doesn't mean that someone goes. We add because we make a commitment to a new person. When I see an artist whose work looks interesting I try to maintain contact with them and see that they come back to show slides in the future. Others I will go to visit in their studio. But I never want to be in a position where we have thirty-five artists again."

Her advice to artists seeking gallery representation is to show the gallery staff "whatever someone feels best represents them.

"They have to do a little bit of homework to see what gallery out there would be most appropriate to approach in terms of sensibility.

"Often what artists do is blanket SoHo, they blanket uptown, they blanket midtown, they just send to everybody. It would save them lots of time and trouble and personal rejection if they approach galleries that would be appropriate. I think that is an absolutely crucial part. And then they have to send in their slides, go in with their slides, make personal appearances. And if they see that someone is interested they have to keep after it. It doesn't always happen first go-around. They have to make the best possible professional presentation available to them either with slides, or slides and a resumé. It should not be a haphazard put-together package."

Nancy Hoffman does not usually deal with artists' representatives, preferring to deal with the artist directly. She recommends that artists approach her gallery by mail first, including a SASE. She also will review, usually in about one hour, slides that are dropped off at her gallery on Thursdays.

It is the art, commitment to that art, and quality that influences Nancy Hoffman.

"You want professionally done slides. You don't want slides with fingers in the paintings—and we get those.

"And if they know anybody we are connected with it doesn't mean a thing to me. Recommendations do not, in any way, influence my opinion of art or the artist."

Nancy Hoffman can be reached at 212-966-6676.

The Successful Artist/ Dealer Community
Alan Bamberger

Successful artists and dealers offer knowledge and experience that can help artists better understand how the art world works. Successful artists are good at integrating art with business; dealers know what it takes to sell art and know what to look for in artists.

The individuals profiled here are representative of the successful artist/dealer community. They're not necessarily rich or famous, but they all make their livings entirely through art—no minor accomplishment—and they're all willing to share their knowledge with you.

Successful Artist Sandow Birk

Sandow Birk is a social realist whose art chronicles contemporary life in the big city. In his third year as a full-time professional artist, he attributes much of his business success to confronting day-to-day challenges as simple as maintaining good records, making himself available, and getting publicity. He stays on top of the little things like where his art is, who owes him money, how much he spends, and when taxes are due.

Keeping his name before the public, he says, means returning phone calls, never missing appointments, writing letters, appearing at his own openings, and maintaining contact with past patrons. In addition to normal correspondence, he regularly cold-calls magazines, galleries, and other places that he feels might be interested in either showing or featuring his art. He knows that if he doesn't make the effort, nothing is going to happen. When asked what prevents artists from succeeding in this arena, he points to characteristics like lack of business acumen, inadequate social skills, and moodiness.

Regarding dealers, he knows that cooperation is the best policy. He understands why a good dealer earns and deserves the 50 percent commission, because earlier in his career he worked at galleries for several years. Among the many benefits dealers provide, he says, are that they have been responsible for placing him in about 25 percent of his significant exhibitions.

With respect to his art, he believes that its appeal lies in its accessibility to viewers. It addresses common concerns and current events. People can talk about it, respond to it, and relate to it without feeling uncomfortable or intimidated. Most importantly, Birk is able to speak about his art not only with dealers and curators, but also with anyone who expresses interest, regardless of their art education. As for the practice of painting itself, he says that an artist must do it whether he feels like it or not—much in the same way writers must sometimes work through writer's block.

Here are some of my personal observations during our interview: Birk returns calls on schedule, is not too busy or distracted to talk, takes the time to provide the information he's asked for, and handles tough questions without taking offense. He has an impressive grasp of what it takes to make it as an artist today and he seems to be pretty much on an unstoppable roll.

Successful Art Dealer Catharine Clark

Catharine Clark, director of the trendy Morphos Gallery in San Francisco, believes that a gallery should be accessible, not intimidating. This orientation is evident in the way she attends to her clients and visitors, by making them feel at ease and that someone has noticed them. Pretension is out; she is readily available to answer questions and respond to individual needs.

Clark expects the artist/dealer relationship to be one of collaboration rather than animosity. She expects the artists she shows to be aware of the financial hardship, hard work, and lifetime commitment necessary to achieve success in the art world. Artists are encouraged to get involved with the gallery to the extent that they are willing to speak about their art, appear at their openings, and even engage in a little selling from time to time.

Clark is particularly informative when discussing behaviors that hold artists back in their careers. Viewing dealers as "a necessary evil" is an obvious problem, for example. Displaying attitudes of entitlement, or demanding more gallery exposure than other artists, also creates conflicts. Inability to fulfill commitments, such as delivering the required amount of art to a gallery in time for an opening, is not only bad for an artist's reputation, but also reflects unfavorably on a dealer's ability to manage a gallery. Betrayal or dishonesty, such as selling to clients behind a dealer's back, are additional acts that usually end artist/dealer relationships, and often the relevant dealer/client relationships too.

Clark never makes decisions about whether to show artists without first visiting their studios. This is important not only for her, but also for the artists. For one thing, artists appreciate the attention and the opportunities to have their work critiqued. They also benefit from the encouragement and learn from the overview her outside expertise offers. With respect to Clark's needs, she finds that artists are often most comfortable in their studios and, as a result, can be candid about their art. They are more inclined to initiate dialogue and offer superior levels of insight into their work.

Clark can tell a great deal about an artist from a studio visit and pays attention not only to the conversation, but to everything else as well. Here are some of the things she looks for:

- Is the radio or TV always on? In other words, is the focus on art, or elsewhere?
- How much new work is in evidence—is the artist productive?
- If little or no work is visible, where is it? An artist should have a body of work, somewhere.
- In what direction is the artist headed, as viewed through the continuity of the art?
- What does the artist collect? This provides insight into his tastes and ways of looking at things.

As is often the case with successful galleries, Clark rarely takes on additional artists for solo shows. She does, however, exhibit new artists' work in a group format on occasion.

Successful Art Dealer Jerald Melberg

Jerald Melberg, of Jerald Melberg Gallery Inc. in Charlotte, North Carolina, places a major emphasis on display and presentation. Every aspect of his gallery is designed to be maximally conducive to the client, including the color of the walls, the direction doors open and close, the way art is framed, and the manner in which one space is partitioned from the next. For a recent Chihuly show, the gallery was almost completely repainted, the floor plan changed, pedestals built, and lighting adjusted in order to highlight the dramatic impact of the glass. Melberg firmly believes that displaying art in beautiful settings helps people understand and appreciate its intrinsic value and meaning.

Behind the public gallery rooms are two private viewing rooms, one of which also serves as Melberg's office. This allows him to conduct two presentations at once, a situation that can arise when clients show up unexpectedly. Conveniences include comfortable seating, facilities for serving refreshments, waist-high shelves for presenting art, a recessed slide projector, and a television for video presentations. Melberg keeps his viewing rooms private and maintains an atmosphere wherein those clients who are invited back realize they are receiving special treatment.

Behind the viewing rooms is the storage area. Unlike many galleries, Melberg does not allow clients into this room. He feels that seeing too much art at once not only confuses viewers, but also reduces the impact of whatever pieces have been specifically selected for presentation.

Selling art is not all that Melberg does. He is a major supporter of the Mint Museum and other art community endeavors. In addition, he presents special events at his gallery including sit-down dinners, barbeques, live music, seminars, discussion groups, and guest appearances by outside experts. And if that's not enough, he also provides special services like in-home presentations, deliveries, framing and display consultation, and convenient payment plans. His success as a dealer is due in no small part to the fact that he makes art collecting much more of an experience than simply buying art.

Artists from all parts of the country have had shows at Jerald Melberg Gallery. They are expected to appear at their openings, interact with collectors, and be able to assist in selling their work when necessary. Unfortunately, getting a show at the gallery is not easy. Of the 200 to 250 new artists whose work Melberg reviews each year, he only gives first shows to one or two at the most.

CHAPTER 3

A Look at "Blue Chips"

"Blue Chip" Spaces: Not for Everyone
Alan Bamberger

Viewing acceptance into "blue chip" exhibition spaces or top-notch galleries as the ultimate measure of artistic success can be a huge waste of time and effort. Far too many artists place too much emphasis on pursuing this form of notoriety when their efforts could be substantially more productive elsewhere. One of the keys to success in any career, art included, is to know where you stand in the great scheme of things and to operate to maximum effectiveness within that realm.

Take baseball, for instance. Only the best of the best make it to the majors (assuming no industry strike). If you play a decent game of softball but that's about it, to do anything more than daydream about playing in the big leagues is absurd, no matter how badly you want it. On the other hand, you can certainly find yourself a softball league with players your speed and have a great time both on and off the field. In the process you'll make friends, cultivate relationships, and possibly get involved in business ventures together. You can either maximize your effectiveness within the softball realm, or bang your head against the wall in the major league realm.

Now take a look at your art. How does it stack up against what shows at major museums and top-notch galleries? Is it similar? If so, how does it compare in quality and originality? If not, should you change the look of your art to better fit in? Do you want to compete for entry into these venues? Can you? Should you even try? Should you even care? These are just a few of the tough questions you must ask yourself in order to ensure that you don't spend your life chasing rainbows or compromising your integrity and your art in order to meet the demands of others.

The good news is that when the big leagues aren't for you, you can leave them behind and achieve success elsewhere. If you paint realistic floral still lifes, for example, and you paint better than most, focus on the realm of floral still life painting. If no museums or blue chip galleries are showing floral still lifes right now, don't worry about it. Go to the center of the floral still life world and make your stand there.

Regardless of what your focus is, the following pointers apply:

- Realistically and honestly assess your strengths and weaknesses as well as those of the competition.
- Get involved with dealers, collectors, gallery personnel, and artists with similar interests and aspirations to yours. Become a familiar face. Get to know people. Introductions from friends and acquaintances often lead to shows and sales.
- Keep abreast of what's happening. Act on opportunities as soon as you hear about them.
- Don't be afraid to take no for an answer. The more feedback you get, the more accurately you'll be able to determine your career path.
- Work within the program or guidelines of your chosen realm. If you're too difficult, museums and galleries will avoid you. If you enjoy being difficult, wait until you're famous.
- Don't isolate yourself. It is a rare artist who moves directly from obscurity into the spotlight. Those who are exposed to your art need points of reference to understand where you've come from, what you're doing, and where you're going.
- Set sensible goals. In the overwhelming majority of cases, reaching the top takes years or even decades.
- Take advantage of every available opportunity to speak with older artists and gallery owners who are well along in their careers. Leave your art out of the discussion and let them do the talking. Finding out how long and hard they had to work in order to get where they are will help you place your agenda for success into its proper perspective.

Although the above pointers generally hold true, feel free to experiment with interesting, unusual, or unconventional ways of attaining your goals. In the art world as in no other, those in powerful positions will at least consider your approach.

PART 2

Exhibiting at
Nonprofit Galleries

Camp, 1997, assemblage, 18" x 24", Will Hildebrandt, LeGrand, Iowa

CHAPTER 4

College and University Galleries

A College Gallery Director Speaks
Harold Lohner

This article first appeared in *The Sage Colleges Magazine*, Vol. II, No. 1, February 1993. In explaining the various functions and needs met by a college space, the article provides a useful bridge from the gallery director to the artist to the community.

If you love art you know the powerful feelings it can evoke and the important ideas it can embody. Your appreciation of art was probably gained through looking, feeling, and thinking. You may know how to make art or understand its theoretical background, perhaps through studying art or art history. Certainly you are aware of art's ability to communicate, beautify, inspire, and enrich the human experience.

Art galleries and museums provide a place for the public to see art in person. Although reproductions allow us to see things that are far away or bring together works and ideas that are far apart, they are no substitute for direct observation. But how exactly art works is a mysterious process; one must be in its presence to appreciate it fully. Compare this to the difference between seeing a great film on a big theater screen and watching it on video at home.

College galleries, situated as they are among the knowledge-thirsty, are in a great position to educate, enlighten, and otherwise influence. For the student of art, they serve as an extension of the studio classroom. When one begins to make art, paint and ink are seen as wonderful, seductive materials. Color and texture become understood as expressive tools. The ability to look at the work of accomplished artists firsthand is invaluable, to observe their use of materials and concepts and to see the range of possibilities that might be aspired to, borrowed from, or rejected. The "real live" artworks in a college gallery make the gallery an instructional tool that grows and changes with each exhibition.

For the student who is not yet excited about art, the campus gallery can be equally important. In that convenient and comfortable environment, he may have his first real encounter with art. As he samples the enormous variety that contemporary art encompasses, his worldview is expanded. The gallery provides a look at what's going on in the outside world, from the immediate region to distant centers. Art opens the eyes to what others see, enables the examination of one's own thoughts and feelings, and becomes fuel for reflection and discussion. Thus a familiarity with the arts broadens one's understanding of everyday experience, yet is seen as a sign of sophistication. A rich cultural life sets apart liberal arts colleges, helping to prepare their students for lifelong learning. Our society is crammed with visual stimulation, and cultural products are an important national industry. What better way to hone one's critical skills than on art?

A gallery might be thought of as a sort of oasis. Set apart from clutter and activity, it's a quiet place where one can focus on art. The essential connection between the viewer and the artwork can be made there. Galleries, like libraries, house information and make available new thought. Members of the greater community look to colleges for that.

The role of the college gallery director is related to those of artist and art professor in that it is both creative and instructive. The artist wants to show people art so they'll like it more; the professor creates contexts for greater understanding and appreciation.

The exhibitions at Russell Sage College Gallery change every month or so, allowing a great variety of media, styles, and subjects to be presented. Some shows examine social issues or aesthetic themes, others are linked by medium. A show might spotlight one artist, the next may bring together the works of several. Shows may be put together in-house or by artists, critics, or other colleagues. Each year at Sage we present hundreds of individual artworks by scores of artists.

College galleries, thankfully, are not dependent on commercial success. We are tied neither to the commercial gallery's inventory nor the museum's collection. Freed from the tyranny of "best-sellers," we can examine less familiar territory.

With that freedom comes the responsibility to refrain from championing a single artist or approach in favor of a broader representation in the field. We bring to light the work of accomplished artists who wish to share their work with a campus and community audience. While some artworks may have limited popularity, this does not diminish their value as objects of study. Each show might be the first one for some students or other visitors, so we must keep in mind both the beginner and the specialist. Coherent shows, supported by printed materials and lectures, make the art more accessible.

Although museums and galleries report increased attendance figures and educational efforts, we are reminded that art and artists remain somewhat marginalized. As it does with popular entertainment, the public seems to view the producers and their products with a mixture of respect and suspicion. The part of the arts community that might be called the avant garde continues to push ideas to new levels and take the greatest chances. When happened upon by casual observers, some artworks may be impenetrable, puzzling, or shocking. Their response may be to ignore, to disparage, or even to attempt to restrict the art. The artists may react by further antagonizing those who would dismiss or suppress them, refusing to explain themselves or to give up their questionable practices. Meanwhile, the press smells a good story, perhaps with sexy details to tease and outrage its readers.

And so is born "controversial" art, which—if television were your primary news source—you might think was the only kind. The label itself has become so overused that movies are now advertised as controversial before anyone has seen them, in hopes a controversy might erupt. Such publicity, whether generated by a press agent or an opponent, often serves both to increase public demand and to create ill will about the art form. For example, long lines formed to see an exhibition of photographs after it was denounced as unworthy of public support. When reading the name of Robert Mapplethorpe, for example, it is now impossible not to think first of the brouhaha and only later of his actual work.

While art is momentarily brought to the forefront, cries of controversy and censorship ultimately serve no one well. Righteous opposition may be countered with trendy support, but this does not translate into an informed audience. Often the art in question is distorted in the process, its content misinterpreted, exaggerated, or glossed over. One begins to look at every show for what might be considered dangerous or obscene. And in a field where subtleties of intent and context are meaningful components, the artworks can be seriously compromised in the glare of public scrutiny.

Art is a form of adult discourse, not in the prurient sense of "adults only," but meaning for an audience of a certain level of sophistication, prepared to meet the artist halfway in order to understand. Fine art has long had standards that are much more inclusive than the media that would follow it, including movies and television. Subject matter is sometimes difficult, and strong opinions are expressed. The element of fantasy in art is vital; by prohibiting certain subject matter the essential freedom of imagination is inhibited. Some would argue that it is exactly those troublesome recurring topics which should be examined, not suppressed. The freedom of the individual artist to create work of personal importance cannot be denied, but it must be balanced with the right of other individuals not to be assaulted by art.

By representing the pluralistic art world, college galleries can moderate the ongoing public debate. Perhaps by giving the artist a limited opportunity for thoughtful expression, fear may be replaced by awareness. Of course such a forum should be seen as endorsement of the free exchange of ideas, not necessarily of the ideas expressed.

So long as stories are not distorted or suppressed, we accept the internal choices of newspapers and magazines as editorial direction, not censorship. Similarly, galleries must choose exhibitions freely but with an eye to what they perceive as their audience and mission. Even the location and architecture of a gallery might influence what it shows. The right to steer clear of potential controversy is part of the right to deal with it. Every artwork and every show cannot please everyone while offending no one; to aim for such consistency and mass appeal would be to seriously compromise art, bringing it down to the level of, say, fast food.

Enter an art gallery with an open mind. Recognize that you might not like or understand what you see. You might be challenged to expand your definition of art, but remember that no work or show is intended to represent what all art ought to be. A reception is an ideal occasion to visit. Often the artists will be there, so you have the chance to talk with them.

Or instead of getting lost in the crowd at an opening, let yourself get lost in the art by visiting when the gallery is least crowded. Avoid the blinders imposed by a first impression and question your own response as part of the artwork. Compare the works to one another to understand a solo artist's style or the connections in a group show. Relate them to things you've seen before. It may be fun to pick a favorite or imagine which one you would most want, but don't be turned off because nothing would look good in your house. While one might decorate to be harmonious or soothing, artworks in a gallery are meant to be seen as foreground, to be individually considered, not viewed as tasteful decor. On the other hand, the daily viewing that comes with living with art may be the best way to get the most out of it.

Because art is primarily nonverbal, look around at everything before reading anything. Then go back and read labels and other printed materials in the gallery, comparing them to what you have seen. Statements by the artists and curators can help you understand their intent.

People frequently ask, "What is it?"—particularly about nonrepresentational works. This will not get you very far because the best answer is always "a painting" or "a sculpture" or whatever. In 1928 the Belgian artist René Magritte painted a picture of a pipe and wrote below it, *Ceci n'est pas une pipe* (This is not a pipe). That painting, titled "The Treason of Images," neatly expressed the difference between signs/symbols and the things they represent, and it echoed throughout the art that would follow.

Artists are aware of art history, and they work with its language of signs. They understand that a picture is essentially something apart from what it might portray and that depiction does not necessarily equal advocacy or approval. The intent behind subject matter may be simple description, reportage, irony, humor, disgust, and so on. You can't read art like signs where an image of a cigarette means it's OK to smoke and a red line through it means it's not. It might be better to read the subject matter of art like that of dreams, assuming it to be metaphor for something else, perhaps less tangible.

Then again, sometimes a cigar is just a cigar. Artists may use subject matter simply as a basis on which to build an artwork. No reading of art should ignore a consideration of the materials, the technique, and such abstract aspects as composition, color, and line. After all, those are the things of which the artwork is made and over which the artist labored, so the form should be considered as meaningful, too. Try describing the artwork to yourself, taking inventory not only of recognizable images, but also of shapes, surfaces, and spaces. Reading reviews may provide additional insight, but keep in mind it is just someone else's opinion, however well informed. Newspaper and magazine reviews allow you to vicariously enjoy art you won't get to see, and criticism is, in itself, an interesting art form. Eventually you may want to study art or read a book about an artist, a movement, or a medium.

If you are not yet a fan or you just "know what you like," consider college galleries as entry points to explore the world of art. New lookers are welcome and encouraged to get past initial responses and search for deeper meanings.

College and University Galleries
Debora Meltz

If you want to show your work and selling it is not a major priority, or if your work isn't eminently salable, then university, college, and art school galleries can provide excellent exhibition opportunities and are very respectable resumé builders. Since sales are not a necessity for them, they can afford to exhibit work that commercial venues must pass up. In fact, they often seek out the avant garde or controversial.

Not surprisingly, there is great demand to show in such places. Exhibitions are often scheduled a year or more in advance.

Consult the *Art in America Annual Gallery and Museum Guide* and the *Art Calendar Annual Artists' Resource Directory* for college, university, and art school galleries. Send a brochure or other inexpensive example of your work, along with a brief letter of introduction/inquiry, to as many exhibition spaces as possible. Or you can purchase mailing lists, preferably ones already printed on labels. The more you send, the better your chances of getting shows. (Two vendors of mailing lists: Caroll Michels, NY, 212-966-0713; or *Art Calendar,* 800-597-5988.)

If feasible, offer to present a gallery talk or a slide lecture about your work. This can be done earlier on the day of the opening, at a specific time during the opening, or on a subsequent day. This will increase your chances of getting a show, and occasionally a school will pay an honorarium to a visiting artist who makes a presentation to the students and/or community.

On the other hand, because schools are often under financial constraints, you might have to pay for shipping, invitations, and/or postage. You must therefore decide whether a particular exhibition warrants the expense.

You might wish to select specific geographic areas before doing a mailing. Some mailing list services will customize lists to target specific locales or markets. Shipping artwork is costly, and you should be certain you can follow through if you are offered a show requiring you to pay part or all of the shipping.

Other than shipping, publicity will be your largest expense—and your largest headache. While some college galleries handle publicity, don't rely on it. Get a list of individuals, businesses, and organizations that are supportive of the gallery, as well as the names and addresses of area newspapers, magazines, and art reviewers. Communities surrounding colleges and universities are generally interested in and supportive of the schools' cultural activities. Turnout for exhibitions is usually quite good.

Send press releases to newspapers at least 6 weeks before your show. Magazines have longer lead times—often 3 to 4 months—so have your P.R. material ready well beforehand. Include a black and white photo—4"x6" will do—with as many of the press releases as possible. Select an image that reproduces well in black and white, even if it isn't your best piece. If you have a good press release, newspapers and magazines will often print it verbatim along with the photo. Be sure the college newspaper gets your press package too, and include a brief note offering to be interviewed, by telephone if that's convenient.

Invitations to the general public are probably not necessary. Find out whether the response is likely to justify the cost. There are many inexpensive, even free, ways to publicize your show. Again, don't rely on the college to do it—the more publicity *you* do, the better. The first time you undertake managing your own publicity, the job might seem daunting. Don't fret. You will soon develop your own style, techniques, and methods of saving time, labor, and money.

If you feel invitations are in order, they need not be professionally printed, flashy four-color jobs. You can produce good-looking invitations inexpensively with a computer and/or a copy machine. If you need more than about 300, it might become cost effective to go to a quick print shop. The price of photocopying is a bargain compared to printing only when making relatively few copies.

The audiences at colleges and art schools are usually enthusiastic and eager to learn about you and your work. They are, however, an impecunious bunch (teachers' salaries being what they are and college students needing their spare cash for beer), so don't expect to sell much.

Find out how the gallery handles sales. To take advantage of sales opportunities that do exist, I suggest the following:

- If the gallery is divided into rooms or sections, or has movable panels, set aside an area for less expensive works such as prints or drawings.
- Have a bin of matted and shrink-wrapped pieces.
- If you have reproductions of your work such as posters, postcards, notecards, etc., make them available. However, never leave small works in an unattended area. School galleries are often left unsupervised. You might wish to offer small works at the opening only.

If possible, attend the opening. For me, the most rewarding aspect of exhibiting at college or art school galleries is meeting the students. They are enthusiastic and welcoming as well as full of questions, curiosity, ideas, opinions, and admiration that will excite and energize you.

CHAPTER 5

Artists' Organizations

Getting Started with Galleries:
The Curator's Perspective
Julia Muney Moore

As a curator, I spend much of my time looking at unsolicited slides. About one-fourth of it is work that I might actually be willing to show, while the rest is either totally wrong or just wrong for me. This is not unusual for galleries all over the country.

With a little preparation, you can ensure that your work gets seen and thoughtfully considered by just the right gallery, and ultimately gets the exposure it deserves. The process takes about 6 to 8 months of effort and encompasses four simple steps.

Step One: Market Research

Before you speak to one individual or send out one set of slides, you will want to do a great deal of research so as not to waste your time and money sending work that galleries will not be interested in. The least favorite pastime of curators and gallery directors is looking at work that is not even close to their focus.

- Galleries. Take at least 3 months to gallery-hop.

Go to as many commercial galleries as you can, as often as you can, and get an idea of the kind of work they show. Don't just go to one gallery once, because galleries have a "stable" of artists producing very different kinds of work and you want an idea of everything they handle.

Another idea is to call galleries and find out when their next gallery artists' show is. Most galleries have a show of all of their artists about once a year, and one-person shows about once a month.

Good sources for gallery information include your city's newspaper, particularly the Sunday edition. Gallery guides are published in several areas, including New York City, Chicago, Los Angeles, the Midwest, California, New England, Washington D.C., etc.; you can obtain this guide at galleries and newsstands. Also refer to the Yellow Pages under "Art Galleries and Dealers." But be careful: "gallery" can mean a frame shop or it can mean a real gallery. Visit the place to make sure.

Gallery hopping can also be done from out of town. Simply call every gallery in a particular area and ask to be put on their mailing lists.

Also, don't forget to check the gallery listings in the art periodicals. If your work is realistic and conservative, look in *American Artist* or *The Artist's Magazine*; the information at the end of each artist's profile usually tells what galleries carry their work. If your work is more avant garde, check *Art Forum* or *Flash Art*. If you make fine crafts, *American Craft* is a good magazine, and there are several single-media periodicals available in the craft arts, such as *Ceramics Monthly*, *Fiber Arts*, and *Glass Art*. Also check your regional art magazines—*Art New England*, *Dialogue* (for the Midwest), *Art Papers* for the Southeast, *Artweek* for California—and your state art magazine if it exists. But always check *Art in America* and *ARTnews*. If you see something you like, again, call and ask to be put on their mailing list. If you use this method, allow at least six months' worth of cards to accumulate before approaching a gallery.

• Nonprofit Spaces. Follow the gallery-hopping schedule listed above. There are literally thousands of nonprofit galleries, art centers, and other exhibition spaces across the country, many of them begging for artists. They are usually found connected to universities, but there is a growing number of independent spaces.

For a listing of nonprofit spaces in your area, check your Yellow Pages under "Museums," obtain the summer annual issue of *Art in America* for its gallery guide—nonprofit spaces are listed in the index—and consult *Art Calendar* for its listings of independent alternative spaces.

Sometimes the gallery's name will tell you what the space exhibits. However, beware of stereotyping: Some of the most progressive galleries in the country have very provincial-sounding names. The best thing to do is—you guessed it—call and ask to be put on the mailing list. If you don't have time to wait for 6 months of cards to accumulate from these spaces, call and ask for a list of the last 2 years' shows.

Some of these spaces are cooperative galleries, which means you have to be a member and share in the work of running the gallery in order to be shown there. Try to avoid these if you are out of town. Although it is technically feasible to exhibit in these spaces, you will usually have to pay a larger membership fee (up to ten times the regular rate!) and the other artists are likely to resent you.

Nonprofit spaces sometimes advertise for artists in the magazines listed above. Sometimes they are looking for artists working with specific themes or media, but sometimes they send out a general advertisement. Do not immediately send your slides; call and get on the mailing list or ask for a list of shows first.

• Competitions. Many museums and galleries sponsor competitive exhibitions, where the artist either sends slides or brings in the work and a jury selects the exhibition from the submitted work. The scope of these can vary from countywide to statewide to regional to national to international, and will feature any number of artists from just two to a hundred or more.

Competition notices appear in *Art Calendar* as well as a number of books and the other magazines listed above. Your research assignment is to write to the ones for which you might be eligible and get a copy of the prospectus, also known as guidelines or call for entries, sent to you.

NOTE: Some of these competitions purchase mailing lists, so you might end up getting calls for entries sent to you for which you did not ask. Do not necessarily enter the show immediately. After the show has been put on, call and ask to be sent the catalog for the exhibition to get an idea of what kind of work gets into the competition. If no catalog has been printed, ask to be sent a list of the artists in the show.

• Other Suggestions. Some cities have odd spaces that have art exhibitions: public libraries, social clubs, shopping malls, lobbies or windows of buildings, etc. Be on the alert for these, and keep your eye on what they show for a few months. Sometimes they are listed in the calendar section of the Sunday or weekend edition of the newspaper, but more often they are not. If you see one, call the management of the location and ask for the name and number of the person who organizes the exhibitions there, and file that number for future reference. Most of these spaces can be had for the asking.

Step Two: Getting Ready

During the market research phase, you can be assembling the materials you will need. Before you approach a single person, you must have the following:

- Slides of your work. The more the better; twenty is standard.
- An updated professional resumé. If you have no professional credits yet, simply list your name, address, telephone number, and where you went to school and for what. This should be typed neatly.
- Copies of any reviews, articles, etc., about your work.
- An artist's statement. This is a paragraph that explains why you do the work you do and what it means. This should be typed neatly.
- Do not send as a part of your packet, but have available, a price list of your works.

It is not necessary to have fancy folders printed to hold these materials. A manila folder will do.

Of all these materials, the most important is the slides. Your slides should be professionally done if you can afford it. If you want to do them yourself or have Uncle Fred try it, remember these tips:

- Use a 35mm camera, good film, and plenty of even light. Set the camera on AUTO and set the shutter speed for whatever the film box says. Use ISO 200 or lower film; if you use a higher-rated film your image will be grainy when projected.
- Photograph the work unframed.
- Compose your shot so that the only thing in the slide is the artwork: not Aunt Suzie (even for scale), not the gallery wall, not your privacy fence, nothing.
- Photograph against a plain white, gray, or black cloth—continuous paper is preferable—to provide a neutral background.
- Take four or five shots per piece; you can get slides duplicated, but dupes are very expensive and the color tends to change. Also, take detail shots that show medium, technique, points of interest, etc., as well as alternate views if your work is three-dimensional.

Your slides should be neatly labeled with your name, the work's title, date, medium, and dimensions (in inches or centimeters, but specify "in." or "cm."). Put a dot on the lower left corner of the slide or put an arrow indicating the top of the slide. Place the slides in a full slide sleeve (available at any camera shop or processing place, usually 10¢ per sheet in packages of twenty-five). There are several different kinds of sleeves, but the best ones are made of thin plastic and can be folded in half and stay folded.

Step Three: The Approach

Here is where your research pays off. You will now be able to narrow your focus to a handful of places where you are reasonably sure your work will get a fair look. But keep these tips in mind:

- Never think, "Oh, they've never shown this work before but maybe they will be so blown away by mine they will leap to show me." A SoHo gallery is never ever going to show wildlife art, period. A community art center that is a regular host of the local tole painters' guild is not going to be interested in sociopolitical work criticizing the current military establishment. Don't waste your time even applying.
- Never walk in unannounced, even if you are absolutely sure this is the place for you. Even if your work is perfect for them, they will resent your attitude and not show you.
- If you are applying for a competitive exhibition or in response to an advertisement, the rules will be spelled out for you. Do not vary them. If it does not say to include a resumé with your entry, don't do it. If it says to send three slides, send only three—do not send two, or four, or ten. Follow all labeling instructions to the letter, and when you send your slides, always send them in a protective sleeve (a partial sleeve is OK) with cardboard in the envelope to protect it. The rules exist for reasons; if you do not follow them your slides may get lost or damaged or worse.
- If you are responding to an advertisement, you should send a cover letter explaining where you saw the ad and identifying yourself as an applicant.
- If you are sending your work unsolicited to a gallery or nonprofit space, you're on your own because you do not actually know if the gallery is even looking for work. In this instance, you can make a phone call. Ask if the gallery is taking new artists and, if so, ask how they prefer to be approached. If there is a set day on which the gallery director or curator reviews portfolios, ask if an appointment is necessary. Find out the name of the person who will be reviewing work.

Most places do not review slides with the artist simply because it is inconvenient to set aside everything else for a whole day. Therefore, you will be going through the mail. After your phone call you must send in your packet with a very professional cover letter identifying yourself as seeking a place to show your work. Be sure to send a self-addressed stamped envelope (SASE) and include some cardboard to protect your slides. Then be prepared to wait. Some gallery directors/curators are very prompt, but others just collect them for 6 months or so before answering.

What to bring or send? Send just ONE body of work. The style should be consistent and identifiable. Do not send a hodgepodge of different styles hoping one of them will strike a chord; this will mark you as an unprofessional dilettante. Your market research will tell you which style is likely to appeal to which gallery; don't waste their time or yours with inappropriate work.

If you have some insider information, now is the time to use it. If a friend of a friend knows they are planning something up your alley for 5 years from now, say in your cover letter, "I understand you will be looking for work like this in a few years; please keep me in mind." This will impress them no end.

There will be one of three answers to your materials:

- "Thank you, but we don't like your work." There are many polite ways of saying this, among them "Our schedule is booked" or "We are not taking new artists now." They all mean NO WAY. If your slides are returned, forget it for now. In 2 or 3 years you can try again. Under no circumstances should you call and badger the decision-maker for reasons, or ask that he or she suggest other places. If they had suggestions, they would have made them in their letter.
- "We will keep your work on file." Maybe they will, maybe they won't. If your slides are not returned, it is fair to call back after 6 months or so and ask for their return if you are not being actively considered for an exhibition. Your work may genuinely be on file; if so, they will tell you.
- "We love your work and want to show you. Here's a contract." You have it made? Maybe, maybe not. Your next task is to look over the contract carefully to see that your rights are respected. For a good overview of contracts, consult the book *The Legal Guide for the Visual Artist: The Professional's Handbook* by Tad Crawford. Never ever send your artwork to a gallery or exhibition space without a contract. If they say they

are not in the habit of making contracts, make one yourself and hand it to them. If they will not sign, refuse to show with them.

Step Four: The Follow-Up

Almost as important as the preparation is the follow-up, even if you have been rejected. If your work has been rejected by mail, retreat quietly and place the gallery/exhibition space's name and address—with the director/curator as the contact person—on your permanent P.R. list. Then, when you get other shows in the future, you can send them an announcement so that your name stays relatively fresh in their minds. Also, you should send them a couple of slides of new work every year or two for the same reason. But make it a casual thing. Enclose a brief letter stating that you would like to update your file (even if they have returned your slides). Do not enclose a SASE: they might throw your slides away, but since you've only sent two or three, it's not a big loss. Also, with no SASE they may be "guilted" into actually keeping them on file (although some directors keep not so much a file as a big drawer of slides). After 2 or 3 years, do the whole approach process again as if you were a new artist.

If you have had a personal appointment with an individual and he has rejected you, always write a letter to thank the person for seeing you and state that you will be keeping them abreast of your activities approximately once a year. Then follow the schedule above.

Final Tips for Success

Accept rejection gracefully. Never, ever bad-mouth a place that rejects you—it may come back to haunt you later. The art world really is very small.

Be easy to work with. Know your rights and respectfully ask that they be respected, but do not push too hard or you will get pushed out.

Be true to yourself. The temptation might be to alter your work to fit the market, but the market will change very rapidly. Better to spend time on the research phase so that you will be matching the market to your work. If you work in reverse, you will get a very bad reputation as a kiss-up artist.

While the above information will not absolutely guarantee success, it will at least mark you as a professional while you are searching for it. Best of luck.

CHAPTER 6

For a Good Cause?

Giving It All Away:
Artists and Donations

Milon Townsend

Artists often wonder—OK, complain—about why they're the ones always called on to give of themselves to support various causes. This is especially galling when you compare the average income of an artist to, say, an attorney's. Yet many nonprofits, from wealthy local philanthropic groups to your own artists' organization, routinely ask artists to donate their artwork, or a portion of the sales proceeds of their artwork, to their auctions and other fund-raisers.

There is a reason why artists *should* be high on the list of these causes. These nonprofit causes are typically seeking to solve a long-term problem that has defied quick and easy solutions. Artists are, by definition, visionaries, and are in a unique position to contribute a vision of the possibilities for a better future.

This is, after all, one of the central and lasting values of art—it offers a new way of looking at things we're all familiar with, and perhaps a new way of dealing with situations we've not dealt well with in the past. An artist may detail his own struggles, suffering, and failures for the edification of others so they don't make the same mistakes.

Tolstoy said, "Art is . . . a means of union among men, joining them together in the same feelings, and indispensable for the life and progress toward well-being of individuals and of humanity."

Everyone gets hit up these days to support some cause or another. Without a comprehensive plan, it's easy to get confused in the dust cloud and end up giving too much or too little. We end up saying, "Why did I do that?" or "Why didn't I participate in that event?"

Just as with advertising or insurance, the only way to develop a strategy that best meets our needs is to sit down and plan. It's highly unlikely that merely leaping at all the solicitations for advertising or insurance that happen to come our way will result in a plan that satisfies us. The same is true of donations.

Decide whom you want to support, and to what extent. Do you want to give of your money, your time, or your artwork? If you want to support a particular group or activity that doesn't actively solicit your help, seek them out! If they don't have a program you can participate in, create one. Another benefit is that when all the other requests for support come at you, you'll feel clear about what you're already doing and you'll be better able to fend off the others with a polite "I'm sorry, not right now."

Do what you do for the right reasons—right for you, that is. Being clearly aware of why you choose to give to a particular charitable organization will forestall dissatisfaction. Here are some of the reasons artists typically support various causes:

- Because it's a good cause. Certainly the noblest and most altruistic of motivations, yet not the only valid one.
- For exposure. If this is the case, be sure of the type and scope of the exposure, and that it will actually benefit you and your work. While *any* kind of advertising, or exposure, takes time to achieve results, at the same time you should establish some parameters by which to evaluate it. If it isn't working, and exposure is the only reason you're giving, then you might want to discontinue participation in this event.
- For a tax deduction. Unfortunately, this is not a valid reason. Many artists think that they can deduct the entire retail value, or even wholesale value, of the work they donate. But the contrary is true—an artist donating his own artwork may deduct only the cost of materials used to create the work. Only a collector donating an artwork may deduct the value of the artwork, and generally a certified appraisal would be required as documentation in order to be able to back up an IRS claim against any such deduction.
- So you may attend the event free. Rules change from year to year. Be sure the perks important to you are still in effect before giving your piece, or you'll feel burned.
- For a photo of a celebrity with your piece. This is very useful to have. This sometimes takes follow-up with the organization, or waiting around with your own camera for the moment of truth. Plan carefully; act boldly.

- A percentage of the purchase price. Fund-raising auctions that return some of the money to the artist have an undeniable appeal.

Being the primary provider of value—in the context of providing the donation—the artist is rightly in a position to state some terms.

- Minimum bid. I suggest that artists require a minimum bid on artwork if that's what is being donated. It does the charitable organization little good to receive only 10 percent of the actual value of a piece, and it does you and the value of your work great damage to see it go for a pittance. I also firmly believe that it cannot be good, spiritually at least, for the people who almost literally "steal" your work for pennies on the dollar.
- A percentage of the purchase price. That artists should receive fair pay for their work is a concept gaining currency today. It's about time! Many charitable organizations offer the artist 50 percent of the moneys generated by the sale of the artwork. (Of course, if you wish you can turn around and donate that amount; you are then entitled to take a tax deduction on the monetary amount you donate.) Receiving 50 percent of the retail price is typical of an artist selling work at wholesale. Many organizations are hesitant, at first, to give a percentage of the receipts back to the artists who donated the work, but the groups that do this will attract many additional artists, generating more net income, and more interest, in the long run.
- Photo. If your artwork is being presented to or bought by a person of note, you can request a photo of this event. This is a relatively small thing for the hosting organization to provide, since they usually hire photographers to cover these events. Be advised, however, that the "photo promise" is the most easily given and among the most difficult to get. You'll probably have to follow up with a series of calls to your contact person—but do persevere. These photos will repay you over and over again for your effort the whole of your professional life.

Leverage plays a large part in negotiation. Before you hand over your donated work is when you have the most leverage. If you happen to have a little form for the organization's representative to sign, with terms and conditions appropriate to the given situation, you will have benefited yourself, and moved things forward a little for the rest of us, too.

I strongly support the idea of artists giving of themselves, in whatever form appropriate, to promote a healthier individual, community, society, nation, and world. I feel just as strongly that only an informed artist with a comprehensive perspective will be able to do so and feel fully satisfied with what they have chosen to do.

CHAPTER 7

How Museums Work

Climbing Museum Walls
Peggy Hadden

Museums are special places. With hushed voices and respectful footsteps, we visit their halls and galleries to view the masterly works that have shaped our educations and informed our theories about art. They house our art ancestors.

Aside from a historical stance, many museums continue to collect artwork made today. But among the myths with which our particular field is burdened, few loom larger or more secretive than the exact process by which one's work is acquired by a museum.

Plain and simple: How is it done? And can it be accomplished by an artist, alone, without clout in today's art world?

Certainly the rewards are formidable. Museum acquisition bestows credibility and accolades on the merits of our work. It boosts our prestige among our peers. And it doesn't hurt the old resumé, either.

So why is the path so obscure?

First, it is rarely written or talked about. Artists who have successfully gotten work into museums aren't talking. Museum curators and staffs, frequently underpaid and working long hours, enjoy the mystique that their institutions bestow in lieu of higher salaries. All of this we can blame on somebody else.

However, it must also be said that many artists, in their reverence for/fear of museums, unconsciously forfeit any participation of their own in the process of getting their work acquired. Beliefs like "the museum will find me" or "you need friends on the board" or "you have to travel in those circles" to get institutional attention for your work might be factors in some acquisitions; but, my dear artist friends, they are also myths that cause you to not participate and to sit in your studio and complain.

So what can you do?

At this point a role model would be helpful. Enter Susan Kaprov, who lives in Brooklyn Heights, not far from New York's highly competitive art world. She is not represented by a gallery, and she rarely goes into SoHo. She is, however, represented in the permanent collections of fifteen museums in this country and in Europe—large museums of national stature. And she did it by herself.

How, I asked, was this accomplished? "Hard work and the direct approach," she said. "Please elaborate," I urged.

First she telephones a museum and asks whether they have an active acquisition policy. (If their acquisitions have been put on hold, or they don't actively acquire new work, there is little that can be done.) Next she gets the name of the senior curator or the person in charge of art in the category into which her work fits. She then determines if the museum has public viewing days.

In fact, Kaprov approached her first museum on a dare. She went on one of that museum's public viewing days without an appointment. Did she take slides, a portfolio? No, she took a small piece of her work, tucked under her arm. She says that this very direct approach is often disarming, opening the doors of even a very busy curator. Often, foreign artists traveling in the U.S. will get gallery owners or curators to give them a quick 5-minute look, and even without a common language it sometimes works.

Having highly original work is one of the things that helps. "If they know they don't have anything like it, that's another reason why they'll take it."

I had believed that museums would expect a significant discount on the price, but Kaprov says that in almost every case the museum paid the price she quoted. The work we were discussing was "under $2,000." She will offer a discount only if there's some kind of a trade-off—an assurance, for example, that the work would be shown and not just buried.

"After one museum buys, there is a cascading effect—you call up another one and even if they've never heard of you, they'll look." For Kaprov, slides are "a big waste of time, unless it's for a grant, then you have to send them, it's the process they use," and large works such as public art, which the curator might otherwise never see if the artwork is in a distant location. Kaprov estimates that about half of the museums she approaches buy her work.

There are many different kinds of museums. I was unable to come up with hard and fast guidelines by which they acquire work. In fact, every museum has its own criteria for what new work it will take, and it can depend upon something as mundane as storage space. Certainly, funding for acquisitions—or a lack of money—sometimes determines policy. A museum may sponsor an exhibition of solicited work, for which there might be one or several purchase awards. The drawback to purchase awards: If your $2,500 piece is selected for a purchase award of $900, you will either have to decline the award, or part with your work for $900 plus whatever the goodwill of having your work owned by the museum is worth to you.

University museums might want artwork for teaching purposes or artwork with particular regional importance. Some museums acquire works only through the bequests of patrons' wills, making for spotty and eclectic permanent collections. There is also the de-accessioning process, whereby museums sell works they no longer want to own. Sometimes, by selling works they are able to continue to acquire new work. So you should not assume that once your work is in a museum it will remain there forever, but you may find that having it owned by a museum opens enough other doors that it is worth the risk.

If you have a patron who is willing to donate your work to a museum, first help him by drafting a letter, for his signature, to the museum director. This letter should include a slide, a description of the work, its provenance (history of ownership), and any particular reasons why the museum might want to acquire it. The tax deductibility of the work is higher if a collector donates the work than if an artist does. To find the fair market value, you will need the services of an appraiser. Often dealers also act as appraisers, but be sure that anyone you choose for this function belongs to an association of appraisers and is reputable.

If you receive an artist-in-residence appointment at a college or art center, they are likely to buy a piece of your work for their permanent collection. Sometimes, artist colonies, as well as print studios and workshops, will ask for a piece of work that has been made there for their permanent collection.

For senior American artists, a fund has recently been established to facilitate the purchase of works and their donation to museums, universities, and other nonprofit institutions that collect and display American art. A letter from the institution, stating its desire to own the work, is required. Deadlines are in March and October. Application guidelines are available from the Richard A. Florsheim Art Fund, Board of Trustees, Univ. of S. Florida, P.O. Box 3033, Tampa, FL 33620-3033.

Moving Toward Museums
Barbara Dougherty

College and university galleries offer some great opportunities for artists. They often print catalogs, conduct sales without taking commissions, sponsor receptions, provide postage, print and address the invitations, do the hanging, provide insurance, and sometimes pay a stipend when the artist gives a presentation in conjunction with the exhibition. Although they usually have a commitment to showing the work of faculty, graduate students, and undergrads, these galleries will also show work by other artists who aren't affiliated with the institution.

I recently had a solo show at a university gallery. Not only was it a great experience, but interaction with the gallery's executive director has given me new insight into my own career.

In 1993, to work more closely with *Art Calendar,* I moved to the Eastern Shore of the Chesapeake Bay in Maryland. One of my former hobbies was collecting baseball cards. I loved the mindless sorting, and I used to do this when life was just too overwhelming. When my four suitcases full of baseball cards arrived with my other belongings, our publisher intuited that, if left to my own devices, I would use these cards to keep my mind off my work. Thus when I said I wanted to look into selling them, he not only encouraged me, he took me to places to find dealers.

The dealer who ultimately bought my collection was—by a strange coincidence—a vice president of a nearby university. When he came to see my cards, I showed him my paintings. He said he would mention my work to Ken Basile, executive director of Salisbury State University Galleries, because he thought my work would be appropriate for a 1-person show. I followed through on this contact and arranged for a 1-month solo show to take place the following year.

The moral of this story is one we hear all the time but feel queasy about acknowledging: Who you know or meet can be more important than the slide presentations we do. Now that the cat is out of the bag, how do we work with fact rather than fight it? To me, this means that we should plan on devoting time to networking our connections, and establishing and nurturing quality friendships within the arts community.

My show was planned for a year ahead. I used the time to develop my relationships in the local community so that when I had my reception it would be well-attended. This included joining some local art organizations and attending receptions as well as getting involved in a few other local organizations. I frequently invited people to come to my home for dinner; this allowed me to share my artwork with them. It is not easy to move from one end of the country to the other, especially if you are an artist who has developed a regional reputation elsewhere, as I had. Thus my task was to start over; I virtually had to begin the process of sharing what I did all over again. I am glad I gave myself a year to do this; as it turned out, the reception was attended by more people than anyone expected.

Ken and his staff were very supportive in the process of planning the show. They included my mailing list with theirs; they did an outstanding job of putting articles in the local papers; they published announcements and invitations. They installed the show with skill; they provided the amenities at the reception. They did all the things that I associate with a blue-chip gallery. The benefit of the gallery's doing all these tasks: I got to concentrate mostly on doing the paintings.

At the reception, I realized that although I was getting what I needed from the situation, I didn't know if my show was fulfilling the needs of the university gallery and its staff. In fact, I realized I didn't even know what the needs of the gallery were. Thus, I arranged to meet with Ken. To my surprise, our talks have been the best benefit to me of this show—I am now better acquainted with the point of view held by institutions like university galleries and other public museums. This point of view, I believe, will help me immensely.

Ken Basile, the university galleries' director, had worked at the Smithsonian as a young man and developed the desire to be a museum director. After completing military service and earning his degree in history and political theory, he pursued a post-graduate degree in photography and museum studies. He chose photography because he was attracted to communication other than by the spoken or written word. He worked at St. Michael's Maritime Museum, and he was the director of the Ward Museum of Wildfowl Art prior to taking on his position at Salisbury State. He stated that as a museum director he was concerned about objects—the stories objects tell, the glimpse they give into life. He said of himself, "I am not an art historian—that is a job for the curators."

He also did not study art extensively, as he was preparing instead to be an administrator.

I had just assumed that a museum director was probably one of the art curators who had excelled in his position. I felt like I had been given a wake-up call. Ken read me the definition of a museum from *Museum Accreditation: A Handbook for the Institution*, published by the American Association of Museums. The quote said that for the purposes of accreditation a museum is defined as "an organized and permanent nonprofit institution, essentially educational or aesthetic in purpose with professional staff, which owns and utilizes tangible objects, cares for them and exhibits them to the public on some regular schedule."

If museums are concerned about objects and culture, and the directors are not art historians, then what can I tell artists about approaching museums or college galleries that consider themselves to be museums? Ken smiled warily and said that the artist whose work is generally of interest to museums probably doesn't have the time to be approaching museums. He continued, "The artist who is of interest to the museum takes stock of the world through the visual image and should play some role in contemporary life. The work of this artist should have impact on the world and on communication."

Ken stated further, "There should be a body of work that will do more than affect people but will in fact act to shape people's lives." He said to think of wartime. "When an army overruns a country in a war, one of the usual acts is to scavenge the objects from museums and take them to the victorious country. This is referred to as cultural theft. The director thinks of this and usually develops a collection as a significant cultural revelation. The artist whose work is shown or collected must fit this requirement."

According to Ken's description, "good" art, significant exhibitions, important sales, patrons, and good presentation are not necessarily important in making art interesting to museums. The terms he proposed give a criteria of a body of work that tends to reveal and affect the culture of the times in which it was created. He said the work of Robert Rauschenberg was a good example of this kind of work.

Realizing that I was naive as to the history of museums, Ken showed me the book *Museums in Motion*, by Edward P. Alexander, published in 1979 by the American Association for State and Local History. One passage, which told the story of Charles Willson Peale, described the beginning of the American museum movement. Peale, perhaps the most significant figure in the birth of American museums, was lent Independence Hall in Philadelphia, where he installed his American portraits, as well as mammoth bones and a variety of biological curios. Peale's four sons served as assistants in Philadelphia and established branches in Baltimore and New York. Eventually, the city of Philadelphia began charging Peale $1,200 monthly rent, which forced the project to compete as an entertainment entity and obtain admission fees as a source of revenue. Finally, after Peale's death in 1827, his museums went bankrupt and were purchased by Phineas T. Barnum. From these collections, Barnum created his American Museum, increased the number of curios, and eventually began sending his exhibitions on tour. From this came his famous circus.

I had never fully realized how close to entertainment the museum project really is. The one side is the serious collection reflecting to America its own culture. The other is the need to raise revenue despite the competition with other entities that charge admission fees and compete for the public's leisure time. I felt a little relieved that my artistic importance is in a sense a hair's breadth away from being an entertaining curiosity; I like life not to be *too* serious.

When one imagines approaching an established commercial gallery, one considers whether the income of the gallery, dependent on sales, will be enhanced by showing the art. As Ken pointed out, the university gallery's budget is determined by grants, foundation and corporate money, memberships, and special events. It may be arguable whether as artists we should or shouldn't be concerned with how others in the art community derive their incomes, but in some important way if we want the art community to care about our income then we should give some care to theirs. This might involve donating works to their collections, which impresses their patrons, or letting them use our work in their brochures and literature.

More than any other project in the last 2 years, my interaction with the university gallery has helped me establish new career directions. I have renewed my commitment to creating not just the next best painting, but a body of significant and integrated work reflecting my point of view. Also, my marketing project of creating a significant exhibition record will include a more determined effort to show at university and college galleries. In approaching these entities, I will concentrate on a dialogue with the directors and staff about the relevance of my work. In this dialogue, rather than present how my art is artistically relevant, I will seek to define its cultural relevance.

I am excited about and committed to this direction, because the quality of support and recognition I felt at this show fed my energy and enthusiasm. That's a nice change from the terrible feelings of loss of confidence I have experienced in the commercial gallery venue lately.

CHAPTER 8

Touring Exhibitions to Museums and Other Nonprofits

Organizing Your Own Touring Exhibition
Raymond Markarian

Before getting into the nuts, bolts, and anecdotes of how my artist friend and I arranged three successful touring exhibits across the U.S. and Canada, I had better cover the question, "Is this for you?" I find there are several reasons why an artist might want to go through all the trouble of organizing a touring exhibit.

First, after you have spent years of study and struggle to develop an art career, which is likely not making you rich right now, it's a very good feeling to have your art recognized and presented to the public by museums, university art galleries, and art associations. The value of the self-esteem and self-confidence that comes from this recognition should not be underestimated.

Second, the business implications of having your work in museum and nonprofit institutions are by no means slight. If you are seeking gallery representation, in addition to evaluating your art, commercial gallery directors want to know, "Who are you?" A resumé peppered with exhibits around the U.S. makes you a "Who."

Collectors see a lot of art they love and frequently must restrict their choices by evaluating the investment potential. Having your work acknowledged by curators demonstrates a level of accomplishment that may determine future value. A curator's stamp of approval may determine future income for you and how your work is handled.

California, for example, has a 5 percent commission to be paid to the artist by the seller if the work is resold at more than $1,000. Your exhibition record could convince a future owner to consider consigning your work to a gallery or auction house instead of being consigned to the attic or worse. The creation of a secondary market for your work, i.e., auction houses and galleries that do not represent you directly, is not likely to occur without wide professional acknowl-edgment and a record thereof.

Our pals at the IRS are very concerned that your art-related tax deductions are for a business, not a hobby. I know of a photographer who was challenged on this point by the IRS because her art was not producing a profit. Fortunately, her extensive exhibition record allowed her to establish that she was building a base for future sales and her deductions were allowed. With government high-speed computers checking more tax records than ever, a record of exhibitions at museums, college galleries, and other appropriate venues might allow you to sleep a little better.

On to the third reason to go to the trouble of organizing your own touring exhibition. If you have aspirations of some day having your art become part of the permanent collection of a museum, you need to create a base of recognition within that establishment.

I know of some artists who are waiting for the Lana Turner experience to happen to them. Lana Turner was discovered while sipping a soda at Schwab's Drugstore on Sunset Boulevard, and, as they say, "The rest is history." I believe you cannot count on serendipity or only slaving away in the studio to get you a footnote in the history books. In the 1920s a soft drink named Moxie outsold Coca Cola. The company directors at Moxie decided to buy sugar instead of advertising. When was the last time you had a tall cool Moxie? I have tried Moxie and I think it was as good as Coke or Pepsi. Halo Shampoo was the leading shampoo brand in the U.S. during the 1950s and early 1960s. Procter & Gamble introduced Head & Shoulders with an advertising campaign that went unchal-lenged. Halo went down like the *Titanic,* and although management tried to regain market share, they never did come back.

Your exhibition record within the nonprofit arena is your advertising bud-get. To find a place in history, you need to develop a good exhibition record and then make others aware of your accomplishments.

If you have gallery representation and your gallery director is making inroads by attempting to get your art into group exhibitions, then you are on your way to achieving your goal. If this is not the case, then you have to do what you can to make it happen. I have a sign in my office that reads, "Nobody Is Coming!" I am reminded daily that my fairy godmother is not going to drop in and take care of my projects.

Fortunately, if any or all three reasons I offered for taking on a touring exhibit appeal to you, the current finances for most institutions of contemporary art make it somewhat easier than you might initially imagine.

It takes about a year to schedule an exhibit and about 2 years for it to complete the tour. The work involved is spread over a 3-year period. If you do a group exhibit, you should keep the group informed as to events on a regular basis and see that everyone receives copies of announcements and reviews.

The first exhibit we organized and promoted was a group exhibition. The exhibit consisted of four pieces each—paintings and/or drawings—by five women artists. Prior to considering the art, we sought participants whom we knew to be reliable and reasonable. I also wanted to use the formation of this group to underline my observation that women are underrepresented in the arts. The exhibit was titled "Five Women Artists: A Southern California Perspective." This approach doesn't always work; one university gallery director said, "Although I like the exhibit, the university had an all-woman exhibit last year."

If possible, get a local art association director or museum curator to curate the exhibit from work by your group. This would add an additional stamp of approval on your exhibit. If you must do your own curating, allow me to paraphrase Ben Franklin: "Surely, because they hang well separately doesn't mean they will hang well together." We avoided having a "theme" because it could narrow the interest and weaken the artistic punch.

Twelve large works or twenty medium-sized pieces work well for most exhibit spaces where your work will be shown. Our exhibits didn't always get the main gallery, but some reviews and gallery personnel indicated our exhibits did occasionally upstage the main exhibit.

Once we had an exhibit together, we needed to locate some curators and exhibition sites. One major source of information for this is the *American Art Directory* (available through R. R. Bowker Co., 121 Chanlon Rd., New Providence, NJ 07974). However, at more than $100, you might want to use the one at the public library. The directory lists museums, university galleries, and art associations along with the names and titles of key personnel. Also, consult magazines like *Artweek* and *Art Calendar*.

You should compile a list of about 500 addresses. By writing to these 500 addresses you should receive replies from about 100. We used a printed letterhead and envelope to convey professionalism.

My contact letter stated we wanted to send a packet of art-related material pertaining to a touring art exhibit. We further wanted to know whom to contact, the title of that person, and when the next review committee would meet. It is critical to get this information, otherwise, the reply will say to send it anytime and your packet will sit around for months until the review committee meets. Before catching on to this "anytime" stuff, we had packets lost in storage and had to send replacements; we had packets unearthed after the review committee had met; we were informed they would have chosen the exhibit and though it was too late we could apply next year. Talk about the urge to kill. So plan for the packet to arrive about one week prior to the review committee meeting to avoid its being lost. Additionally, we inquired how long the material would be needed. This gave us a legitimate reason to telephone them if they dropped the ball. We used this otherwise negative phone call to build rapport.

We sorted the reply letters by ranking them according to where we would most like to have the exhibit shown and then re-sorted the letters according to the month they indicated to send the packet. This gave us the mailing order in which to send out our packets.

You should use a minimum of twenty-five packets, because some will be lost, some will be kept by the booking institution to document the exhibit, and you want to have enough to contact institutions in a timely manner.

If the information within your packet is concise, organized, and labeled, and you tell the curator or director why they need you (don't tell them why you want them, that's not how to sell) then you should have similar positive results. Our group exhibit was shown at four university galleries, two U.S. and one Canadian museum, and two art associations. The next solo exhibit was shown at ten university galleries. The last solo exhibit was shown at four U.S. museums, four Canada museums, and one university gallery.

Costs So Far. You will be sending a letter to about 500 institutions. Your letter will say you would like to send a packet of art materials pertaining to a touring art exhibit—you want to know whom to contact, his title, and when the next review committee will meet.

Your first expenditure will come from compiling a list of sites to contact. The *American Art Directory*, *Artweek*, and *Art Calendar* are all you should need to form your list. Free arts newsletters (available from state arts councils, listed in the *American Art Directory* and in *Art Calendar*) are also great sources of announcements of exhibition opportunities. Your outlay in compiling the list will consist mostly of time.

I recommend using professionally printed letterhead and matching envelopes for the most polished look. You will pay around $40 for 500 letterheads and $60 for 500 envelopes. Be sure to get some blank matching paper for second pages and other materials.

Postage for 500 letters is $160.

Your exhibit might cost you more or less depending on how gold-plated you make your proposal and how much you're willing to trade time for convenience. Of course, if you have a group of artists in your exhibit you will divide costs.

Once the responses to this initial pitch begin coming in, it's time to send out the more complete proposal and slide packet.

Your Packet. The first item in the packet you want the contact person to see is your cover letter. If he has a title, use it. This is courteous—besides, everyone has an ego. Thank the institution for inviting you to submit your work. This is a nice way to establish that your packet is not unsolicited mail; unsolicited mail can easily be ignored or, worse, discarded.

In your cover letter, refer to your exhibit by the title you've selected. A title provides an intellectual focus and makes it easier for curators to discuss the exhibit in conference and with you.

When my friend and I organized our touring exhibitions, we stated the number of participating artists, the number of works of art, and that there was no fee for the exhibit. Their only cost, beyond printed announcements, was one-way transportation via common carrier.

We also enclosed a self-addressed, stamped postcard for the curator to use to let us know the material had been received. If the card did not return within 10 working days, we phoned to verify that they received the packet. As long as you have them on the phone, if it seems appropriate ask about the museum, other exhibits or programs, and build a little rapport.

The closing statement of your cover letter should instill a note of urgency. We let them know the dates the exhibit was available and we stated that a prompt response would enable them to reserve the dates of their choosing.

Following the cover letter and the self-addressed stamped postcard, we enclosed a slide sheet. Each slide sheet holds twenty 35mm slides. Slide sheets are available at camera shops. There are two kinds: cheap and archival. The archival type will help to prevent deterioration of your slides. Camera shops also carry small computer labels ($\frac{1}{2}$"x$1\frac{3}{4}$"). Use two labels on each slide: provide the name of the artist and the artwork's title, medium, and size. This will prevent problems in identifying the work of individuals in your group; it can also help the viewer determine where the top of the image is.

After the slide sheet, provide a slide list. This has the same information already on the slides, but it is easier to use, photocopy, and pass around the conference table, especially if your well-labeled slides are in the slide carrier. Remember that booking an exhibit is often a group decision in a museum or other nonprofit institution; make it as easy as possible for the curators and committees to view your proposal smoothly and completely.

Send all the support materials that seem appropriate. Do not send original materials or original slides—only copies or duplicates.

A resumé for each artist is a must.

Artist statements are helpful if you have something to say.

Newspaper or magazine articles are good. Cut and paste the articles to fit onto 8$\frac{1}{2}$"x11" pages and make copies; highlight with yellow markers the areas where you are mentioned.

Postcards from past exhibitions are good, even if they show work that is unlike your current work.

We circulated a 5-minute video of the art for one of the solo exhibits. Although this had some art that wasn't part of the touring exhibit, I believe it reinforced the show.

More on Our Costs. The cost of compiling our slide/proposal packet—cover letter, self-addressed stamped postcard, slides (three per artist), slide sheet, slide list, support materials and photocopying thereof, round-trip mailing envelopes, and postage—amounted to about $14. Our twenty-five packets cost our group a total of $350.

You might be wondering why we charged no booking fee. There are professionally curated exhibitions available for modest fees. Also, we were trying to do what I hadn't heard of any group of artists doing on their own, and I felt we needed the advantage of not charging a fee. In retrospect, had we made more contacts and charged a modest fee, we could have found the same number of exhibiting sites. It may be possible for a group or individual, depending upon the level of accomplishment, to charge $150-300 per site. It certainly is reasonable.

Here's how we arrived at our "one-way transportation" arrangement. We paid the freight to our first exhibit site. But, after that, the institutions paid the freight to the next site, and so forth, until the work was returned to us 2 years later. Each of our three touring exhibits traveled over 20,000 miles, but we footed the bill for only the first few hundred miles.

Here's a ballpark idea of shipping costs—you might also wish to give the curators this information. Currently, based on a 2,000-mile journey, one can expect to pay about $225 for a 500-pound shipment, the approximate weight of each of our exhibits. However, it is highly unlikely your exhibit will be shipped to and from the most distant corners of the country. Because our exhibit consisted entirely of paintings, the freight companies informed us that they would ship the exhibit under Class 110—the classification of the freight determines the cost per hundredweight. Yellow Freight and Roadway Express were the two common carriers we used—we didn't use art shippers because the costs were prohibitive. I discovered that we were not alone; many museums use common carriers to ship art. Air freight companies, LEP Profit in particular, can often be even less costly than the common carriers.

The curators will usually work with you to adjust scheduling to lessen the shipping distances. We did encounter some curators who wanted to book our exhibit but seemed nervous about making scheduling arrangements; we made saying "Yes" easy by phoning the curators at the next sites to work out the shipping schedule.

It would be lovely if life went exactly as planned, but suppose—realistically— that you're left with a hole in your schedule and neither shipping company nor receiving museum has room to store your art for a month or two. Solution: You can get a trucking company to store your shipment for about $30/month. This beats having the art shipped back to you.

Insurance is one topic that should be discussed with everyone in your group. Document the decisions so everyone is smiling and talking to each other at the end of the tour. The institutions that selected our exhibit had insurance within their buildings, but would not or could not insure the exhibit in transit. Some of our group chose not to carry insurance. Others got coverage through Artists Equity (National Artists Equity Association, P.O. Box 28068, Central Station, Washington, D.C. 20038, 800-727-NAEA, 202-628-9633), whose underwriter is Trinder & Norwood Art Group (6 Corporate Park Dr., White Plains, NY). This is inexpensive insurance that covers your work against loss from fire, theft, vandalism, or accidents in your studio, at art venues, or in transit. With common carriers, you will probably be required to sign a statement that you will hold the carrier responsible only to the limit of the insurance of the freight classification—Class 110 is only 50¢ per pound.

Although I wouldn't dispense with insurance, I believe one's best protection against loss is a well-constructed shipping crate. Shipping crates will cost about $20 each, or $480 for 24 works of art. See the article in this book about building shipping crates.

Don't forget to throw in $100 or so to cover telephone calls and other miscellaneous expenses.

So far, from start (the solicitation letter) to finish (shipping the work) we've spent around $1,400. Divided up among a few artists—say, six—this becomes affordable: $233 each. If you got into ten juried exhibits, which don't have the same cachet, at an average cost of $23.30, I'd say you got a great deal. But, isn't $1,400 expensive if you have a solo exhibit? You get not one, but ten or fifteen or more solo exhibitions; you get back some of your materials; your slides can be used elsewhere; you can re-use your crates. And we landed sales of three paintings from one solo exhibition and received two generous and unexpected honoraria. I believe the possibility of sales are best in photo and print exhibits because the art can be sold and taken home on-the-spot without changing the structure of the exhibit.

Someone Bites. As soon as we obtained our first venue, we wrote to all the other institutions who still had our packets to tell them the name of the institution that had booked the exhibit and the time slot which was now unavailable. This was done partly out of consideration, but primarily for the psychological effect. The value of an item often increases the instant someone else wants it. I call this the "Me, Too!" Factor.

The first two venues to commit were listed in subsequent cover letters. Remember, you're sending out twenty to twenty-five packets initially; as the curators who do not select your exhibit return your packets, you must change the cover letter and start over again.

By the time we had three venues, we were asking them to check the newly enclosed exhibit schedule to find the booking dates that were still available.

Progress occurs at the speed of paper. We waited about 7 weeks before responses started coming back. The response rate should also increase as you progress through the list. This is because (1) you are applying to your first-choice venues first, and (2) curators feel more confident in booking the exhibit as soon as they see others committing to it.

After 7 weeks, it's time for a polite call. We found that the longer they held on to the materials, the less likely they were to choose the exhibit. Beware of curators who are too polite to say no. Their "kindness" can cost you valuable time. Also, don't get caught in the limbo of summer vacation that comes up every year at universities.

Keeping the Project Rolling. After you have the exhibit shipped off, you'll need to be sure the sending and receiving museums are in contact with each other. It's also not a bad idea to have each site forward a form, which you provide, to enclose in the shipping crates that describes the condition of the work when it was received. A copy of this form should be sent to you at the end of each show; you can assess any need for repair along the tour or, if you don't get your work back in a condition close to the way it was shipped out, you will have a record of where the damage occurred.

At this point you should have a good overview of how to create the events that go into a touring exhibit. I will close with what was, for me, the biggest surprise connected with this project. The surprise came when we informed curators that the art would arrive in foam-lined wooden crates and all they had to do was have staff open the crates, wipe off the paintings, and hang them on the wall. On three occasions the attitude of the curators changed so dramatically from reserved to relieved, it was almost palpable. We booked those three venues, and I suspect several others were won over because of the ease in handling the artwork.

I sincerely hope your own unique background and perspective will allow you to build on the information I've provided and you achieve even better results.

PART 3

Running Your Own Gallery and Conducting Studio Shows

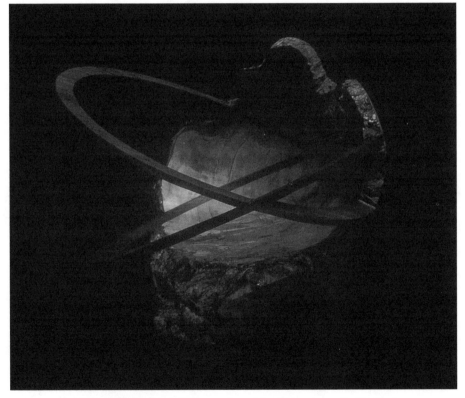

A *Turned Wooden Vessel,* 1996, turned wood, Joe Dickey, Annapolis, Maryland

CHAPTER 9

Operating a Gallery Smoothly

Owning Your Own Gallery
Barbara Dougherty

There is a breed of artist I call the "working artist." This is essentially an artist-entrepreneur who does not do art as a spare-time activity or support himself with income from another source. The working artist creates with the hope and aspiration that the art will pay the bills and more.

This artist is always looking for information and techniques that will enable success, and is constantly deciding which entrepreneurial activities will promote sales yet leave time for creating the artwork that is to be sold. Owning and operating a gallery is a viable alternative for the working artist.

This is a more formal activity than showing work at your studio. The general public seems reluctant to visit the studio of an artist. There is a mystique of privacy about an artist, and an invitation to an artist's studio can be felt as an invitation to interrupt. Take the same space and do exactly the same things (work and display) in that space and call it a gallery, and the public is not reluctant to visit. I have always painted at my galleries and I have always called them galleries.

An artist can create a gallery of his own and be successful. My recommendation is that an artist who takes on this project must embrace some business tasks in a creative fashion:

- Staffing by cooperative efforts with other artists
- Investment capital through trade and patron participation
- Low cost alternative advertising
- Keeping track of sales and inventory with a simple system.

Before I opened my first gallery in 1975, we held some art shows in the homes of some collectors and I approached people who attended these. I told them I was intent on opening a gallery. I had chosen a location and needed to raise about $500. I offered these customers a certificate that could be purchased for $25 and was worth $50 in merchandise the moment we opened. I also proposed that their names would be carved onto a special plaque. This patrons' plaque was to become a permanent fixture in the gallery. Within one weekend twenty-five certificates were purchased.

Many of our customers never redeemed their certificates; they simply liked being part of the project. Other certificate holders crowded into the gallery as soon as it opened, redeeming their certificates and purchasing even more. Thus, we had a profitable beginning. Essentially, the certificate holders walked into the gallery being able to purchase anything up to $50, and they were not hindered by a psychological barrier against spending.

Later I used this technique in offering gift certificates, where the certificate was redeemable for a higher dollar amount of art than what it originally cost to purchase. Ninety percent of the time more was spent by the redeemer than the original value of the certificate, and the certificate helped the original customer overcome their reluctance to buy art as a gift. I considered the dollars given away in this project advertising dollars. Essentially, the gift certificate was one person bringing another to my gallery.

My first gallery was closed when my family moved from New York to California, where I opened my second gallery in 1985. This time, the funds for renting and remodeling the space were not raised by certificates—I traded artwork for help and materials.

Both of my galleries operated at a good profit margin. I was able to pay expenses, keep producing art, and pay bills at home with the money brought in by the gallery.

Part of the success I could attribute to making the environment of the gallery a remarkable place. I don't think an artist maximizes the sales potential of a gallery by hanging pictures or setting up sculptures without decorating first.

Both of my galleries were decorated similarly. I brought in large, old garden fountains that I bleached; around these I placed plants and large chips of rock salt. They became central display units that gave a museum courtyard ambiance to the gallery. Each wall of the gallery and the separate standing display units were done with different materials. For instance, on one wall I nailed wooden roofing shingles, and on another wall I applied a ceiling plaster. First I embedded in it a fixture from which paintings could be hung and then I swirled the plaster with my hand in a texture over the rest of the wall. (If you try to do this do not do the whole wall at once—the weight of the wet plaster can bring it down.) Pedestals and shelving were either in unfinished timber or upholstered (not in burlap). *Decor* is a good magazine to subscribe to for gallery decorating ideas.

I always had a specific sales counter and well-lit window displays. I found that many sales happened by attracting the casual window-shopper.

Track lighting was by far the largest and most important investment.

Next was the installation of a stereo unit. Sales occurred more often when there was music.

I staffed my galleries with my family and with other artists whose work was hung and sold in trade for their time. The gallery sales commission was diminished by the amount of time they were willing to spend. An arrangement was made to calculate the dollar amount of an artist's work sold against the time spent by the artist in the gallery. If hours or sales exceeded the standards I had created, then an adjustment was made.

In neither gallery was I able to afford insurance that would pay an artist a full dollar value for the loss of their work, but in the second gallery I installed a theft and fire alarm system. I found that the monthly cost was around $50 for a competent system.

In my gallery I did not have opening receptions. Instead, I tried to create events. The difference was that I could really profit more from free advertising by creating an event than I could from the listing of a gallery opening. Newspapers, local magazines, and radio stations are usually very willing to publish or broadcast materials that come to them in the proper format. My technique is to send a publicity package. To newspapers and magazines, this includes black-and-white photos, a written press release, and supporting documents.

For instance, an artist came from Switzerland and we installed his paintings in my gallery. I wrote a story about his obsession with experiencing the West as he had seen it represented by Frederic Remington and Charles Russell. I sent it out to the local media with a black-and-white photo of him and his work. This package achieved a wonderful feature story in the local newspaper.

Then I had him paint a portrait of then-President Reagan; he hoped to achieve portrait commissions while here in the States. He presented the portrait to the director of the local Republican organizing committee. We took a photo of him making this presentation and submitted this again to the newspapers with the announcement of an event at the gallery where many artists would be present with their work. At this event my Swiss artist was accepting portrait commissions. Again we were pleased to achieve a good, large story highlighting this artist who was becoming a local star. The publicity helped us achieve attendance at our event and sales at the gallery. The public liked the idea of one artist sponsoring another and the whole publicity package helped sell my work as well.

Advertising expenses can bankrupt a gallery. My attitude is that advertising is all-important but should be accomplished as inexpensively as possible. The Yellow Pages is a wise expense only if the gallery is going to offer additional services like framing, art restoration, or art lessons. My best advertising was having my husband carve some creative wooden signs for our vehicles.

My experience also was that any advertising solicited personally by someone coming to the gallery, especially for directories, newspapers, and magazines, was high-cost and not profitable.

One problem of owning an art gallery is that usually only one in every four people who come in are customers. One of the four is an artist looking for representation, another is a salesperson selling anything from advertising to disability insurance, and the third is a good-willed philanthropist seeking endorsement or a donation. Many of the people who walk into the gallery have no intention of being your customer and have no respect for your time and your need to consider your paying customer. Thus, I posted two signs: "No Solicitations" and "Artists Seeking Representation Seen on Thursdays."

I did not create a gallery specifically for the sale of my work and my husband's work, even though between us we could produce enough inventory for a gallery. The initial reason I included the work of other artists was the need for staff. Then as artists presented work to me for possible representation, I found myself viewing art I liked and knew I could sell. Including the work of other artists was a benefit that did not diminish the sales of our own work. This may not fit a marketing approach by other artists, but an art gallery usually needs to represent the work of more than one artist to be successful.

There are other tasks that one cannot ignore in this project, like accounting procedures. A system that allows for updating inventory lists, i.e., by price tags that contain numbers which must be recorded on sales slips, eliminate many headaches caused by lost or unaccounted-for items. Careful accounting of expenses and the saving of expense receipts is an absolute necessity for tax accounting. Contracts between the artist/owner and others represented by the gallery must be made.

I liked having my own gallery and closed it in 1994 when I moved back East. I found the project successful and exciting and it is a marketing strategy that I will use again someday.

Competing with Galleries
Alan Bamberger

Although some collectors buy directly from artists, many don't. When those who don't are asked why they prefer gallery buying to patronizing artists, the most common complaint is that artists present too many problems to deal with directly.

The good news is that artists can fight back and increase studio sales by adopting techniques of the galleries and by learning not to let personal feelings and opinions get in the way of making sales.

Following are some suggestions. Some might not be suitable for your way of doing business and are certainly not required for successful selling, but if your goal is to increase studio sales, the more you implement the better. If none are for you, at least you'll come away with a deeper understanding of why galleries exist.

- Keep regular business hours. Whether for 1 hour a week or 40, have standard times when you are open for business. This alleviates the time and effort potential buyers must go through to make appointments.
- Make collectors feel welcome and comfortable. Answer their questions, show them what they want to see, explain how you work. Place too many restrictions on what they can look at, where they can walk, or what they feel they can say, and you'll alienate them.
- Set aside a portion of your studio in which to display finished work. The more you can approximate gallery viewing conditions, the better. Collectors have an easier time understanding the impact of a finished work when they see it in a clean, well-lit, uncluttered setting.
- Don't talk down to collectors even when you know more than they do. Lecturing to someone who doesn't want to be lectured to generally turns them off.

- Allow collectors to see the full range of your work no matter what you personally think of it. If they like something you don't, that's fine. Not everyone's tastes are identical. If they're more interested in your early work than your current work, that's OK too.
- Don't be overly sensitive when collectors express their likes and dislikes. If you become visibly offended, you decrease your chances of the collector becoming your patron. Remember that everyone is entitled to their opinions.
- Collectors might mention names of other artists in their collections. No matter what you think of these artists or their work, don't get negative.
- Be sensitive to buyers with modest budgets. Try to work with them and find art that suits their needs rather than tell them that for the kind of money they have to spend, they won't be able to buy anything of consequence.
- Have a return policy and allow collectors to take works home on approval. Deciding on what art to buy is not easy for most collectors and they appreciate this kind of consideration on the part of sellers.
- Be flexible about your prices. If a collector wants to negotiate and is capable of doing so in an inoffensive and appropriate manner, seriously consider lowering your prices. You're under no obligation, however, to work with anyone who is rude or insulting or wants to buy your work for nothing.
- Don't base selling prices on your current financial situation, whatever that may be. If, for example, your studio rent is due, don't decide that's the minimum amount of money a collector must pay.
- Set all prices ahead of time. If you go back and forth about how much you want for a piece, expect the collector to go back and forth about whether or not to buy it. Hesitancy or uncertainty in pricing gives collectors the idea that your prices vary according to your whims or that different people get quoted different prices for reasons known only to you.
- Don't confuse the selling prices of your art with your level of self-esteem. Expect problems if you get too involved or emotional when the time comes to hammer out money issues.
- Avoid overemphasizing the significance of the work of art a collector is considering buying. Don't act like he's ripping your heart out or

absconding with the best thing you've ever done. The collector isn't buying your body, your soul, or the essence of your being. He is buying your art.

- Allow collectors to pay over time or make cash/trade arrangements if you have a use for what they have to offer.
- Don't be shy about collecting money that's past due. If this is something you might have trouble with, plan ahead as to what your policy will be should this situation arise.
- Provide buyers with written statements, explanations, or other written information that give them insight into who you are and what the particular piece of art being purchased is all about. Galleries can only give receipts and secondary documentation—you can give much more, especially of a personal nature.
- Don't be abrasive. If you have difficulty relating to collectors, better skip the studio sales and go directly to the dealers.

The one huge advantage you have over dealers and galleries is yourself. You are the number-one person qualified to provide insight into who you are, why you do what you do, and what your art is all about. Make every studio visit a joy, an experience, an education, and an adventure for your collectors. They appreciate this, and the better you can demonstrate to them how buying from you is more advantageous than buying from dealers, the more studio sales you will make.

Taking the Credit: Getting Visa and MasterCard Merchant Status
Barbara Dougherty

By 1977 I had been selling my artwork at various exhibitions nationwide for 5 years. I remember feeling left out of the twentieth century because I was not able to allow my clients to use their charge cards for purchases. In fact, I lost sales more than once because "folks don't like to carry cash."

An artist friend once suggested that when an item cost too much for a cash or check purchase I could be my own credit provider. One method: taking the sales amount in a series of post-dated checks. Problems: the handmade chess set I had sold in this manner was never paid for, because none of the checks after the first one were any good. Furthermore, I found out that I couldn't collect on them, because it is illegal to accept post-dated checks.

With this loss in mind, I went to talk with my local banker. I had developed a good relationship with him by banking there and by hanging pictures in the bank lobby. The bank showings gave both of us good publicity, and I had made sales there.

Although I could not recoup my loss on the chess set, he said he would try to help me with my desire to accept credit cards for sales transactions. He said that the main problem in becoming a merchant was that banks tend to frown on merchants who do not have stable storefront retail locations. However, a few days later he informed me that he had gotten permission to make me a credit card merchant.

I have made more sales as a result, and other artists who can accept credit cards feel the same way.

If you have not been able to get approval to be a credit card merchant, this article provides some information and advice that might help you.

There are various credit card providers. These include Visa, MasterCard, American Express, and Discover.

There are drawbacks to American Express. First, it can take up to 2 weeks for the funds to be credited to your account after you make the deposit. Second, the amount charged by them as a commission—called the "discount rate"—is usually higher than what Visa or MasterCard charge.

Yes, merchants pay a percentage too, not just the consumer, for the privilege of making transactions using credit cards.

Despite the drawbacks, I found that the best place to start is with American Express. Their system does not lend itself to the same abuses that have occurred with Visa and MasterCard; thus, they are more willing to allow merchants without storefront retail locations to accept sales from customers. You can apply through the American Express Merchant Service (800-528-5200). Also, once you are an American Express merchant, it is easier to qualify to accept the other cards.

One of my artist friends reported to me that her sales increased by 30 percent once she became an American Express merchant. She, however, never sought the ability to accept the other cards; she feels that anyone who has other cards has this card too.

I never sought to accept Discover—I only gained the option when I purchased the electronic machine for my gallery that automatically verifies transactions. Personally, I dislike what I've heard about the tracking and use of merchant sales information that I've heard Discover uses in their promotions.

Visa and MasterCard acceptance can be authorized by commercial banks, or some separate providers. Each bank has its own standards in qualifying merchants, with guidelines from Visa and MasterCard. In addition, a recommendation from a higher authority in the bank can supersede some of the usual requirements.

However, recent mail order and telemarketing scams have made many banks leery of nontraditional merchants. A "traditional" merchant has a storefront location, has been in business for a certain number of years, has been at that location for a certain period of time, and has a demonstrable track record including tax returns and lack of formal complaints. After all, if a mail order merchant makes deposits but then withdraws the money and skips town, the bank may be liable for the funds if the transactions deposited were not legitimately made or the orders were not legitimately fulfilled. As usual, the ramifications of crime tend to be widespread. In this case, crooks have made it difficult for legitimate, but nontraditional, merchants to qualify to offer credit card acceptance.

The most important thing to know about applying to become a Visa or MasterCard merchant: It is up to the bank. Each bank makes its own policies. One bank, or several, might turn you down—another might not.

When you apply, put your best foot forward. There are several things you can do that will help your application. The best approach, of course, is to have a working relationship with the bank in the first place. Doing displays, having accounts, knowing bank personnel—all these factors help.

Find out which banks have helped other artists, craftsmen, antiques dealers, and others who sell at exhibitions who are credit card merchants.

When you apply, think of it as any other kind of loan/financial trust application: You must look creditworthy. A list of the last year or two's sales will help. Looking like a reliable merchant might help also, although I can't say I have ever done anything but look the part of the artist through-and-through.

Besides banks, there are independent merchants who advertise and extend to you the ability to be a credit card merchant. In doing research for this article, I called Larry Schwartz, president of the National Association of Credit Card Merchants. It costs $349/year to belong to this organization, which offers a host of services and protections to the merchant, no matter who extends credit card capability, the bank or an independent. Mr. Schwartz strongly recommended that an artist or craftsman would be better off procuring credit card merchant status from a local bank rather than a card service provider. Specifically, he points out that any problems with collections are nearly impossible to resolve when your card service provider is out of your local area. Schwartz also said that the credit card industry has been riddled with clever scams and it is absolutely imperative that you select a provider with utmost care. The National Association of Credit Card Merchants is in Boynton Beach, Florida (407-737-8700).

There are many ins-and-outs of becoming a merchant who accepts credit cards: service charges, equipment, invalid or stolen cards, charge-backs, etc.

Credit card merchants pay the bank or the company providing this service a service charge, which is a commission called a "discount" rate—this is a percentage of the total sale including sales tax and shipping and handling. The discount rate varies. Some of the factors affecting the rate are your monthly sales volume, the length of time you will wait to receive your funds, and whether you have manual or electronic equipment to accept the transaction. The discount rate is usually between 2 percent and 5 percent. Sometimes the rate will vary from month to month or even transaction to transaction, and the rate will vary depending on whether you do charges manually or electronically. Thus the equipment you need is another consideration. All the equipment, whether it is a manually operated imprinter or an electronic station, can be leased or purchased, either from your provider or an independent source. The costs vary widely. When I first became a credit card merchant, I paid $25/year for the bank's manual Visa and MasterCard imprinter. However, American Express provides the imprinter at no charge (but their discount fees are much higher).

The electronic equipment can come with a variety of gadgets, including a mini-printer which can generate a receipt/signature record of the sale. My first electronic device, a Trans 440, I leased for $7.95/month last year; yet I have heard of others with this same device paying leases-to-own adding up to more than $1,500. One independent card provider approached me at my gallery, offering me a discount rate of less than 2 percent if I leased my machine from him. But when I figured out the cost of the machine on his program, it amounted to more than $55/month. The difference in a 1 percent discount fee versus the equipment lease did not make his offer a good deal for me at that time.

The next consideration: the possibility of accepting cards that might not be valid. Larry Schwartz talked with me extensively about this, since people in our profession tend to make sales in nontraditional retail locations. We might not have access to authorization devices or phones. Thus, Larry recommended that after looking carefully at the card and the hologram (the special symbol on the card), it is important to compare the signature on the back of the card with the one on your sales slip.

If you have any doubts, if it is legal in your state ask for other identification such as a driver's license. Check the described characteristics of the customer like hair color, eye color, and height.

As a further protection against bad transactions, once you have accepted a card, using the authorization service will help guarantee you payment. However, always remember that a customer can charge-back the sale for almost any reason for up to a year, or even 2 years, after the sale. You should know that customers can challenge the validity of a charge at almost any time.

I had a few bad sales because of bad cards, until I began providing a registration card for my artwork with each sale. This is a large index card-sized title agreement that informs my customer that I reserve the copyright on my work (unless it is specifically transferred). I have the customer, in his own writing, print his name, address, phone number, and provide his signature as purchaser and/or registered owner. I fill in information about the artwork: its size, title, completion date, and medium (watercolor, oil, etc.). Since I began doing this I have not had a single bad transaction. I believe there is too much of a personal commitment involved in filling out this form than a person with less-than-honorable intentions would be able to handle. I have had potential customers walk away from the sale when they see the form. At this I am always a bit chagrined, but it is better to lose a sale at that point than to lose the piece of art and the sale.

So here we are again. Sometimes I just want to divest myself of all these practicalities and be an artist anarchist. At those times, I regale myself with tales.

One of my favorite tales is about Ma Jones, the woman who brought child labor laws to this country. Coal miners were on strike in Pennsylvania, and strike busters were marching to the mines. The main road was blocked by striking miners and Pinkertons. Ma Jones was helping the striking miners. Suddenly, it appeared that the scabs were fording the creek to get to the mine. Ma Jones and a few wives of the strikers ran to the creek. She ran up to the leader of the scabs and blocked his way. She said, "Cross this creek and the water will run with your blood—there are five hundred miners in the hills behind me!" The scabs retreated. Later she was asked whether there really were five hundred miners in the hills. She said, "Naw, but the *souls* of those miners were sure there!"

Somehow I want sometimes to call on the souls of living and dead artists to protect us from all this, as Ma Jones did with the souls of the miners. I would call on these souls to protect us from registration, verification, and so on and on and on.

And yet, find me close to a potential sale and you'll hear me mutter, "Do you have a Visa card?"

Helping Galleries Help Themselves:
Interview with Nina Pratt, Art Market Advisor
Caroll Michels

Finding gallery representation can be a long wait. In New York, for example, many artists are led by a gallery's carrot for as long as 10 years. After several rounds of annual studio visits and more rounds of appointment changes or no-shows, finally a commitment is made—an actual exhibition date is scheduled. But the exaltation of gallery status can quickly dissipate when one discovers that being a gallery artist is not all that it is cracked up to be. What's going on?

Nina Pratt is a New York-based art market advisor to contemporary art galleries, private dealers, print publishers, and art consultants. Her clients include established businesses as well as newcomers. She advises clients nationwide on strategy planning, marketing and sales, and operations.

Nina owned a gallery in Massachusetts, but it was not until she moved to New York and worked for a gallery that it become apparent that her peers needed help in developing sound business practices, including marketing, sales, and planning skills. Thus, her advisory service evolved.

I met Nina a few years ago, and while comparing notes about our respective occupations, she isolated the main reasons why so many dealers sink or barely keep their galleries afloat, neither living up to their own nor to artists' expectations. As she ran through a list of gallery weaknesses, I felt flickers of *déjà vu*. Many of the reasons dealers fail, or never attain success, sounded very familiar. In fact, for the most part, they are the same reasons that prevent artists from achieving career goals, with or without gallery representation.

Nina believes the root of the problem is that many dealers buy into the myth that art and business don't mix, a prejudice often shared by artists. "Dealers are terrified of being viewed as used car salesmen," she said. "They go to great lengths to disassociate themselves with the 'business' aspects of art." She also pointed out that many people open galleries naively believing that selecting an arts-related profession will automatically make them successful. Parallels can be drawn between those artists who believe that the ability to create art is the only talent necessary to guarantee a constant stream of dealers, curators, and collectors knocking at the door.

If one can be convinced that professionalism is not synonymous with "Crazy Eddie-ism," Nina assists clients with formulating a business plan, looking at the overall picture, including marketing and sales goals, and organizing or reorganizing their methods of operations.

To help readers understand more about why they might be disenchanted with the performance record of their dealers, and to give those looking for a gallery some pointers on good gallery management, I asked Nina to elaborate on specific gallery weaknesses related to business strategy and savvy. Following are some of the key issues she covered.

• Advertising. She faults dealers who use "tombstone" ads, those without visual information—or what I refer to as generic advertising. She pointed out that basically galleries lack an overall or specific advertising strategy, and rarely employ important target marketing concepts. Ads are repeatedly placed in the same art periodicals without analyzing whether the readership is actually the market or the only market a gallery wants to reach. She emphasized the excellent potential market in non-arts publications. For example, if a dealer already has collectors or wants to develop a clientele from the business community, it would be advantageous to advertise in publications that business people read, such as *The Wall Street Journal*.

• Sales Techniques. Over the years Nina has observed that a dealer's selling style matches his personal buying style, and that dealers frequently hire staff who possess the same style. This lack of flexibility can be the kiss of death. "Collectors come with a variety of backgrounds, tastes, and buying power, and they also come with a variety of ways they behave as consumers. A gallery must be able to adapt to the range and differences in consumer habits." She finds that during personal encounters with the public, dealers tend to go to an extreme either by not talking at all, or talking too much. The cool, nonverbal approach can be perceived as intimidating, and by talking too much a dealer is not listening to what the potential collector is saying. Nina emphasized that important data can be gleaned from listening, including aesthetic leanings, price range, style of buying, and sincerity of interest. She also faults dealers for not asking visitors for their names and addresses. Although not everyone will cooperate, attempts are rarely made to solicit this information, and opportunities are lost for developing future business relationships.

• Mailing Lists. Most galleries strive for quantity rather than quality. Nina would rather see a gallery maintain a mailing list comprised of 500 recognizable names rather than a list of 5,000 unfamiliar names.

• Greed. One of the most self-defeating business practices shared by dealers is the unwillingness to split commissions. "Dealers should be willing to pass up a commission in order to show a client that you can get them what they want. This can most definitely strengthen a working relationship with collectors, stimulate trust, and encourage future sales." A cooperative spirit between dealers, and between dealers and art consultants, is at an all-time low.

Nina agreed that if those considering opening a gallery or entering a related profession were presented with a checklist of qualities and skills necessary for a successful career, the majority of people reading such a list would have second thoughts about entering the field.

If your dealer or art consultant could use some help, Nina Pratt can be reached at 116 Pinehurst Avenue, New York, NY 10022.

CHAPTER 10

Studio Shows

Mohammed to the Mountain:
Getting Collectors to Come to Your Studio
Carolyn Blakeslee

Rather than getting your artwork "out there," this article is about bringing collectors to you.

Some people have psychological barriers against coming into a studio vs. into a gallery. Many people feel that an artist's studio is a mysterious and private place and are reluctant to intrude. Others might fear being cornered into buying if they are alone with you in your studio.

Here are some tips on how to defuse those tensions and to get potential clients to come to your studio.

Hold a Regular Open House

David Breeden, sculptor, holds an open house/open studio/potluck gathering every Wednesday evening at his home and studio complex in Charlottesville, Virginia. Marvelously fun, the evenings offer people the opportunity to meet other creative sorts. People bring their specialties, so tasty food is a draw too.

Breeden has been doing this for nearly 2 decades and has never missed a Wednesday—it works. Despite the rural location, lots of people come. There's cleanup involved, and a commitment for someone to be there every week, but minimal expense—people bring their own booze as well as their own food. It has become an event people look forward to.

Whether you offer your open house weekly or monthly, the benefit of holding a regular event is that when the event occurs regularly it becomes a habit for people to consider it as an activity for every week or month.

Sponsor Special Events

Have a concert or a jam session once a month.

Sponsor an art-food potluck—everyone brings his/her specialty dish, presented in the style of a famous artist.

Host a poetry/literature reading.

Sponsor an evening featuring all of the above, call it a "salon," and insist that all attendees wear black clothing and berets. Peculiar accents are optional.

Hook up with your local winery or wine distributor and have a wine tasting.

Offer a free demonstration. If you're too shy for that, make a video of one or more of your artworks in progress and show it during your event. There's no need to make it a feature presentation, you can just keep it looping in the background and people will gravitate to it when their conversations falter. Museums offer videos in conjunction with major exhibitions of living artists; generally these videos alternate the interview format with in-studio work.

Hold a show featuring artwork by you and some of your friends and have a formal opening. They can help you with the work. All of you could demonstrate your techniques—or you can rotate your lecture/demonstrations as the series continues.

Make It Easy to Buy

Offer installment sale terms.

Offer rental, option to buy, or even approval programs. William Turner, a sculptor, offers an "on approval" arrangement from his Onley, Virginia foundry/gallery. He has never been stiffed even though he doesn't have a signed agreement. Personally, this arrangement makes me nervous, but it works for him.

Allow a trade-up with no expiration—anyone who purchases an artwork of yours may trade it in on something else later and you will credit the total amount to the later sale. This is another goodie Turner offers his clients. Only a small percentage of his collectors have taken advantage of it, because they like the work they bought—and even if they do they're purchasing more of his artwork anyway.

Get credit card capability. Some banks are becoming more flexible about letting artists offer credit card acceptance. While most artists do not have a storefront commercial place of business, some banks now accept trade show and fair/festival attendance as evidence of *bona fide*.

At your studio events, put out a small flyer or brochure that has ideas for people to consider. If you offer installment sale terms or any of the other arrangements I've outlined here, list them in your brochure. Let them know if framing, shipping, delivery, or installation services are available. If you have a portable portfolio that you would be happy to show a corporate art committee, list that in your brochure. If you're available for lectures or demonstrations, say so. If you invite people to come to your studio for private showings, mention that too.

Basically, you want people to know why and how they may get to own your work. If you or your potential collectors are uncomfortable about discussing these things then a brochure will make it easier for you and for them. If you are uncomfortable with selling, have a "designated driver" handle sales for you—your spouse, a friend, an employee.

Make Your Artwork User-Friendly

Whether you're making paintings or wearables, people need to know how to clean them and otherwise take care of them. Photographs can fade with exposure to light, heat, and humidity; gold resist in painted wearables will disappear in dry cleaning, so they must be washed by hand; oil paintings collect dust like everything else and they need to be dusted—tell how to do it, and give special instructions if your paintings have texture or other fragile elements.

Besides protecting you from liability in the event of future deterioration, a simple tag or brochure on care is also a good P.R. device: It gives your collector something to file and it is a keepsake for getting in touch with you later. The more documentation you provide, the better.

Get Press

Regular events might take a while to get going, but pretty soon your open studio could be the talk of the town and the event people really look forward to. Regular events are publicized largely through word of mouth and your personal invitations, but news releases don't hurt either, especially when you have a special event.

If you can write, submit how-to articles to art magazines.

Don't overlook the value of letters to the editor and other forms of personal non-event-connected communication with people.

Send out an occasional newsletter to your collectors and to others on your mailing list. Tell them about publications you've appeared in, workshops you're giving, exhibitions you're participating in, personal news, upcoming events at your studio, and so on.

If you make your art fun to view, easy to buy even if it's expensive, and straightforward to care for, then you have a winning combination. If you have good food and drinks, good company, and a handsome studio, all the better.

More on Open Studios
Peggy Hadden

Recently, a fellow artist invited me to an open studio event she was planning. Knowing of this artist's success in selling her own work, I frankly wanted to see how she did it. Here are my observations.

The guests were a mix of about fifty people of different ages and included children. The feeling was casual, with music, lots of "finger foods," sodas, and wine. There was no evidence of any pressure to buy. But people did.

By presenting a variety of work and mixing older pieces with newer, she offered a selection of sizes and price ranges to her guests. In all, there were about thirty works exhibited. The work was hung erratically, some pieces higher and some lower, all contributing to a loose and temporary atmosphere. The feeling was conveyed that this work was not permanently installed, but would soon be going out the door in the hands of happy collectors. I have also been in this artist's studio at other times when she had framed works placed on the floor, neatly stacked against a wall. Other visitors with me were drawn to look through these works and I realize now that a "ready-to-be-bought" atmosphere was consciously created in both kinds of studio visits.

In organizing the event to occur from 5–9 P.M., the artist had bridged the natural gap between work and dinner. Guests drifted in and out easily, and things seemed to move fluidly. Weeknights are better for this kind of affair in our city (New York), as many people go away on weekends. This might not be the case in other areas where a weekend evening might be an ideal time for a relaxed get-together.

No titles or prices were posted. On reflection, I am sure this was deliberate. When prospective buyers were forced to ask about a work, the artist was alerted to their interest. This gave her an opportunity to talk about the piece more fully. She could mention details that enhanced the work and gave it more background. Example: "Oh, do you like that one? I'm so glad! It's one of the best of my early collages and it led to so much of my later work . . ." You get the idea.

Parts of her work area where guests were not allowed had been blocked off with plain muslin stapled across doorways. White boards were propped up to close openings. Simple, but these deterrents kept works-in-progress, and machinery which could have been dangerous, off-limits.

Some of the pieces she was showing were quite large. She had lined up a burly friend to help lift, wrap, and carry them for buyers. I was impressed that she had ready and at hand the appropriate materials: tape, bubble packaging, and a stapler. No interrupted conversations to grope around in search of packing materials. This reminded me of seeing, in another artist's studio, a fat roll of brown wrapping paper on a wrought iron stand. It was situated directly under his drawing table. My immediate reaction was, "This guy must sell a lot of art!" Maybe yes and maybe no. But he convinced me and probably a lot of prospective buyers as well. It is important to make it look like your work sells. Not daily, perhaps, but often enough that you've thought about how to package it for carrying away from your studio.

Once an artwork was bought, a piece of white paper tape was put next to it on the wall with the buyer's name on it. As the walls were also white, the result was more subtle than using the traditional red dot employed by galleries to indicate a work has been sold. The tape also did two other things: (a) It committed the buyer to follow through with the purchase as the evening concluded, and (b) It kept prospective buyers from falling in love with a piece that was no longer available.

My artist friend encouraged taking pieces on approval. Remember, she had invited these people and had a phone number, so she could always track her work down. But she told me later that for her, a trial period always resulted in a sale—even if the original work taken on approval was not the one that sold. The relationship established in taking an artwork on approval bestows, inherently, some responsibility on the person who does the taking. He has borrowed a work to try, causing you extra work in packing it for them, in your paperwork keeping track of the piece, and further, by removing it from possible sale elsewhere while in their possession. Most prospective buyers will bend over backwards, if not by buying something else right away, at least by keeping up with the artist's future activities. As we are all in this for the long haul, it is good to have a few collectors waiting in the wings for future endeavors, who feel themselves to be in our debt.

I did not see any money change hands. Negotiations involving payment for art were kept out of sight. I think this was also part of the artist's desire to keep the atmosphere of the evening light and non-pressuring to the other guests. Another thought: I believe it is good policy to have, and consult, a price list. You will seem more businesslike about the sale of your work and buyers won't feel that you are arbitrarily inventing prices as you go along, contingent on the buyer's ability to pay.

Finally, the artist had invited several of her artist friends. This was done, I think, to give her confidence and support. It was also to add color to the evening—we artists are such colorful types!—and to keep the subject of the event where she wanted it: on art. Of course, she had invited artists whom she knew she could trust not to undermine her evening. We discussed our own work, naturally, but also engaged in conversations with other guests about her work and were genuinely pleased whenever a work sold.

By the end of the evening, a significant amount of work had been sold. I think all of the artists who were there were encouraged by the success of the event. It was clear to all of us that this artist had worked from the beginning with a definite plan and had succeeded because she had given every step serious attention.

CHAPTER 11

Art in the Home

Art Appreciation in Real Life
Sharon Reeber

On a recent business trip to Portland, I visited my sister, a professional who has lived there for a long time. As I had never spent time there, I quizzed her about the area's galleries. She is interested in a variety of art, is well-educated, has disposable income, and owns original art, so I assumed she would at least be familiar with the more prominent ones. But all she could do was provide me with a map. She doesn't like to go into the galleries.

"Why not?" I asked.

"They make me uncomfortable," she replied. "I don't feel like I can just walk in and look around without knowing about the artists or intending to buy something." For the same reasons, she has never gone to an opening, even when invited.

For the working artist it's easy to forget just how much of a barrier the formal setting of a gallery poses to those who are interested in art but have not formed the habit of seeking out contemporary art. My sister is but one of many who feel out of place in a gallery. With her taste, income level, and the fact that she is now building a large home, she should be an ideal client—yet she steers clear of galleries. Our conversation gave me a fresh insight into what I perceive to be a stark contradiction between the standard gallery context and the way people really like to look at art.

I have just added two rooms to my home. The room above the new studio serves as a large dining room, dance floor, and gathering place. It was also designed with an informal art gallery in mind: It is light and open, sparsely furnished with expansive wall space.

At a recent party my paintings were illuminated by soft lamplight and candlelight. There was food on the table, music in the air, people were talking and dancing, and the rich colors of the paintings glowed from the walls. The guests were not focusing on the paintings, as at a museum, rather, the art was part of the atmosphere, adding a unique presence and emotion. The paintings were available to be looked at or glanced at or ignored. Like the savory hors d'oeuvres, they were there to be nibbled on visually all night. While some guests tuned them out, others could sample them in little snatches.

This is a lovely way to encounter art. Aesthetically, this is a vastly different experience from the walk/stop/look rhythm typical of a gallery or museum visit.

One of the guests I've known casually for a year or so apparently took advantage of the opportunity to enjoy my art. Although she knows I am an artist, it wasn't until late in the evening that I realized she had never before seen my work. She would classify herself as neither educated about nor interested in art. But she looked at my paintings that night. I thoroughly enjoyed hearing her reaction to my work, and I was honestly challenged by her questions. When my art was presented in the right context, she had no trouble confronting and responding to it. And we both benefited from the encounter.

Another surprising incident has caused me to focus on this quality of art experience. One of my paintings is on loan to a friend and hangs in the main room of her house. Her father, who lives next door to her, told me he sometimes stops in, sits in that room, reads, and enjoys that painting. He is having the glancing/glimpsing experience that allows him to savor the work. He had first seen this painting at a gallery exhibit of mine, and was attracted to it then, but since he spent less than an hour at an exhibit of twenty pieces, he couldn't do more than get an impression of it. To my surprise, he told me one morning over coffee that if his daughter didn't buy the painting, he would.

The surprise was because I've never thought of Dick as an art person. He does not read about or ponder contemporary visual art. He does not seek out exhibits in the city. He has visited the closest major museum maybe twice in the past 40 years. He does not care in the slightest about the art world and has no idea where my work fits into it.

Yet he is, upon closer consideration, an ideal art collector. Dick is somewhat eccentric, intellectually curious, and well-traveled. Last year he sold his dairy farm in order to enjoy his retirement. He is mature, experienced, and wealthy enough to confidently pursue his own interests. This month he is in Russia attending the Bolshoi Ballet several times a week and learning the language. Although he doesn't imagine himself an art collector, he does look at and occasionally buy art on his travels. Though he doesn't have a gallery goer's habits, when given the opportunity he turns out to be an art appreciator and supporter. I suspect there are more like him out there.

The gallery's context as a viewing and sales venue, along with the behavior patterns that the gallery scene implies, will not serve many artists or many potential art patrons. Personally, I love going to museums and galleries, and I do this joyfully and frequently. As an artist I have embraced this art habit.

But many people who have seen my work in my home or the homes of people who collect my work do not do galleries, yet they can and do appreciate the work. They relish it. They think about it. They ask me intelligent, insightful questions about it. They respond to it, and I love that, because a response from a viewer is the other half of the communication link that I initiate by making art.

In thinking back on my own aesthetic experiences, I have most fully enjoyed, appreciated, and considered pieces that I have encountered in more intimate settings like private homes because of that context. The world surrounding the experience of seeing the work is filled with many other positive impulses: being with people I like, doing something enjoyable and comfortable, seeing the work integrated into a room with life. Especially important is the opportunity to glimpse, notice, or study the art as I want, over an extended period of time. It is rewarding to visit with art at a leisurely pace instead of in the intense atmosphere of an exhibit where you may confront several years of an artist's thoughts and efforts packed into one large, well-lit room. I assume most art collectors, major or minor, like to live with their art where they read, eat, cook, socialize, or play, and do not set aside an exclusive art-viewing room. So that's where I want my work to be—in the home and in the heart.

As I continue to evolve my goals for my work and my life, one recurring theme is, simply stated, "Get the work out." Corollaries are "Get the thought out" and "Get the message out." Don't hold back. What a waste to have artwork in storage where it cannot be shared. So I actively pursue opportunities to exhibit my work through existing avenues: commercial and nonprofit galleries, juried shows, corporate exhibit spaces.

But I'm beginning to think that this leaves out many of my potential appreciators. In an ideal world I would always get compensated for putting my work on display. But based on past experience, it rarely happens. So when my work is not in an exhibit, I offer to hang it in the homes of interested friends and supporters. One could argue that there are two elements to my viewers: those who just look, and those who buy and support my work. But to the degree that these are distinct elements, I need both. I have a lot to give and so do they.

CHAPTER 12

Studios at Art Centers

Creativity on Display

Roberta Morgan

The Torpedo Factory, named for the original use of the building, states boldly in their visitors' guide, "There are more than 150 artists working here, on three floors, in a fantastic variety of styles and media . . . . We invite you to join us, observe our creative processes, ask questions and learn."

Art centers, like this one in Alexandria, Virginia, are places where art is brought to the public through performances, gallery exhibits, and educational programs. Often they're also places where art is created in spaces set aside for individual artists.

These studios offer many benefits to artists, including sales, increased exposure, and the opportunity to work with other artists. But artists need to weigh their needs and the needs of their work before choosing such a studio. "An artist needs to consider the fact that art centers have different types of traffic, and they need to match that with the work they are doing," said Richard Zandler, director of Montpelier Cultural Arts Center, located between Baltimore and Washington.

The opportunity to make sales can be an attraction to having a studio in an art center. With 750,000 visitors annually, the Torpedo Factory delivers on that expectation. Collage artist Gwendolyn Graine confirms this, though she avoids commercial emphasis when marketing her art. "I generally sell two works a month, though some people sell much more than that here. A couple of galleries have seen my work here, and picked it up, but I didn't sell as much through them as I have through my studio here." Graine will correct anyone who thinks her studio at the Torpedo Factory is an added expense: "I have always paid all my art expenses plus through the studio. It supports itself and makes a little more."

This matches the experience of David Daniels, a sculptor at The ART-WORKS at Doneckers, in Ephrata, Pennsylvania. "It's always been profitable for me, and you get a lot of exposure you wouldn't get otherwise," he said. Like the Torpedo Factory, ARTWORKS has four floors of studios and galleries in a building that used to be a shoe factory. However, this center is less fine-arts-oriented than the Torpedo Factory, with about forty studios, and more space devoted to commercial use.

Smaller art centers, with less traffic, are focused differently. They give artists recognition and publicity, but don't aim to make their spaces commercially viable markets. Artists working in them readily point this out. Montpelier, with a traffic volume of 30,000 visitors a year, takes this approach. Fiber artist Roslyn Logsdon said of her studio there, "It has given me recognition, but actual sales from the place haven't been many." Her sales come from other sources: "I exhibit the wall hangings nationally and in craft galleries in the Northeast—so I more than break even."

Like Montpelier, Rockville Arts Place is oriented away from commercial marketing. A small art center, R.A.P. has two galleries and a handful of studios, and it has wasted no time establishing itself as a place where quality in the visual arts can be enjoyed. For painted-furniture maker Michael Pollack, the situation at R.A.P. is structured to prevent exposure from becoming commercialized. "The purpose is not so much to sell as to have a place to work where the public can see you working," he said. Sharing studio space with Pollack, goldsmith and designer Lucinda Callahan added, "I did not come here to sell my stuff—I always have more than enough to do, I never need a job."

Artists stress interaction with other artists when asked to list the advantages of an art center studio. "You have a community," said Logsdon. "Even though I'm the only weaver, there are other fiber people here." Graine agrees. "I get a lot of good feedback here . . . artists come in and they tell you a lot about technique."

Other benefits include having a workplace away from home. "Having a studio here helps me to structure myself," Callahan said. At home she "would get into bad routines, like working late at night and then getting annoyed when people call at nine A.M." Painter Betsy Anderson at the Torpedo Factory added, "At home I tend to think I have to do the wash or do something in the yard, and that distracts me from my art. It's good to get here where my only job is my painting."

Such advantages shouldn't obscure the fact that this arrangement isn't for everyone. "A public facility is not a private place," said Logsdon. "You have to have a side of you that's ready to work with the public." Adapting to visitors is possible, though. "People ask me how I can stand the traffic, but I've been here from the beginning [of the building's use as an art center] and the traffic built up gradually. I don't mind it," said Graine. When asked if the traffic requires supplementing work done at the art center with work at a home studio, Graine reported, "I do the most creative part of my work here—it's the boring laborious parts I do at home. I really create everything here."

Some artists need to locate where traffic is lighter. Callahan started out in a retail situation where traffic was heavy, like the Torpedo Factory. "I found that grueling—what happened was you worked there all day and then came home and worked more seriously all night." This resembles Daniels' experience at ARTWORKS. "I still maintain another studio a block away," he said. "I bring work here to finish it."

Art centers recruit prospective artists through similar methods. Normally the management of an art center will supervise the selection process to make sure that a variety of work is being done on the premises. Usually an outside juror is hired, and sometimes a selection panel, to screen applicants for the quality of their work.

Rent for studios is set at a dollar amount per square foot of space per year. ARTWORKS has the highest rent of the centers reviewed here, $12 per square foot as of this writing. Montpelier charges $5 to $5.25, the Torpedo Factory $6.93, and R.A.P. charges $8 per square foot. Occasionally R.A.P. sponsors a competition that awards a studio for 6 months rent free. Additionally, some art centers have special equipment, like printing presses, available for an extra charge.

While creativity starts with the individual, it is part of a dialogue with a wider community. Diverse art centers bring varied opportunities to artists seeking to link up with an artistic community as well as with the public at large.

CHAPTER 13

Commissions

Commissions: Some Considerations
Barbara Dougherty

An outdoor show for sculpture had a statement posted on their announcement board that addressed the issue of "how to be an artist." It said things like: chase moonbeams, build forts with blankets, hug trees, cultivate moods, plant impossible gardens, and refuse to be responsible.

At the bottom of the statement it should have added: Beware of all commissions.

The last commission I accepted turned into a problem, of course. When I accepted it I had a feeling that this would be the case. In the arrangement I agreed to receive phone calls for 3 months from my customer whenever the sunset sky in Santa Barbara had a particular vibrant look. It was expected I would view this sky so it would be the essential ingredient in a watercolor I was to render. My client wanted two paintings. One was to have this sky and one was to have a buttermilk sky. These phone calls came usually at the most inopportune moments. My customer would then talk for so long that by the time I viewed the sky the strong color had faded to dusty hues. Despite my instincts and this evidence of peculiarity I kept the commission—I was charmed by this woman who had studied art and worked at an art museum.

When the day came to deliver the paintings, I called my client to relate the fact that I had not yet done the work. I am like this with commissions. I have a hard time getting to them and usually start only hours before they are due. I was calling to admit this. However, my customer never gave me the chance. Her concern was that she had expected to close escrow on the sale of her home, but the close had been delayed. She was anxious about her own lack of funds. Without telling her of my own situation, I agreed to an extended delivery date.

Again I procrastinated until just hours before this new delivery date. First I painted the sunset sky and then while that dried, I began the smaller piece with the buttermilk sky. I was not familiar with the term buttermilk sky but my customer had carefully described it. A visitor came to the studio just as I finished laying in the colors for the second piece and commented, "That's not a buttermilk sky—it's too white in color."

During every commission I have ever accepted (including a multitude of commissions when I was a production potter), I always have had a particular frantic moment of total loss of confidence. This was the moment. I agreed the sky was white but somehow my rendering fit the description I had recalled. If I called to verify with my customer I would also have to admit that I was just beginning the work. So I painted the buttermilk sky again using a butter color instead of a white.

The next day I called to arrange delivery and was again delayed by my customer because of circumstances beyond her control. (Circumstances beyond control are also part of a commission.) This time I went out and finished the pieces and set them aside. Three months later I went to deliver them. My customer looked at the smaller piece and said, "What is this?" I said (thinking I would prefer to be elsewhere) "Oh, a buttermilk sky." She said summarily, "No, it is not!" Then we looked at the next piece. She loved the sunset sky but asked me to change an element in the landscape. I refused. She decided to take the sunset piece anyway, but only on the grounds that I accept a further deposit and take the painting home to protect while she moved her household.

It is a year since I accepted the commission, she now has the piece on her wall, and she still owes me $150. At least my own obligations are complete. Sometimes this is the only satisfaction that comes from a carefully drawn contract.

The moral to the story is that I am as much a problem as my customer when it comes to doing commissions. Nevertheless, last week I ended up in a conversation with a potential customer over a potential commission. I never completed the contract, though, because all I could think of was buttermilk skies.

When I do agree to take a commission I use a contract because it accomplishes these important tasks:

- Discovering if I can negotiate with a potential client
- Resolving the issues of description, price and payment
- Resolving the issue of ownership of copyright for the finished pieces

- Resolving the issues of extra costs (travel, materials, etc.)
- Defining schedule of production, delivery, and installation
- Defining obligations in case of failure to perform by either party (including taking into account circumstances beyond control)
- In the case of certain commissions, resolving the issues of royalty, resale, limited use, distribution, supervision, and quality of reproduction

Sample contracts have been published and these can help you confront and declare the resolution of most of these issues. But often, sample contracts fail to give you the essential warnings. These are:

- The state you live in may have laws on "work for hire" and other state-specific laws that are not dealt with in the contract
- Tax responsibility is rarely declared in these contracts and should be
- Legal language is very particular—an "and," an "or," or an "and/or" can make an immense difference
- It is not easy to take a customer to court for breach of contract

There are two basic categories of commission customers. The first category is corporate and/or public commissions. These entities may have contracts for you to use but you should not assume that the contract or those making the contract have really carefully analyzed or researched their, or your, position. If you seek this type of work remember to find out if your payments might be delayed due to corporate accounting procedures.

The second customer category is the private commission. These are usually from a person wanting something they cannot make for themselves or cannot find anywhere. Sometimes they are the result of a person wanting something they cannot afford from someone else and you are a less expensive alternative. With these customers I spend a lot of time and effort getting swatches of color and pictures of similar images. With private customers, I adjust the deposit. I do just the opposite of what you would expect. If the customer gives me an indication that they will be hard to please, I charge a smaller deposit so that if the situation becomes impossible it is easier to end. Also, a smaller deposit keeps me from spending an inordinate amount of time and energy on a commission without verifying that I will be compensated as I go along.

Remember in a contract to specify if the framing or pedestal for the piece is your responsibility, and whether or not you will deliver the piece. Also remember that although most sample contracts for commissioned work have terms for the artist to retain the copyright, you can sell the copyright for additional consideration (money). You can give a customer a limited right to publish and distribute work and retain the copyright, but you must be very specific. Warning: Do this with caution—in some instances you may have in effect transferred the copyright without knowing it.

Arrangements between the artist and the customer, the gallery, or the public entity have lately been examined and reexamined on the basis of resolving difficulties before work begins or before the value of finished work is risked. Communication on these subjects and sharing new information has to be a task for all of us especially since basic human agreements have become so complicated.

In the process of adapting the contract technology to suit your needs, don't forget that when you accept a commission to fulfill the vision in another person's mind it is in itself an impossible task. Even a commission that allows you to create your image for a specific site can be problematic. Any time someone else has an inclination towards the look of a project then the root of the project is shared vision. And that is the essential difficulty in commissions.

PART 4

Fine Art Expos, Fairs, and Festivals

Woman in Mid Life, 1993, silver gelatin print, Jan Camp, Berkeley, California

CHAPTER 14

An Overview of Booth-Style Shows

The Benefits of Exhibiting at Booth Shows
Michelle T. Carter

Artistic visibility and career support through meeting collectors and dealers are the benefits of exhibiting your artwork at booth-style shows. Shows are worth the time, money, and effort if the artist is willing to do the homework regarding the profile of the exhibition and the preparation for being an exhibitor.

Before sending your check to reserve a booth space, research the show's reputation and profile as stacked up against the following ten questions:

- What does the fee include?
- What is the show timeline?
- How many times has it been presented in its current location?
- How many exhibitors have participated in past shows?
- What is the location of the show in terms of existing buyer traffic?
- What is the advertising and promotion plan to attract buyers?
- What is the profile of the buyer?
- What are the categories of artwork presented?
- What has been the success of other exhibitors in past years?
- How did they do it?

The Show Profile

One of the first questions always asked by an artist is, "How much will it cost me to exhibit at the show?" Shows are an obvious investment of time and money, so once the booth fee is determined a more realistic question to ask might be, "What do I get besides a 10'x10' space for the time and money I spend?" The abbreviated marketing term is "ROI," or return on investment. A related question to ask is, "What is included, or not included, in the booth fee? How much are the extras?"

Find out whether the show has been presented in the area before, how many exhibitors there were, and how many people attended. It is always more desirable if a show has created a prior show reputation to attract quality buyers and exhibitors. The designated booth fee is usually based on the promoter's ability and reputation to bring qualified buyers into the show to create sales opportunities for the exhibiting artists.

A seasoned show promoter knows timing and location are important factors supporting sales for the exhibitors. If the length of the show is only a few days, it will probably be scheduled on a weekend. If the show is several weeks or months long, the promoter will probably schedule the show to coincide with a tourist season, holiday celebration, or other event.

Always consider other activities in the area. Determine if the activities will enhance customer traffic or detract from attendance.

Also consider the current economic status and demographics of where you intend to show. The sales will only be as rewarding as the discretionary income available in the show's geographical area.

A show's success for an artist will depend on the number of sales and contacts made during the exhibition. Sales is a known numbers game; therefore the show promoter's job is to bring the prospective buyers through the gate. Be sure the location has existing customer traffic, and/or the promoter has an advertising and promotion plan to attract buyers to the show site. Current trends show people have less available time and are looking for brief escapes within a convenient time frame and distance for their busy schedules.

The promoter's responsibility is to attract buyers to the location with an effective advertising message and promotion plan. An artist should be able to determine the reach and the depth of the communication plan by assessing the placement of print advertising, public relations stories, and broadcast announcements.

A key factor when marketing a product or an event is to "know your buyer." The promoter certainly knows the profile of his potential buyer; this knowledge enables him to know how to reach his desired audience to build the gate numbers. The promoter will know where to target direct mail announcements, designate advertising, position promotional posters, and place broadcast announcements.

It is also vital for the artist to know the buyer profile prior to deciding whether to become an exhibitor.

Of equal importance is to know the price point and artistic profile of the other exhibitors. For example, it could be a waste of time for an artist doing original paintings to exhibit where only posters are being exhibited. It might also be a waste of time for an artist to offer ceramics at $1,000 or more per piece if the average buyer at the show spends a total of only $100 or so.

Knowing who attends the show and who exhibits at the show is a good indicator of whether the exhibit is right for an artist, especially if he is able to attain show feedback from a previous exhibitor. "I'm going to school on you" is a golfer's term for watching the other player on the course. The purpose is to learn from the fellow golfer's experience in a particular situation. Networking with other artists is an added bonus of exhibiting your art on the show circuit. If the situation presents itself where a fellow artist will generously share the road map of his successes and failures, TAKE NOTES!

Upon determining a particular show is a good fit, an artist must address the show preparation to maximize the benefits of participating.

The Groundwork

It is important to review the exhibitor package supplied by the show promoter to establish an effective timeline for show tasks and to determine what booth materials need to be ordered. The exhibitor package is usually self-explanatory regarding placing orders for display walls, electrical outlets, lights, furniture, floor covering, and signs. The artist may also be required, or opt, to provide his/her own booth. If that is the case, it is wise to consider a lightweight, easy-to-assemble display unit.

An artist can simplify pre-show tasks by outlining a list of tasks to complete before the exhibition. The list might include items to be shipped with the booth and artwork, such as a toolbox, printed sales materials and invoices, calculator, stapler, breath mints, pens, guest book, etc. To support an organized show effort it is vital that an artist adhere to the directed timelines designated for ordering equipment and shipping inventory.

Booth Design

The design of the booth is an important consideration for attracting potential buyers. A common mistake when selecting art to place in the booth is to "show everything." A cluttered booth only confuses the buyer. Artworks should be grouped to create a visual dialogue with one another, enticing the viewer to join in the artistic conversation.

Installation height and placement is important for establishing a relationship with the people approaching the booth. Pedestals and shelves will allow the artist to create better viewing opportunities for the buyer. A tall director's chair can be placed to the outside of the booth, so if the artist wishes to sit he will still be at eye level with buyers.

Also of importance for attracting interest is color and lighting. The color of the wall-covering and the sign need to avoid competing with the work for the buyer's attention. It is proven people react to color. Many artists will opt for a subtle color combination to highlight certain qualities of their work.

Proper lighting will attract and focus the attention of the people walking by the booth. It is always advisable to investigate and select booth lighting with careful attention to heat and safety factors.

Visual Aids

Printed visual aids in a booth serve the purpose of educating potential buyers about the work. An artist might be expecting too much if he hopes to transform himself into a salesman during the show. His job is to create the quality artwork and present it to the potential buyer. Art sales involve 90 percent education and 10 percent sales skills; people buy art because they love the work. An effective wall installation of visual aids can educate the buyer and support sales.

A printed brochure can also support sales. A color reproduction representing the best of the work, with an artist statement (about the process) and biography (about the artist) could be framed and installed in the booth. Also next to each work of art should be a title card giving the artwork's title, size, medium, and price. An alternative is to leave the price off the title card and simply group all the prices on a separate piece of paper. Extra copies of the brochure and price list should be available for interested buyers.

Publicity and Communication

The show promoter will have his marketing agenda to create visibility and awareness for the show, but a show's success can be enhanced by promoter/artist teamwork. The artist should have a communications plan for creating a rewarding show experience.

If the show is in an area where he has exhibited before, he should send a postcard announcement to his buyers and potential buyers in the area, inviting them to visit the booth to see the new work.

Before the show, local dealers should be researched. Appointments with dealers representing a compatible art portfolio bring the opportunity for new representation.

A presentation package would consist of slides, slide and price list, bio, statement, and SASE. The contents can be placed into a pocket folder and a 9"x12" envelope for mailing. Send the package with a cover letter to the prospective dealer requesting an appointment. A follow-up phone call would confirm the appointment or personally invite the dealer to the artist's booth.

Some artists exhibit at booth shows because they are interested in licensing opportunities, or in having work reproduced into a limited edition or an open edition reproduction. If this is the case, send a letter of invitation with a color visual aid to exhibiting publishers/distributors inviting them to stop by your booth.

Show Time and After

During the show, the artist's job is to welcome buyers and to be available to educate potential buyers/dealers about the work. On occasion, an individual may enter the booth and decide to critique the work with negative comments. This can adversely affect the buying atmosphere for other interested people. Rather than attempting to avoid the awkwardness of the moment, it is advisable to address the situation.

One option is to say to the outspoken individual, "I appreciate your reaction to the work. Perhaps there would be a more appropriate time for this discussion. A group of artists and I are meeting for coffee later. Perhaps you would like to join us and express your views at that time."

Art acquisition is a very personal choice, so a rule of thumb is to "agree to disagree" when discussing personal views about a particular work. There is, however, a time and place for constructive commentary. If the source is knowledgeable, the feedback is helpful to an artist. However, rude comments about the work in your booth are unacceptable.

If someone refuses to leave your booth, inform him that if he does not leave you will be forced to find the show promoter and have him ejected from the show. Then do it.

Remember: Your booth, like a temporary home, is your domain.

Regarding sales, an artist should have a copy of his business license and resale tax license at the show. The need for sales invoices and a cash box would depend upon the show's sale format. If the artist is handling sales independently, the ability to offer credit card acceptance would be an added support for sales.

During the show the artist should have interested individuals fill out 4"x6" client prospect cards for the purpose of post-show telemarketing and direct mail contact. The cards would ask for name, address, phone, and area of art interest. If an artist is considering future advertising in the show vicinity, as a marketing survey he should also ask how the individual found out about the show and what publications the prospective buyer reads.

The final success of a show is measured in its totality during the weeks and months following the exhibition. The artist's ability to contact the interested potential buyers and dealers will support a greater return on the initial investment of time and money for show participation. The obvious importance of remaining in contact with prospective clients in the months after the show is future sales and representation opportunities.

If an artist is willing to do the homework regarding show profile, and willing to prepare the groundwork for exhibition, booth shows have the potential of bringing to the artist the buyers and dealers able to offer career visibility and support. With that in mind, here are some last tips:

- The design of the booth is an important consideration for attracting potential buyers. The color of the sign and the wall-covering need to avoid competing with the art for the buyer's attention.
- A common mistake when selecting art to place in the booth is to "show everything." A cluttered booth only confuses the buyer. Visual sales aids and a well-prepared portfolio serve the purpose of educating the buyer about the artist's complete body of work.
- Attend one or two of the shows you're thinking of participating in before making the commitment to participate. Attend the expo in the city where you plan to exhibit—the Chicago experience, for example, might differ from the New York show. Virginia Beach might be different from Coconut Grove.
- Take detailed notes. What do you like about the show? What do you dislike? Observe what works and what doesn't appeal to you: displays,

selling techniques, the way exhibitors are dressed, booth locations, etc.

- If possible, talk to exhibiting artists and find out how they're doing. Just be sure you do not get in the way of their interactions with attendees.
- Be sure you know precisely what you want to accomplish. Set goals, figure out strategies, make plans.
- Begin planning at least 6 months before the show. Set up ways you can maximize the benefits of participating in the show.

CHAPTER 15

fine Art Expos

Onstage!

Barbara Dougherty

Last September I exhibited *Art Calendar* magazine in the publications pavilion at the Las Vegas Artexpo. I had set up my booth; it was the first morning of the exhibit. I had arranged my table, straightened signs and products, and directed the lights.

One of the first people to approach my booth was an artist. She and a group of other artists had formed a gallery and had taken a booth at Artexpo to display their art. None of them had ever been to an expo-style art show, and they were not confident. At her request I went to view their booth.

Arranging Your Display

Nothing had been set up with an eye to the needs of potential patrons or clients. They had paperwork laid out in an unsightly fashion. There was no crowd-stopper, a particularly significant piece that would stop people in their tracks during their treks around the displays. The chairs were set for their own comfort; care hadn't been taken to preserve access to the artwork. Viewing distance had not been imagined at all.

In other words, though these artists had poured their hearts and souls and pocketbooks into the show, they hadn't spent sufficient time thinking about customer interaction.

First we rearranged the booth. We pulled the print rack out of the way; we got rid of the chairs; we put paperwork out of sight. We re-hung the artwork by grouping artists. We moved the table from the back to the side so it didn't block the entry and traffic flow to the back wall.

Opening Lines; Continuing the Conversation

In my experience, the worst greeting at an art exhibition is a question, even something like "Hello, may I help you?" Questions put viewers immediately on the defensive. Unless someone has approached your booth with great determination and a hunger for your work, the best response you'll get is "Thanks, I'm just looking." So remember the tendency for people to respond tentatively, and create your approach accordingly.

I like to start with "I am the artist if you have any questions." Then I immediately follow this with information, like "These are watercolors and I like to paint them on location." Information tends to direct the viewer's attention to the art; I know he *wants* to look at it, and it's my task to make it comfortable for him to do so.

I cannot assume that the new viewer will, in one glance, truly be able to see the artwork. Thus, I prepare something else more personal to say, almost as if I'm sharing a secret. For instance, I might say "This painting is of the late afternoon. I wish I could have captured the light as it was that day." Sharing something intimate about your work, or something about the creative process, is the kind of information that show attendees like to glean from contact with artists. This information is among artists' best-kept secrets.

I try to reveal my feelings about the piece. Very few of my paintings are completely comfortable to my eye. By revealing the ways I desire better execution, I find myself in successful conversations with potential clients. I simply present myself sincerely as an individual trying hard with doubts and failures just like everyone else. This attitude opens many doors for me.

Practice greetings and opening statements about your pieces.

Besides the verbal approach, the physical approach to a viewer can be very difficult in such limited space. For example, if you are sitting down, rising to face the viewer is confrontational. On the other hand, if you *don't* rise your behavior could be interpreted as rude or uninterested. Yet without doing *some* sitting at your display, you will physically stress yourself. The solution? Obtain a nice-looking tall director's chair that allows you to sit, yet be at the eye level of most of the people who approach your display.

How to Deal with Typical Viewer Responses

If you can create a comfortable approach to viewers, and if you find yourself in a conversation with a seriously interested party, you must be prepared for the inevitable directions art-world conversations take:

- "Yes, I would like to buy this."

- "I'll be back."
- "I might be back," or "I'll have to check with my wife."
- "Not now but perhaps in a few months."
- "Are you interested in showing with our gallery?"
- "I would like to publish your work."
- "Hi, I'm an artist too . . . [I have no intention of buying anything.]"
- "Talk, talk, talk, talk, talk. [I have no intention of buying anything.]"
- "Well, your work evokes and redefines the meaning of life, but frankly I think your technique and composition show some *blah blah blah* . . . [I have no intention of buying anything.]"

If someone wants to buy something on the spot, great. Calmly complete the transaction. Accept the check or the credit card, do any verifications you need to do, offer to hold the piece until the buyer is finished walking the exhibit hall or until the show ends, and fill out the show pass which allows the person to take the piece out of the convention center. Be sure to have them fill out a client card.

Actually, "I'll be back" is the most common response. Generally someone will say he is going to look at the rest of the show and come back. Though it isn't likely he really will, you can help to entice his return. One way is to hand him a brochure of your work and say that when he comes back you will give him a pre-printed list of your show specials. If you have a list of already prepared show specials, you won't look like a bargain basement, you will convey the impression that this show is a special setting for your special sales. If a potential client walks away knowing that a pre-printed list of show specials is available, they have the warm impression that you are negotiable within ethical boundaries. And if the "I'll be back" wants to see the list of your specials right then and there, give it to him—you just might make a transaction on the spot.

If someone says "I might be back" or "I'll have to check with my wife" he's an unlikely prospect. Nonetheless, before *anyone* walks off, make sure you get his name and address.

Besides dealing with direct purchasers, you might also find yourself in the position of being approached by a gallery or a publishing company. Do not find yourself surprised by these people—be prepared. Know what commission rates and other terms you will and won't accept. Have your questions printed and ready for these potential inquiries. Also, many of these trade buyers will ask to make an appointment with you rather than talk to you on the spot; think about times and environments you would be comfortable in setting appointments.

For gallery owners, list questions like:

- How do you promote a new artist during the first year or two of representation?
- Do you use contracts?
- Do you require geographic exclusivity? What is the region?
- Do you do the framing?
- Who is your insurance company?
- How many artists do you represent?
- What is your commission structure?
- Do you charge the artist any other fees for any gallery services?
- Who pays the costs of the opening reception?
- Do you print invitations? how many? Who pays for the printing and postage?
- What P.R. do you do?
- Do you share the names of purchasers with the artist?

You may have many more questions. The point is, if you have a questionnaire ready for gallery owners who approach you, you present yourself as someone prepared for that opportunity. I ask dealers to take a questionnaire with them and return it to me later during the show. That gives them a reason to return to my booth—we have a chance to think about each other; he has a chance to see the rest of the show and evaluate my work again; I have the chance to see more clients and evaluate him again.

Here are some questions you can ask publishers:

- What style of reproduction do you publish?
- How many artists do you currently represent?
- How many images do you produce each year?
- What are your catalogs like?
- How many catalogs are printed?
- How often does your catalog come out?
- Do you offer an advance against royalties?
- What is your distribution network?
- What do you do to promote the artist?

Some conversations won't require printed materials or questionnaires. Nonetheless you should think about them before you go.

For instance, you will be approached at the show by other artists. While dialogue with other artists can be the best part of the event, it can also destroy the potential for other conversations that could lead to a transaction. If you allow a situation where a potential client has to interrupt, then it will be extremely difficult for you to make a successful contact. Let your fellow artists know that you want to be a part of the community, but you are serious when it comes to representing yourself and the visiting time is after-hours.

That said, think of what you *do* wish to discuss with other artists; think of the information you would like to learn from them while you're at the show. For instance, if you are a sculptor you might want information on foundries. If you're thinking about getting published, you might wish to discover other artists' experiences with publishers. Maybe you want information about other shows.

You'll also need to be ready to deal with time-gobblers. I have found that they are generally accompanying someone else and think they're being polite by engaging you in conversation. You would like to end the conversation. It is tough, but you can still say it kindly: "Excuse me, but the hours of exhibition here are limited. Though I enjoy conversation it's not appropriate for me to have extended conversations at my booth." Your booth is your domain.

In the case of the person who thinks he's a critic, he is behaving absolutely inappropriately. You should interrupt him immediately and say, "I'm sorry, but this is not the appropriate time or place for this discussion. Here's my brochure; if you will leave your card I will be happy to talk with you after the show."

Other Important Show Preparations

Know your aspirations. Define your goals before you get to the show. Do you want to be a fine artist represented by galleries and museums? Do you want a publishing company to reproduce your images—and if they do, will it help you achieve your professional aspirations? It is not enough just to want to make money; you need an exceptional kind of mental clarity to do well at a competitive venue of this kind.

You also need to know clearly the amount of production you are really capable of. You might be asked, for example, to enter into a contract that will require you to produce twenty pieces each year. Are you capable of it? Do you want to do that? Know your strengths and limitations before you go.

Also, before going to the show you will need to attend to many details such as shipping your work to the show, ordering booth supplies, and so on. Your exhibitors' manual should have all the information you need; read it carefully at least a couple of months before the show, and flag pages you're fairly sure you will need to consult as the show approaches. The promoter's manual will be your bible in terms of the mechanics of preparing for the show. And, if you have questions about dealing with the union or any of those mechanics, call the promoter and ask; they have staff there to help you have a successful show.

Preparing for and Initiating Follow-Up

Many people come to fairs and expos with business cards—collect these. If no card is available, write their information on pre-printed 4"x6" client cards. Spend some time with their contact information and rate the potential customer. I use a scale of one to ten to mark my intuition of the potential for a successful transaction to that person. Your list of names and addresses, with your ratings, will help you determine what kind of follow-up to do with all your potential clients after the show. Also, the little bit of time you spend imagining the nature of that person will help you remember his name and face—if that person *does* come back and you recall his name, you have created a wonderful potential for a successful transaction. "People do business with people they know."

Whenever you pass out literature—whether it's brochures, tear sheets, business cards, questionnaires, order forms, or catalogues—always have your name and contact information on all the sheets. When people collect literature at a show, it's easy for them to misplace literature that is supposed to go together.

Each day, as the show ends, it is important to ask yourself these questions:
- What was the best contact I made today?
- What was the best conversation I had today? Why?
- What did I learn today?

Immediately after getting back home, write notes to the people you decide were the best contacts you made, and express your feelings about the contact or conversation.

There is a lot to do and a lot of preparation when you take on a project of this magnitude. It's hard and rigorous, and the risks are large—but so are the potential rewards.

CHAPTER 16

Art Fairs
and Festivals

Outdoor Art Shows

Barbara Dougherty

The 1990s are heralding changes in the economy of the entire world. It should not be a surprise therefore that the business environment for art should be reassessed. Artists, rather than agents or galleries, must be the ultimate source of marketing direction and stamina. The opportunities to meet the public and exhibit art must be recognized, revitalized, and adapted.

The first project in marketing for an artist should be the identification of goals. Personal goals must take into account the number of art projects an artist can realistically accomplish in a given time. Then an artist begins to describe a plan or plans for marketing that art.

After defining goals, a list of projects and activities can be made that will foster and support success.

A viable project often overlooked by fine artists is to participate in outdoor art shows. I accomplish three objectives this way:

1. Adding the names of potential customers to my mailing list
2. Advertising and becoming better known as an artist
3. Selling paintings

However, sales are never my primary objective when I exhibit at outdoor art shows. I confess that I expect the public to be skeptical of the credentials and the quality of the exhibited work. Therefore, in that particular environment, personally extending an invitation to potential customers—to my gallery or other more formal upcoming exhibits—is my primary objective. The honing and limiting of my expectations of sales has led to the initiation of many successful negotiations. Sometimes an attitude of anticipation of sales can actually keep them from occurring.

Preparations for attending outdoor art shows include first and foremost getting ready to meet the potential customer. The first task then is to form an image of this person. To do so, I must find out the description of the community that attends the show. This is essential homework. It includes knowing the type of homes in which the customer may live, and the basic economic activities in the area. It also helps to know the number of years that the show has existed, and the style of art that is advertised in show promotion materials. In other words, who will come to see this art show? What do they expect to see?

I will soon be attending a show in Newport Beach, California. I have never been to this show but in talking to the promoter I found that tourists, not local residents, will be expected. This means that I must include in my presentation materials a clear indication that I am willing to offer shipping for purchases. This is an effort I would spend little time on if I had found that the expected public was primarily local residents.

In speaking with some local hotels and the Visitors and Tourists Bureau, I found that over 60 percent of the tourist public at Newport Beach were actually from inland areas no more than 100 miles from this popular seacoast resort, that the average income of the tourist was $32,000, that married couples were the most likely visitors, and that the average age was between 40 and 62.

The average age description of the purchaser of my paintings over the last 10 years matches the age description of the tourists expected at the Newport show. So I have decided to take on the extra expense of hiring a friend to help me at my display. The most important task for my friend is to help me gather the names and addresses of potential customers. For this I provide a form. The form contains a brief statement of my experience and commitment to art as well as my name and address. Many times it is more effective to encourage that the form be mailed back to me than to have it filled out at the show.

On the form, before I give it out, I note what I believe to be the age of the customer and my intuited sense of the likelihood of that person making a purchase. A rating of 10 means it is unlikely whereas a rating of 1 means it is very likely. In other words, a rating of "50+4" means a person older than 50 with a more than casual interest in my work. This rating process later helps me make decisions regarding customer follow-up.

Even though selling is not my first objective at outdoor art shows, I nevertheless do not exclude the possibility. Because of the information I obtained before the Newport show, I decided to purchase two exhibition areas rather than just one—I wanted to show more of my larger works. If the description of the public had been tourists from a further distance, I would have probably planned a smaller display with more transportable pieces.

When I plan a display for an outdoor art show, I plan my "crowd stopper." This is the piece(s) of extraordinary impact. The main impact of an extraordinary piece at an outdoor art show is that it helps the exhibitor gain a public identity. It also tells people the highest price of the work available at your booth. When I was a potter at outdoor art shows, I created a sculptural fountain that was powered by a car battery. As an agricultural artist, I use at least two 48"x72" framed watercolors as crowd stoppers.

When you go to display a work of art, you have to ask yourself the question, "Why would anybody look at my work?" If you have a really nice display and really nice work, the question is, "Do I have a crowd stopper?" The crowd stoppers are exciting in terms of artistic development because they let my imagination loose with what I can create that will stop the crowd.

One crowd stopper that worked exceptionally well was a 300-piece spiral wind chime composed of one large and many small pottery Gabriels blowing on trumpets. The piece sold instantly to the owner of a newly opened restaurant that happened to be called "Gabriel's."

When I set up my display, whether it is for an outdoor exhibition or an indoor setting, I make sure my display booth is organized and uncluttered. I use only one sign. It is a simply designed banner of self-adhesive vinyl letters. The letters are attached to a plastic tarp about one by three feet. The banner notes "shipping available" and that I accept credit cards. Mostly it contains my name and a statement of my art as a commitment to the vanishing agricultural lands— a statement that helps the public know my identity.

An overlooked but important ingredient of outdoor art display is the chair that will accompany the display. I use a tall director's chair. The taller chair allows me to engage in conversation without either being rude or too forward with my customer. Countless times with regular chairs I have experienced the customer back away when out of politeness I would simply rise from my seated position.

I never put price stickers on artwork. I prefer to be attentive to the attitude of a customer looking for a price, and I prefer to provide a catalog. Do not wait until someone asks you for a price; a physical gesture of even just looking for a price should be responded to immediately. I usually say something like "I am the artist if you have any questions." When I do give the price of a piece of artwork, I then immediately begin to share some "inside" information about the piece. Inside information can be a statement of technique or inspiration. It should not be a canned or practiced phrase but more a personal response to the interest of the viewer. The inside information statement can then be followed by assurances like guarantees about originality and the artwork's permanence.

Attitude decisions, display plans, and the formation of objectives are the basic work of preparing to exhibit at an outdoor art show. As these tasks are accomplished and the costs are encountered, the all-too-familiar questions surface: "Is the effort worth the cost? Can I sell some artwork to defray the expense?"

I must earn at least $500 to cover travel costs and overnight lodging. Some of this cost is just the time to prepare for the show. Often at outdoor shows, problems with the weather, particularly wind and rain, exclude the possibility of earning enough to cover the costs. I find that despite the risks and the costs, which I include in my budget as advertising expenses, the rewards generally justify the risks.

One of the most important benefits of this type of show is that I have the opportunity to meet and converse with other artists. This unique environment has been the greatest resource in my career for obtaining information on technique—both for the art and the marketing.

In fact, one of the greatest shows of my career was in Kernville, California. There was intense rain through all 3 days of the exhibition and I spent most of my time underneath an umbrella with an artist whose work I admire. While under the umbrella he shared with me a sense of his attitude towards his work and marketing which for me has been a constant source of inspiration. Although at this show I made no sales, countless sales have been made since then because of our conversation.

I have exhibited at outdoor art shows on the East and West Coast for the last 20 years. The following are some of the practices that work for me:

- Even if I have to rent a canopy, I prefer this for display.
- My display stands are always painted white and I keep the art at eye level.
- Display units that are slightly tilted rather than strictly vertical are more effective.
- Business cards are not left to be grabbed—they must be requested.
- There are always better areas for exhibition and it is worth paying more for these areas.
- A good show takes a great effort—thus, overnight accommodations should restore rather than exhaust me.
- A display plan should include an area where the viewer can easily stand away from the traffic flow of moving crowds.
- Most of the paintings should be framed.
- Display bins for prints or unframed paintings should be stable and easy to access.
- Extending the ability to make purchases by accepting credit cards will improve sales.
- Some credentials are essential such as an award, a well-displayed article, or a recommendation. Credentials must be carefully displayed.
- Use accessory lighting whenever possible.
- Always have packaging materials available so people can take your artwork, safely, with them.

The success of participation in this type of art marketing event can never be measured by the amount of sales made at the event. The real work of a show begins when you get home. If you take the time to add names to your mailing list and write thank-you letters and notes to potential customers as well as follow through on leads for other exhibition opportunities, you may find that you gain a greater respect for the effort. Essentially, the outdoor art show can then become your most effective advertising program.

Use Your Display to
Project a Positive Image
Constance Hallinan Lagan

When I present seminars teaching artists and craftspeople how to improve their professional image, I advise them to use effective merchandising displays.

There are two old adages I always share with students: first, we don't ever get a second chance to make a good first impression; second, we seldom improve when we have no model but ourselves. The points I make when I refer to these two timeworn bits of wisdom are that we must perfect the first image we offer the public, and we can improve that first impression by modeling successful exhibitors. Since our first encounter with the public is often at art and craft fairs and trade shows, where our display speaks for us, we should utilize the very best display setup we can afford.

There are two invaluable sources for effective display information: those who sell displays, and those who buy them—specifically, professional display manufacturers and suppliers, and artists and craftspeople.

Those Who Sell Displays

Begin your search for the best display setup for your business with professional display manufacturers and suppliers. Write or call them for their catalogs. You can find their contact information by reading advertisements in the Yellow Pages and art/craft trade publications.

After you receive their catalogs and supplemental promotional materials, compile a list of questions to ask each one on your list, and call them for the answers. Designing and purchasing a display setup is a big investment that can make the difference in just how successful you are on the fair/trade show circuit, so take the time now to contact these suppliers, gleaning as much information from them about their products and services as possible.

Some questions you should ask sellers of display setups include the following:
- What guarantees accompany your display setups?
- Do you have a showroom in my area where I can see them?
- Who are some of your customers, and where do they show their work? (Call these individuals and ask if they are pleased with their setup. If possible, visit them if or when they are in your area.)
- What are your payment terms?
- Do you service your products? If so, do you service it at my studio or must I return the display to you? Who pays the postage if the display must be returned to you for servicing?

- If you do not service your product, do you have authorized dealers who are trained to work on your product?

Those Who Buy Displays

The second source of information on displays is other artists and craftspeople who you know are successful marketers. Attend art and craft fairs as an observer, taking notes on which displays are attracting the most customers. Note the size and style of these display setups. Look at the shelving and lighting. Ask exhibitors where they purchased their displays. Many artists and craftspeople purchase the basic arrangement from one company, the shelving from another company, and the lighting from still another. Ask for details. Most exhibitors will share this information with you if you approach them when they are not busy serving customers and in a manner that is friendly and non-competitive.

Some questions you should ask buyers of display setups include the following:

- Where did you purchase your display?
- Did the shelving and lighting come with the setup?
- Is the display easy to assemble and take down?
- Have you had any problems with the product?
- Have you noticed an increase in sales since you have been using this display?
- Is your display guaranteed by the manufacturer or dealer?
- Has the manufacturer's or dealer's service been good?
- Have you bought from this company more than once?
- Would you like me to mention your name if I contact the company? (Sometimes businesses give commissions to old customers who bring in new customers.)

Anthony Robbins, author of *Unlimited Power* and *Awaken the Giant Within*, and one of the most popular motivational speakers of the 1990s, believes that all any one of us needs to do to be successful is to find out what successful people do and do it ourselves. So purchase your display setup from a successful manufacturer/supplier who has been recommended by a successful artist/craftsperson and you should be on your way to creating a great first impression—and to becoming successful yourself.

Protecting Yourself from Thieves and Shoplifters

Carolyn Blakeslee

If you have a gallery or participate in art festivals, you face the unfortunate possibility of theft. If you're aware of shoplifters' methods and stolen goods receptacles, you're in fairly good shape where preventing theft is concerned. You're in even better shape if you have a way of reviewing the events of the day if something *does* go wrong. The trick is to develop awareness without shutting down your clients', and your own, enjoyment of your booth or shop.

Be knowledgeable of the receptacles shoplifters use. Their carrying materials can be commonplace or creative—from diaper bags to sophisticated containers with false bottoms. Containers in which your goods can walk away include pockets, pocketbooks, briefcases, knapsacks, duffel bags, carry-on travel bags, baskets, shopping bags, loosely collapsed umbrellas, loose sweaters/coats/other oversized clothing, boots, wheelchairs, shopping carts, luggage carts, strollers, baby carriers, baby blankets, ponchos, backpacks, slings for broken arms, fake gift boxes, fake hollowed-out books, fake FedEx and other kinds of shipping boxes with false bottoms, and so on.

Keep thieves' methodology in mind. Some will simply pick-and-pack while you aren't looking. Some will try to lay a coat onto your countertop and scoop up whatever the garment covered. No matter what the method used, the thief is only able to take something if you're not looking or if you're not paying attention. It only takes a second for a thief to accomplish the deed.

If a shoplifter thinks you're paying too close attention, he might try to distract you. If a hubbub occurs nearby it could be an accomplice. The shoplifter might "accidentally" knock something over in your booth. He might ask to see something on the shelf behind you—you'll have to turn around to get it. She might point and ooh-and-ah at the object on the shelf above eye level, and you can't help but look at what she has pointed at. Maybe you'll be handed a large bill, causing you to root around in your wallet, money bag, or cash register to make change. Perhaps you must turn around to call in your credit card verifications. Then there are the old second-grader classics like "Your shoe is untied," "You have a run in your stocking," "Is that twenty-dollar bill over there yours?", "Look!", etc.—and your stuff vanishes as you look toward the phantom crashing airplane. Some thieves will puncture a tire or otherwise disable your vehicle, ask you for help, or use other tactics to lure you away from your display, your work, or your loaded vehicle. Refuse to be distracted by something loud and immediate going on—respond slowly and keep your stuff in your peripheral vision.

Besides basic awareness, other precautionary measures include the buddy system, locking up your goods at all times you're unable to directly watch them, disguising your money carrier, and having insurance.

The buddy system is a good idea whether you're a diver or an artist. If you're called away from your display to help someone, if you're distracted, or if you simply want to wander around the show and look at others' displays, you should have at least one teammate in charge of your display. Some shows provide booth-sitters.

Use locks to your advantage. Small and/or expensive items should always be in cases. One distraction tactic used by thieves is to disable your vehicle; if your vehicle seems to be disabled, lock your stuff in it before you examine it. Lock your cash register and display booths if you have to turn your back to approve a credit card.

Keep some of your cash in an innocent-looking receptacle like an empty Marlboro flip-top box of cigarettes in your Velcroed-shut pocket, and keep only change-making cash in your regular cash register. One of the principles here is to avoid putting all of your cash in one basket.

Have adequate insurance. I dislike insurance, and it's often difficult to collect, but nothing else substitutes for it when, God forbid, something bad happens.

Another protective device is a camera. If you have a video camera with a wide angle lens, you can plug it in via your adapter and record videos all day. It might take a few videos to capture footage of the entire day, but if at the end of the day you realize that something has been stolen, through your videotapes you might be able to discover who the shoplifter was. You can keep your camera in the open, mounted in a corner at ceiling level—this might be a deterrent to theft in and of itself. Or you can choose to hide your camera—if you are the victim of an out-and-out robbery hopefully the hidden camera won't be discovered and you'll have a tool for use in catching the robber and possibly in a criminal trial later.

Precautions must be balanced with courteous and professional behavior. If you come across as too watchful or careful, you run the risk of losing a customer for all time. For example, last year I was hunting for a dressy outfit for the Ray Charles concert we were planning to attend. Upon entering one shop I was asked to check my shopping bags and my pocketbook at the sales counter. They smiled when they said that, and they said it was the store policy with everyone, but I was still quite shocked. I didn't like the idea that someone thought I looked like a potential thief. Besides, if I checked my bags and my pocketbook at their sales counter, that would have given them the chance to steal *my* stuff. I will never go into that store again.

Your street smarts and precautionary measures will help you protect yourself against theft. But your caution must be balanced with your own level of enjoyment and the spirit of generosity and helpfulness that you communicate to your clients.

PART 5

*Juried Exhibitions
and Group Shows*

Content, 1991, watercolor, 11"x14", Barb Dougherty, Upper Fairmount, Maryland

CHAPTER 17

Juried Exhibitions

When It Comes to Competitions:
Interview with Nedra Tornay
Barbara Dougherty

Nedra Tornay, California watercolorist, past member of the board of directors of the National Watercolor Society (NWS), markets her work exclusively through juried-by-slide competitions.

Nedra Tornay is over 50, married, and has raised her family. She had no art instruction in high school or college; she attended business school and was a secretary. Her first art instruction was a landscape architecture night class at a California community college in 1983. After that she took only four more art courses.

Tornay began to enter juried competitions because she felt it was a way for a person without a traditional art background to gain credentials. She discovered that besides gaining standing and recognition, she could also win cash awards and make sales. Between 1987 and 1993, she has entered forty-nine competitions, been juried into thirty-two, won thirteen awards, and sold four pieces for as much as $9,500. She won her first award in 1987, and in 1989 she won a $2,000 award from the Adirondacks National Exhibition of American Watercolor. Her work has been published in national art magazines including *American Artist* and *The Artist's Magazine.*

She says she can overcome her fear of rejection and involve herself in a disciplined effort to enter juried competitions with slides, yet when it comes to approaching galleries she finds herself intimidated. Her fear of galleries is more a fear of interference than of rejection. Tornay feels free to experiment with her subject matter, technique, and creativity with her current strategy; her fear of galleries is that they would demand an amount of production and a similarity of style that would interfere with her artistic expression and growth.

Her success is partially attributable to good slides. She commented that as a member of the board of directors of NWS she got to see slides submitted by other artists. A large percentage of the slides were in violation of the slide criteria or of such poor quality that they could not even be considered.

Tornay showed me a plastic sheet of twenty slides of the work with which she has been successful. The slides, brilliant and clear, are done by professional labs—Tornay instructs them, "I want saturated color in my slides." Her work is photographed out of frame and mat, without cropping—the labs use black backgrounds. If necessary she has the lab mask the slide with photographic silver tape for clean presentation.

It occurred to me that maybe there was something in Tornay's artwork that actually helped the photographers produce the brilliantly clear slides. With this suspicion I questioned Tornay and other winners of competitions. I uncovered three factors that tend to produce better photographs for competitive entries:

- Color clarity of the original artwork
- Avoiding textured surfaces
- Making sure the slides project well before sending them out

The process of jurying by slide demands more attention to factors such as color in the execution of the original work in order to compensate for the fact that a slide is a second-generation representation. Tornay has spent a great deal of time experimenting with color to find the cleanest colors to use in watercolor. One of her techniques is to use only those colors that aren't "chalky" in appearance. The colors she likes include cobalt, scarlet lake, and new gambouge. She avoids earth tones and cadmium colors.

Competition winners pay particular attention to preparing and creating smooth surfaces for their artwork. They are concerned about not having brush strokes, or chiseling or fabricating in the case of sculpture, compete with the image of the art in the slides.

Tornay said that when projected for NWS jurors, the tiny 1-inch slides are blown up to about 4 feet. To experiment, I took various slides and projected them. Sure enough, once certain slides were projected bigger than 1 foot square, they seemed to lose quality; this was especially true when the original piece was smaller than the projected image. Also if the colors were soft, the image lost quality. No matter what pieces one wants to enter in a competition, the artist should first project the slides and reject those that do not project well in larger dimensions.

Here are more slide tips from Tornay: label your slides neatly with a fine point Pilot permanent marker (she never uses tape for labeling for fear of the slide getting stuck in the projector), and replace the slide mount when sending a slide that has been used before.

Other factors are important too. For example, Tornay does research on the jurors listed in the prospectus of the event. She does not enter competitions wherein the jurors do mostly nontraditional art. Tornay's work is photorealist, often close-ups of flowers and plants. Upon looking at the results of some shows that were held between 1989 and 1992 and reading the jurors' statements, I found that they were concerned with choosing art that was of good quality and representative of the kinds of art submitted. An analysis of forty top-prize winners in NWS art competitions showed nineteen winners with traditional styles and twenty-one with contemporary styles, while the jurors themselves were 80 percent traditionalists. This sleuthing might not be the best guideline for everyone, but Tornay has found it useful.

When an artwork is accepted, practical problems confront the successful artist. Tornay talked about unexpectedly selling a painting and having it accepted for an award at another back-to-back show, and having to borrow the piece back from its purchaser. The solution involved shipping the art from the collector in Colorado to the show in California. For this, Tornay discovered a company called Airfloat Systems Inc. (800-445-2580), which sells a Strongbox. The box is, according to the company's brochure, "a shipping container designed especially to transport framed art, prints, canvas, precision instruments, and other valuables safely and without added unnecessary weight." They cost $12-$250 depending on size and quality. The reusable boxes are "self-closing with locking tabs." Due to the Strongbox the collector was able to easily pack the painting in the box for safe shipping. With these boxes Tornay is able to get her work to exhibitions and home again, and she has never experienced any damage.

Tornay recommends Federal Express for shipping even very large pieces. Federal Express will ship almost any size (they have recently changed their dimension and weight guidelines), and their prices are very competitive. The one drawback: Federal Express has a $500 insurance limit for artwork.

There are other costs associated with entering competitions, of course. For example, organizers sometimes charge a handling fee above the entry fee. Tornay says that some of the competitions are beginning to charge unreasonably for this service and she avoids them.

Another expense is framing. Tornay invests her money in clean, large mats rather than in expensive frame moldings; she uses metal moldings. Her average cost for matting and framing a 22"x28" piece is $70.

The first time Tornay sold a piece, she had priced it at $1,500 because she had not wanted to sell the work and thought that would be a prohibitive price. The next time she put a supposedly prohibitive price on a piece—$9,500—that piece sold, too. Now Tornay sometimes enters "Not for Sale" works; she finds that this does not affect the work's acceptance rate.

Tornay enters only competitions offering prizes of at least $3,000. She always sends a SASE for her slides even if one is not required, and she has never had slides lost. She also sends a special thank-you letter to the sponsors of a cash award when she receives one.

Tornay is a careful and dedicated artist who in a short period of time has become a major player in art competitions both as a participant and as an organizer. She has derived an income and a resumé of participation, awards, and collectors. Tornay cites a statement made by one of her favorite art instructors: "OK, you think you see it, look at it again!" That is what she does with listings and prospectuses of art competitions.

CHAPTER 18

Invitational Group Exhibitions

The Etiquette of Salons and Other Group Shows

Peggy Hadden

Having just been through a jam-packed salon-type show, I've been thinking about how artists see such an opportunity. This show was a result of a gallery inviting all artists in the area to participate.

Actors refer to such a wide-open event as a "cattle call." That is, everyone—professional and amateur alike—may audition for the part. In our case, all the work that was delivered was hung. This time, artists were not juried. Thus the range of technical expertise and subject matter was somewhat uneven, as one might expect.

But there is joy in an event like this, a democratic attempt to give every artist, whatever the extent of their training, professional ambition, or experience, a fair viewing.

A hundred years ago, our art ancestors joined in salons, and the fruits of their labor fill museums around the world today. Then, as now, salons were, for many, the only place where they could show. We even read about the *Salon des Refusés*, or salon of those refused for the salon. Many elements of those old salons haven't changed at all. The art is still hung ceiling to floor, with the frame of one work often touching the frame of its neighbor.

But because today's events are often organized by overextended artists' groups offering little supervision, the manners of the participants and the presentation of their work is often appalling.

Consider the following:

1. Work submitted is often too fragile for the rough-and-tumble atmosphere. This is not the place to exhibit egg shells and tissue paper. Be sure your work will hold up in the atmosphere in which it finds itself.

2. If you plan to enter a piece of sculpture in the show, be sure there will be pedestals on which to mount your work. Don't expect them—call in advance to check and make plans to supply your own stands just in case.

3. Be sure your work is ready to hang. This means screw eyes and wire attached to the back, an arrow indicating the top, and all the necessary labeling information attached to the back of the piece. Wires should be fairly rigid when stretched between the screws; otherwise, the work will lean out and protrude from the wall once it has been hung. If your artwork is in two or three parts, the parts should be joined together by you to assure correct positioning.

4. Because the hanging of such shows is often done by rushed and harried volunteers, you should never assume that they will read, or even see, the precious instructions that you've attached to the back of your piece. Artists, because they are so intimately involved in the creation of the work, assume others will regard it equally carefully. That the hanging committee is faced with several hundred works and limited time to get them hung never seems to occur to the artist. As a former hanging committee member, I can tell you that all those works and their installation instructions, lined up like new campers with notes pinned to their T-shirts from anxious moms, will not be read. Many instructions will most likely have to be ignored for the good of the group as a whole. We had an artist whose note requested that his piece be lit by candlelight. Nice. Sentimental. Not feasible. Not in a salon show, with the needs of the other artworks that would flank this piece, to say nothing of the fire hazards and distraught insurance agents which would also result. In fact, lighting in almost any salon show will be, by its very nature, arbitrary. The variety of heights, with some works hanging high and others low, makes any type of lighting treatments end up utilitarian, rather than evocative. Think of a bus station.

5. Take the time to think about how your piece will get seen. As to size, our show put only marginal limits on what sizes of work would be exhibited. The results were as you might expect: bigger was definitely assumed to be better. But this year I psyched things out. With the

visual cacophony that always occurs in these situations, it came to me that a smaller piece with a larger mat surrounding it would stand a better chance of being seen. By setting the work off within the frame, it wasn't out there begging for attention next to the neon colors of whatever might be hung next to it. When I saw the completed installation, I knew my instinct had been right.

6. Don't enter unfinished or wet work. I'm recalling the artist who arrived with her artwork wrapped in towels. I have two thoughts about situations like this. First, the show was announced 2 months in advance. While I'm all for spontaneity, this artist is running the risk of damage to the work. Second, is it fair to the group operating the show to enter work requiring special handling?

7. "Etiquette" is an old-fashioned word. But sometimes the unthinking rudeness these days makes saying these things necessary:

   a. Under no circumstances should a work be removed from any show before the show is over, even an hour before the closing. It is thoughtless and callous behavior.

   b. Artwork should be removed promptly when the show ends. Leaving work to be stored invites damage and will require someone else to move, wrap, and secure your work.

   c. Unless provisions have been spelled out otherwise, there will probably not be room for packaging to remain on-site during the exhibition. Take it away and bring it back when the show is over.

   d. There are always a few artists who offer to help hang the exhibition. Then, after hanging their own work—very advantageously—they disappear. These people get a reputation in a hurry and are deluded if they think no one notices.

8. Set realistic prices, or specify "Not for Sale" if you don't want to sell it. Here's another tale from the show I've been talking about. One piece was very high-priced—its price was several times that of anything else in the show. During the exhibition, the gallery director noticed that this piece attracted the attention of several very well-known gallery owners who attended; however, upon seeing the price of the work, their interest died. One dealer complained to the director, "I couldn't get those prices for this artist's work even if I took him into my

gallery." Our director knew that the artist was fairly inexperienced in exhibiting, so she called him for clarification on the price. "Oh," he responded, "I just didn't want to part with that piece, so I made it so expensive I knew it wouldn't sell." By so doing, the artist had destroyed the interest of several gallery owners who might have taken him on in their galleries. This piece should have been marked "Not for Sale." Don't outsmart yourself—if you are unsure about your pricing, talk it over with someone who has more experience.

So far, this article has stressed what *not* to do at large salon-type shows. However, there are some do's.

Do get involved. This kind of group endeavor is a wonderful chance to swap information, meet new people, and, yes, see some really interesting art. The organizers will probably need some gallery-sitters, a hanging committee, someone to help keep up the appearance of the gallery (yes, sweep!), and bartenders for the opening. If up to now you've been more of a bystander, this is a good time to make your presence known.

Do realize what a show like this is and isn't. If your feelings are a little fragile for the style of a salon show, don't set yourself up for a disappointment. There are other places to show and other environments for your work. Maybe reading this will help you to see the advantages and disadvantages of showing with a group.

Finally, do say "thank you" to the people in the sponsoring organization for giving you some wall space. They deserve your thanks.

CHAPTER 19

Creating Your Own Group Exhibitions

Curating/Organizing a Group Show
Peggy Hadden

One of the most enlightening, fun, and career-advancing things I've ever done was to curate a group show. By placing myself on the other side of the fence from where I usually find myself, I came to see artists, including myself, in a different light.

Group shows are called for by sponsors far more often than one-person shows, so the effort is more likely to succeed than trying to get a solo show for yourself. However, there is a distinct difference between curating and organizing an exhibition.

A curator selects the work for the exhibition, names the show, secures a space and funding, is responsible for mounting the event, and handles a million other details. He also reaps the rewards, kudos, heartaches, and glory, what there is of it, for being responsible for it. A new category is born for the resumé and the possibility of being asked to curate more events arises. You are seen in a new way, by artists and other art world professionals alike. Suddenly, you have taste, intuition, and a keen eye, all things that were supposedly missing when you were "just another artist." While these qualities that you have sprouted overnight may seem a bit ephemeral, they can be used like the coin of the realm for getting closer to the people who can help your career move ahead. They can also make more palatable the long hours and low pay that a curator usually gets. There is very little, if any, financial gain; for almost a year of work, I received $200. But I still think it was worth doing.

However, should this endeavor seem to be more than you are willing to tackle alone, try organizing a group show. An organizer gathers a group of artists together and they each determine what they want to exhibit in the show. Or a group of artists who have decided to show together may select one person in the group to be the organizer. Another alternative occurs when the group plans the show together. Duties for preparing the show are divided among the artists and each one is responsible for a different chore.

The first thing is to find an exhibition space where you would like to have your show. There are many different kinds of spaces, from a full-time gallery space offered by nonprofit organizations, to a local business such as a bank, hotel, or restaurant which may want an exhibition up for only a few weeks or as long as a year.

Whatever the site, you will need a proposal. From a straightforward phone call to the person in charge of exhibitions, to a formal multi-page document, a proposal will always get more consideration from those who make decisions if it appears to be well thought out.

It helps to have a title for a framework. If the people at the space like your title, you're halfway toward the goal of getting your proposal accepted. Try for something more original than simply "Paintings by Five Artists." While this title may truthfully tell what viewers will see at the exhibition, it lacks the exciting quality, the pizzazz, that will sell your show to an exhibition committee—or, for that matter, to prospective viewers. Find out what these five artists have in common ("Five Views of the Maine Landscape") or how they differ ("Five Points of View from the Lone Star State"). They may all be art world veterans ("Five Masters Explore the Portrait") or new and emerging ("Five New Points of View in Cartoon Art"). For the group show I curated, which was all collage, I chose the title "Spare Parts." Like the headline from a New York newspaper, "Headless Body Found in Topless Bar," the title should make your audience curious to explore further.

If you have not yet decided what the thrust of your show will be, giving it a title will be a big help in focusing yourself. Selecting artists you want to include will suddenly become easier as you evaluate their work in relationship to your title. If you haven't selected the artists for your show yet, go to nonprofits' slide registries where you can see the works of many artists and gauge how they will look together. For my show, I set a limit of twenty artists. To arrive at this figure, I had already visited the space where I wanted to show, estimated the amount of work necessary, and ascertained that the space's owners would soon be looking for work, as they had announced a call for proposals and set a deadline. I went to three different slide registries and selected artists from all three.

Art Calendar also welcomes calls for submissions from artists who are curating or organizing shows. Give the title, theme, media/size/geographic/ other rules and restrictions, the kind of space you're seeking to show in, and a contact name, address, and phone number. If you decide that artists will be responsible for any costs of the show, clearly state how much and for what.

Of the twenty artists I selected, I knew only one of them personally. It's not necessary to know the artists; in fact, it could even turn out to be a handicap. You don't want to give the impression that you have a clique around you.

Everyone needs to understand that you are the curator or organizer and that they have certain responsibilities because they have work in the show. Once you've invited everyone, ask the artists for a sheet of slides with information about the availability of each piece, since size limitations or content restrictions (e.g., a request by the bank or restaurant for no nudity or political art) may cause you to need more than your original choices of artwork. You should also ask them for a current resumé. Double-check that their mailing address hasn't changed, and get the best day and time to reach them. These artists are your exhibition's foundation and you will be communicating often. It's a good idea to make up a complete roster of artists and phone numbers to distribute to everyone so that each phone call or message doesn't have to pass through you.

Work with a floor plan. If this is a regular exhibition site, they probably already have one. If not, make a simple drawing, and measure for all dimensions. Include ceiling height. Note where stationary ceiling lights and other fixtures are located. Note if they are fluorescent or incandescent.

This floor plan, however crudely drawn, will become the basis from which you work. By the time the show is to be mounted, you should have a pretty good idea of which works will go where and know from your measurements that they will all fit. Between the slides and your floor plan, you should be able to work out that certain pieces relate well to each other. Thus you should be able to work largely from your studio, eliminating extra visits to the site. By the time you hang the exhibition, it should be just a matter of art handling and hardware.

Look at the entrance and imagine your viewer or critic entering the space. Will your show be in an area by itself, or will it have to work with other signs, colors, and graphics that are part of the business? Will any of the work be partially obscured by poor lighting or daily activity? Our show was in a bank and several of the works hung behind the tellers. They were not obscured, because all of the protective caging around the tellers was clear Lucite, but their distance from the viewers caused several of the artists justifiable concern.

Certainly, all of us would like our work to be shown in clean and well-lighted spaces. Sometimes when a business offers a space, we have to think realistically about the compromises that will be necessary for our exhibition to coexist in their space. You must first acknowledge and work with the limitations that may be found. If this is something that you feel would ruin your exhibition, look for another space. Second, you must explain these limitations to the other artists who will have to adopt a pragmatic attitude about the space, or they won't be happy being part of the show. Discuss the site's limitations among yourselves. Talk about the pros and cons of having artwork there. It may be worth having a less-than-perfect exhibition in a spot that gets a lot of traffic (and potential sales) or a site that is in close proximity to upscale galleries or a museum. A restaurant that has classical music and a calm, unhurried atmosphere with waiters attuned to talking about the art with customers may do more to sell your art than a beautiful white gallery space with low traffic and indifferent gallery personnel. Appreciating these trade-offs is what makes artists in the nineties different from those who existed before us. The ivory tower approach to purity about where art should be shown just doesn't work anymore. It's lonely in an ivory tower anyhow.

A letter of agreement should be written by you and a copy sent to all of the artists. State delivery dates, the dates for the show, and when and how the show will be dismantled. Ask the artists to sign and return a copy of the letter to you. At our exhibition, one of the artists removed artwork a week and a half before the show was over. It left a gap in the exhibition and left the rest of us very upset. A letter of agreement would have prevented this from happening.

Now that you've selected your group, if you are going after a space that hosts group shows regularly, your next step will be to write a proposal. While much has been said here and elsewhere about proposals, a proposal comes down to three main sections:
- What you are proposing and to whom it will appeal
- Your method—an outline of the project in four to six short sentences—including the artists' names and a short description of their work
- The budget for bringing the project to fruition and where you hope to obtain funds

Ideally, the proposal should take up a page, but depending on the group to whom you're proposing, the length of the proposal may vary. Certainly, the "what" section should take no more than a page.

An easy way to begin is with a relevant quotation. Then, show how your exhibit agrees with, differs from, or challenges this quote—or, why it is still true and relevant, 50 or 100 years later.

Discuss how your show will demonstrate a point or offer a variety of points of view around a central theme.

Tell "why now." Why is your exhibition relevant now? Anniversaries of events or movements are good reasons, or maybe you notice a trend developing which you want others to see, too. If you need help with this part, don't hesitate to ask for it. College professors, who read a lot of term papers and do research themselves, are good people to approach for assistance.

This "what" section is the first thing your exhibition committee will read, and it should pique their interest. If it fails to do so, your second and third parts—who and how—won't matter.

Assuming you've sold them on the "what," you must now move on to the "who." Show slides of the artists' specific work you plan to use. Include their resumés, as their successes will strengthen your proposal. Reading a stack of resumés is time-consuming, so in my proposals I include a single sheet to introduce the artists and highlight their careers. If they want to know more about a certain artist, the individual resumés follow this highlight.

Finally, tell "how." Budgets are never pleasant to read, but if you plan yours out in broad terms without using too many categories, it should read smoothly and total up neatly at the end. Do not include minute things in your budget, clump them together. For example, a category like publicity for the show can include expenses for the invitation card's design, typesetting, printing, press release, and press kits. Other categories could include mailing, insurance, advertising, shipping, installation costs, documentation, opening reception, and proposal preparation.

Proposal preparation can be time-consuming and costly. Preparation costs can include phone calls, slide duplication, word processing, mailing, etc. However, do not include babysitters, soft drinks, or the time you spent.

With your budget, include a statement recognizing the sizable amounts of money that can be replaced by volunteer services and contributed goods. This points out that you and your group will be able to contribute much at little or no cost. Ask the proposal committee to think of your budget as a working list that is flexible in terms of size and detail.

When you are preparing the budget, it will help you to know what they have provided other artists in the past. Start with that figure and work backwards. If they have been generous, plan your needs accordingly. If, however, they have provided only part of the funds necessary, state where the rest of the necessary budget will come from.

You may need to ask a nonprofit organization to act as your fiscal agent. Acting as your "umbrella" group, they won't become involved in or sponsor the actual event; they will receive the funds for you, disburse funds, and keep records about how everything is being spent. Many business sponsors feel much better about giving you the funds you are requesting if you have an umbrella organization. Any nonprofit group can play this role for you, whether they are an arts group or a nonprofit service, religious, or civic organization. Some nonprofits charge a small fee for this service; be sure to itemize it in the budget as administrative costs.

It is OK if you still don't have all the funds. Maybe the sponsoring group or business will feel your idea is worthy of their help. It's a good idea to show that you have located some of the funds, however, as it indicates that you have a picture of the whole cost and have made an effort toward raising funds. Divide the funds under two categories, "funds on hand" and "funds needed." Even if your Aunt Tilly has given you $50, list her with contributors, as her faith in your idea is in your favor. Or you may indicate that certain funds you have in savings will be used for the project. This is not a loosely planned scheme; you believe in it, and it has some outside support, however small. Include a timetable for major parts of your project, so they will see that you have an overall picture of the work that must be done and where each part fits in the sequence of events leading up to the opening night.

In figuring out your budget, don't forget artists' fees as well as your curator's fee. Try to keep this amount proportionate with everything else. For instance, if your total request is $5,000, a curator's fee of $1,000 may be too high. Unfortunately, curating an exhibition is looked on as somewhat of a labor of love, and you will not be able to think of your curating the way you think of pricing an artwork. After all, it's something you are asking to take on. Go over these arguments in your mind before you ask for too large a fee and get turned down. In spite of what you're thinking, I am on your side, but someone has to tell you what others may be thinking and what their rationale is. Curating is a category much like museum work and everyone knows that museum employees are underpaid.

The sponsoring group may offer to provide your opening night reception, and if so, this does not need to be part of your budget. Find out if they will be inviting special guests, such as business clients or executives from their parent company. Those invitations should be handled separately, as they may wish to include a note or mail the invitation card in a special envelope. Ask if they want particular city officials, such as the mayor, invited. You will be responsible for these invitations; be sure that your officials meet the right people and say how truly terrific they are to be sponsoring the event and backing local artists. This kind of connecting may seem a long way from art and the studio, but it will serve you well the next time you are seeking support for a local project.

Documentation of the project is critical. This is a category you may feel can be skimped on. However, it is probably the most important category in your budget for two reasons. First, for yourself, documentation will help you launch future projects more successfully. It's evidence that you were able to do what you proposed, and can be trusted to oversee upcoming projects. The second reason to have good documentation is that it may be needed by the very people you are applying to, in order for them to secure funds or approval in the future for more projects, or to account for the funding they're offering you for this one.

If your sponsor is a business, they may need your documentation to have future funds allocated to such projects, or to prove to higher-ups that their sponsorship was a good idea. The use of videotape coverage, as well as black-and-white photographs or color slides, professionally made, will be adequate documentation. But don't skimp.

Send one copy of this documentation to the sponsor, along with a thank-you note, after the exhibition is over. Tying up loose ends after the show makes good sense for many reasons, including that you may want something else later. For example, I went back to the bank where my show had been exhibited, and I borrowed video equipment for a panel discussion I was doing. The fact that I had finished up everything on my first project made it possible for me to go back and ask again.

And, keep them on your mailing list—they are in your corner now.

All in all, curating/organizing a group show offers you a chance to grow as an artist and as an art-world professional. You will learn things about mounting exhibitions, knowledge which is sure to increase your respect for the people in museums and galleries who do it as a matter of course. You will definitely come to see your own artwork in a new light. I think all artists owe it to themselves to have the experience of putting on a group show, and I know the opportunities are out there. Just do it!

PART 6

Public and Architectural
Art Competitions

Oliphants, 1993, ceramics, 16"x18"x10", Elvi Jo Dougherty, Upper Fairmount, Maryland

CHAPTER 20

The Power of Community Involvement

The Making of an Outdoor Sculpture

Patricia Meyerowitz

The purpose of this presentation is, first, to share some of the solutions to the financial difficulties I encountered in having a small grant to make a large, outdoor sculpture; second, to demonstrate how important and rewarding it can be to involve the local community; and third, to show how one can continue to get mileage even after the work is completed.

First a little background. My husband and I moved to Easton, Pennsylvania from New York City in 1986—much to my surprise. I am a big-city person. Having been born in London, England and having spent 16 years in New York, it hardly seemed credible that I would one day land up in small-town America. However, having run out of money in New York, that is exactly what happened.

We were fortunate to have bought, for a very small sum of money, a 2,300 square feet loft in New York in 1975, only to see its value increase significantly over the next 10 years. When the time came for us to move—we were being assessed out of all possibility of remaining in our co-op—we heard about this small town 80 miles due west of New York.

Easton is an old, historic town with many downtown commercial loft buildings that had been half-empty for years. The area had also been run down for years and the city had been struggling to recover from a depression. The mayor and some other enterprising people in City Hall, together with a visionary artist who had already moved from New York, suggested that one way to improve downtown Easton would be to encourage artists to come visit and rent or buy downtown property. To cut a rather long story short, a seminar was arranged, phone calls were made, some judicious advertising was placed, and slowly the word got around. Artists came, saw, and bought or rented. And that is how we moved from a fractious co-op in New York to our own building in Easton.

Easton already had in place an arts program that offered small grants to individual artists each year, with matching funds from the Pennsylvania Council on the Arts. After being here two years, I wrote a proposal and sent it to city hall at the appropriate time. The first year I applied, the proposal was rejected, but the following year, knowing that the committee would consist of different people, I simply changed the date and sent it in again. This time it was accepted.

Although my proposal naturally included a budget, it was an incredibly skimpy one since I knew that city hall had very little money to dispense. But since this would be my first large outdoor commission, I was, like many artists in similar positions, prepared to go to some extra trouble to get that first monumental outdoor sculpture in place.

The first thing that happened was that city hall found that it had less money than it thought, so each of the three accepted grants—mine included—were cut short by $107.10. This left me with the bureaucratic sum of $3,832.90 to construct a monumental, 12- to 13-foot sculpture out of redwood. My budget called for a concrete base, a reinforcing rod which needed some welded attachments, labor to cut the redwood units with which I was to construct the sculpture, and two helpers. I had a small contingency fund, but it seemed I would be over budget before I even began. It also seemed obvious to me that I would have to do a little fund-raising of my own.

I had already befriended several people who had lived here for many years. I spoke to one in particular and asked her who she thought I might contact for donations. Through her, I made a list and proceeded to write a letter to send out. The letter explained my position and stated what I needed. I didn't ask for very much—$50-100 would be just fine.

The next thing was to approach all the merchants from whom I needed supplies. I asked them if they could either donate the goods, or the mark-up on the goods. They all agreed to the latter and this saved me quite a bit of money. Meanwhile, the checks started coming in, and I managed to collect an extra $400.

During this time, the local newspapers had begun to cover the story. Another friend of mine, a woman with public relations expertise, had offered to write a professional news release for me and made lists of people to whom this should be sent. Since the press was writing about me during the period of my fund-raising, this helped to bring my name and my project into the public consciousness and no doubt helped the fund-raising efforts. Also, when merchants and other people are being approached to help in fund-raising efforts, they will very much appreciate a personal thank-you from you the artist; also ask if they would like to be included in your press releases and possibly earn a mention in the newspaper.

I tried to make it clear to everybody that this was a community effort and that the sculpture—the first contemporary work for the City of Easton—would belong to all the citizens. This approach and attitude were very helpful and people began to get involved and excited by the project. I made sure that the local press knew who would be directly involved with helping me and suggested to them that they visit the workshops to photograph the various stages of production. This had the marvelous effect of making it an exciting event for my helpers, as well as advertising them and their particular skills. They all appeared in the local newspapers at one time or another during the process. The ironworker I had selected to do the welding actually donated his time, which was a wonderful surprise and gift to me.

By a lucky coincidence, the City of Easton was in the process of building a new amphitheater about 100 yards from the sculpture site. Since concrete was being poured all the time for the amphitheater, it was obvious to me that I should approach this same contractor to pour my concrete base. I explained to him over the phone what I wanted and arranged to meet with him on site. He asked who was going to pay for it; I was about to ask him whether he might consider donating some labor or a percentage of the material when he offered to donate the whole thing. This was wonderful and came entirely out of the blue.

After the base was poured and I saw what a great job his workers had done, I realized how much I had underestimated the cost of such a base. However, I also realized that by this time I was slightly ahead of the game as far as finances were concerned. Also, the actual construction time turned out to be shorter than I had anticipated so I saved money there too.

The newspaper's photographer was on site almost every day, and so everyone in town got to see the work in progress even if they were unable to get to the actual site in person.

I had another plan up my sleeve to save money and get more mileage. After the sculpture was completed, I put this plan into action. I had intended to have a postcard made showing the sculpture. A postcard is an advertising tool that can fly all over the country and the world—but one needs to have a good photograph taken and that, too, costs money. I approached the local newspaper again and suggested that they run a photographic competition for the best photograph of the sculpture. I had to talk quite hard to convince them, but finally they agreed that it would be a good idea to sponsor an "amateurs only" contest and subsequently ran some ads for it. I had figured out beforehand what the prizes might be. The newspaper could either give some cash prizes, or they might persuade the local photographic store to give away some equipment. They chose the former. My prize contribution would be to use the winning entry as the photo on the picture face of the postcard, with credit given to the winner. It worked out very well since everybody turned out to be a winner. The newspaper gained publicity, the entrants had a good opportunity and incentive to enter the competition, and I gained more publicity—and a free photograph.

The winning entry turned out to be a perfect shot for a postcard, which was finally made with the name of the prizewinning photographer printed on the stamp side. Two thousand were printed; part of the cost was covered by the extra money I had collected through my personal fund-raising efforts. I proceeded to give a few away to all the people who had helped me with the project. The rest are available for sending to art dealers, galleries, and museums—and some are selling in local stores for 50¢ each.

In conclusion, I feel that it is quite important to get the local community on your side when a public work of art is concerned. People get to know you and really feel that the work belongs to them. And an added benefit in my sculpture's case is that there has been no vandalism.

The Project Just Begins
with Getting the Grant

René Joseph

I got what I wanted: money to spend on painting! Doggedly trying for years to get a grant, any grant, I sent Arts Midwest a proposal that included previously rejected slides.

When they awarded me a New Partnership Matching Grant, I thought the work was over. Compared to the labor of writing a polished application, the rest would be easy. The image I was going to paint was so strong in my mind that it seemed it would paint itself. I hadn't a clue about the extra work involved to accomplish the project goals. I quickly learned there was more work than art involved.

How did it all start? Elliot Park, a downtown Minneapolis neighborhood organization, wanted a mural. A badly peeling and decaying 60'x16' wall in the community garden needed care. Knowing more than a wish was needed to get it done, the neighborhood gave me much good advice and help on my first draft of the proposal. When the guidelines came, the text had to be shortened to fit the format. Having previously volunteered for an arts panel, and having seen winning proposals from the viewpoint of a judge, I had learned to evaluate my own documents. This extra work spent in refining makes a clear statement to the jurors. A well thought out and presented proposal says immediately that the artist can do what he plans.

Once the good news came, there wasn't time to be relieved. A grant is a big responsibility, and I was accountable for getting the mural done within a strict timeline: after the last freeze and before the gardeners planted—a period of only 90 days. I was able to do what I wanted, but there were countless demands on my time and energies that had nothing to do with painting and everything to do with a successful project.

Besides the job of designing and putting up a 60-foot outdoor mural in Minnesota's rainy season, my additional responsibilities included conducting workshops, locating and hiring help, recruiting volunteers, doing most of the press releases, going to meetings, putting up posters, fund-raising, and ultimately tuck-pointing the wall with cement one final time.

Somehow the ability to make snap decisions was quickly learned, priorities were organized, and everything worked precisely. Everything fit into its own time frame—a matching cash amount and a space to exhibit documentation of the project were locked in before the official starting date of the grant.

What I learned about making a project successful is shared here.

Rule number one is commitment. Be prepared to spend all your time and mental energy on your project. Expect 14-hour days. Plan to get up and immediately start working. When a break is needed, that's when to take a meal or a shower. Some days will be more demanding then others, but don't expect a normal, leisurely schedule. You have to be able to relax and keep yourself on a treadmill all at the same time. It's important to take care of yourself.

Allow more time to get a project done by scheduling a built-in time delay of several weeks.

Needed supplies were raised thanks to my background in telemarketing. One must learn how to say what is important concisely, and in a manner appropriate to several situations. Fund-raising is basically projecting your belief in your project to others. An honest, positive attitude is what sells.

The project began by walking door-to-door distributing a press release announcing the importance of the project to the community. Copies were made of a more formal but still generic letter explaining the project and requesting funds and in-kind donations. These were given with a hand-written note to key potential contributors. Those expressing interest were given a copy of the proposal that included the budget. They took the project seriously because I came prepared.

Learn to listen carefully to people, divide your solicitations realistically, and don't get greedy. Base your decisions on finding a proper compromise solution. In a fight over funding, another neighborhood organization initially got upset over possibly losing the donated paint they usually get. In my formal presentation to a local manufacturer's contributions committee, I explained that the paint would not be wasted because the other group would get the leftovers, avoiding another request for paint. This impressed the committee, helped me get the paint, and kept everyone happy.

Following up on all donations, big and small, with a thank-you letter and a promise to invite them to any openings is a nice gesture. If you get donors, plan to send them copies of the final report and copies of any significant press coverage. For the big donors, think about presenting them with photos in a commemorative portfolio.

Because the National Endowment for the Arts (NEA) supports Arts Midwest, I thanked my senators and representatives. Local politicians such as the mayor and members of the city council, as well as the press and TV and radio stations, should also know about the grant. For the price of a stamp and some time, it's all free advertising for your project.

By making these contacts early in the project, word gets around that you are professional. In my case, the in-house newsletter distributed at city hall mentioned the project and local newspapers, radio, and TV all carried repeated stories of the mural. The businesspeople who were later asked for help already knew about my project through these channels. Politics is part of any community-based undertaking. By politics, I mean dealing with people and making contacts in a respectful but successful way.

Keep your granting organization informed of your progress too. Often they won't ask or tell you this because their experience is that artists fight any attempts to make them accountable. But it helps the organization get more funding for additional projects through their board. And if you keep them updated, they can and will promote your project. That is an important aspect of working with people: Being considerate of them helps them accommodate you and it can be an all-win situation.

Attention to details is extremely important. Two things will immediately become apparent when you stay on top of details: You will be worn out by it, and it will probably put you behind schedule. But—and this is a big but—the rewards are worth the effort. By recording the names and hours of each volunteer at the end of a long day while the facts were still fresh, I could proudly, and easily, prove that sixty-three volunteers logged over 1,000 hours on my project. It's also helpful to keep notes as the project progresses for a final essay report to the funding agency. Rigorous record keeping will provide a valuable mailing list and give you the facts to plan your next project accurately.

Details include checking the calendar daily and faithfully recording changes and additions to plans, as well as separately recording expenses. Use an adding machine. Begin by making a strict timetable and faithfully stick to it. I did things I would not otherwise have had the courage to do, simply because if I didn't, I couldn't proceed on schedule. As crazy as it sounds, three separate calendars were kept so I always had a quick reference of publishing deadlines, personal deadlines, and the deadlines promised in the original grant proposal.

A filing system is mandatory. Thankfully, no one took a photograph of the piles that completely covered every available flat surface, including the floor, before I discovered that file cabinets are not for storage but for filing current information.

Keeping on top of details will also prevent damage to your project and reputation. Two examples are helpful here. In another similar public art piece which had a much larger budget, someone forgot to get the historic preservation committee's approval and the whole project almost stopped. In my mural project, my member organization failed to tell me until the last minute of an important detail—the building owners wanted to approve of the design before we started painting.

There were other close calls that can't be traced to any one person's fault, just the situation. Since it's impossible to tell which detail will be most critical at any given time, you have to be committed to taking care of all of them as they come up. When dealing with a nonprofit organization, they may need statistics to help you. It is your responsibility to compile them because you have the information.

When a task presents itself, don't put it off—there won't be time later and you won't be able to backtrack it. At the very least, record it for future reference. Rainy days aren't wasted days. If you can't do what you'd hoped to get done, that's the day to get ahead of the paperwork by planning press releases, making posters, making phone contacts, and tidying up loose ends. So be prepared, and if you can't be prepared, be organized. This just might get you out of some tight spots and keep you from being overwhelmed.

Working in the traditional manner with stencils, the painting of the wall was easy. After making the equivalent of a 60'x16' drawing, the rest was pretty much paint-by-numbers. A strong structural drawing allowed flexibility on blendings and allowed for the little mistakes that personalize a picture. The groundwork made the rest of the painting easy—anyone can paint within lines.

Volunteers, once found, can be helpful here, and were an important part of the proposal and budget. An inner-city neighborhood, with a mix of businesses and people of all financial and educational backgrounds, has a wide variety of skills and funding sources to pick from. Some volunteers made the small, handmade sketchbooks that were designed and handed out for input on the mural. Others offered professional photography skills in video and still prints.

Contacting people personally helped more than posters; I connected with a lot of people in person at the mural site. Some people were reached through stories in the papers. By stressing the positive aspects of a community self-help project, there was repeated coverage on all four local TV channels.

To allow for more youth involvement, and to get the press interested, a community paint day was held for children to paint their own flower designs on the bottom of the mural. That also brought out bored adults who were willing to help paint all day. The neighborhood has several soup kitchens and shelters for the homeless, with lots of transient foot traffic. Statistically, most of the neighborhood residents are low-income and single. They were grateful for a new and interesting activity to fill up a lonely day.

In all, six separate press releases were sent and sometimes hand-carried to the media. At the opening reception, all four local TV news stations carried our story on both the early and the late news. One of the volunteers made a photographic record of the project for the cost of the film and developing; that enabled me to document the entire project in a display at the local library. During the month it was up the exhibit was seen by an estimated 72,000 people.

The project had a lot of positive results. It caused businesses to become aware of their importance to their community. Some businesses hadn't found a way to help before, some had never been asked, while others hadn't any idea they were even in a residential community. Money was brought into the neighborhood and for the most part spent there, and the project employed several neighborhood people. Because the neighborhood is an urban community on the edge of downtown, it has many needs. The mural has a lasting psychological and spiritual reward in an otherwise distressed area. Bringing a hopeful enchantment to a district with an uplifting project undertaken by the community is a positive step in an inner-city environment and makes it a better place to live and walk or drive through.

Even though the work was harder then planned and the budget tighter than anticipated, I got a lot out of the project. Besides getting my name out there, and adding to my professional portfolio, I now have no fear of tackling an even larger public project. I know I can do it. More importantly, receiving the recognition from the grant has given me a sense of self-respect as an artist that I've never possessed before. As someone recently said to me, "You take yourself seriously and now others do too." The mural created an atmosphere within which I had to solve visual and other problems fast, and that helped me define my artistic thought processes. Forced to do my own P.R., I found I was able to articulate what my art was about. I got to solve the problem of pictorial space and to play with a whole new range of colors and to make it public. In other words, I had a lot of fun.

All well and good, but how did the budget go? Well, it's hard to say because it's not all in yet. Right now, expenses were around $2,500, so I didn't pay myself. I received $700 from the grant, $850 in cash contributions, and roughly $1,000 in in-kind donations of materials and labor. The repair to the wall took more funds than expected. In the original proposal, I wasn't responsible for the wall preparation, but no one else wanted to deal with it and it was important to me to make the mural last as long as the paint.

On the plus side, the neighborhood is very happy with the mural and is seeking more funds so I may get paid in the end. They're also working to find funding for me to do another mural soon. And even if I don't get paid, the exposure has already brought me a number of interesting projects including consulting for the local transit authority on another project and an invitation to submit designs for a project to decorate the city buses.

Planning, hard work, and dedication can bring about a successfully completed public project and leave behind a very positive image of the artist. I believe anyone can do what they set out to do if they are willing to accept responsibility for getting the work done. The true value of a grant is that it allows an artist to do something that would otherwise not be feasible without other seed money or a rich uncle.

Meet the Mural Makers: CityArts
Peggy Hadden

Seeing a nice blank outdoor wall always makes me start composing the image I would put on it—the imaginary muralist—though to tell the truth I've never done a wall-sized mural. But I think large clean spaces like this beckon to the artist, and my response is probably typical.

OK, so if you're thinking seriously about a mural project, how do you start?

This question took me to CityArts, a nonprofit organization dedicated to the creation of murals and other site-specific artworks such as sculpture and mosaics in the varied and diverse communities that make up New York City. Using teens and young adults from the neighborhood as apprentices, CityArts oversees, and stresses the importance of, community involvement all the way through the project. About 150 murals have been created under CityArts' administrative guidance since its inception in 1968.

CityArts' executive director, Tsipi (pronounced SIP-ee) Ben-Haim, took me through the process of who funds murals, what the community contributes, and how artists are selected. I asked Ms. Ben-Haim, "Who wants a mural, and why? Where are they initiated?"

I think her answer applies to cities and towns all over the country: "Neighborhoods want them—they give communities a sense of pride, identity, and ownership. It says who they are." She outlined several kinds of groups who initiate projects:

- The local board of education, for a new school or the renovation of an older one
- The local youth department—mural projects can be included in an after-school curriculum
- The local parks department, for playgrounds or parks that have a space that needs brightening
- The state criminal justice system, which funds projects that can help at-risk young people by giving them a worthwhile alternative
- The Housing Preservation and Development Board, for the commissioning of temporary or permanent murals in new buildings or around construction worksites
- Politicians who want to give people a better understanding of who they are
- Corporations such as banks and supermarkets who do business in the neighborhood and want to contribute something to the culture or economic development
- Individuals who have seen murals at other locations and want to organize something similar in their own neighborhood

I asked Ben-Haim how CityArts finds their artists.

"We have a slide registry that is being added to constantly. Artists can write to us for an application—enclose a SASE—and send it back filled out and with slides. And please tell them *not* to put 'See attached resume' on it because there might be five to six panelists sitting at a table looking at applications and it's difficult to keep going back and forth to their support materials—things do not stay together. They need to fill out the application as fully as possible. We look at everything in our slide bank regularly, and we also publicly call for applications through mailings and in publications and bulletins for artists. The slide bank is used also to recommend artists to collectors, corporations, or communities. Then, after we've narrowed down our search, we interview the artists we're still considering, to be sure they would be able to artistically bring the mural to fruition."

If an artist has a site and a project in mind, "we accept unsolicited proposals for review, too. If it is feasible and the community wants it and the funding is there or can be found, we're always ready to go ahead."

Once selected to produce a mural, the artist's first step toward production is to conduct "meetings with the community. Being introduced as a professional artist is important. He will be a role model for the children and we stress this. The artist is not serving the community, but is a guide. There will be several meetings, among everyone who is interested. They will make drawings of things that are important to them. Usually the artist will introduce a theme—say, the environment—and they will express themselves around that theme. "The artist then takes these hundreds of drawings back to the studio and integrates them into his style and creates a whole drawing which will be transferred and enlarged onto the wall."

At the same time the drawing meetings are taking place, the wall at the site must be prepared. Ben-Haim pointed out that up close, a surface that looks ready might turn out to have holes, cracks, or broken concrete that wasn't noticeable before. Wall preparation is critical, and you might need to consult a construction person to tell you if there is a water shaft behind the wall or if the brick is a type that won't dry, once wet, for weeks. You can acquire this kind of expertise—both your own expertise and knowing when and whom to consult— by assisting another artist on a mural project before you set out on your own. Better to learn from someone else than to have gigantic problems, like paint peeling, 2 months after you've finished the mural.

A mural's costs vary. "Renting scaffolding is expensive, and the higher your site rises, the more scaffolding you will need. Scaffolding also raises insurance costs. So a ground-level mural might turn out to be less expensive. On the other hand, it will be susceptible to graffiti and won't be as easily visible as one that is higher up. Our projects cost about $15,000 per wall, but they can be as high as $30,000 depending on size and the amount of supplies needed."

Ben-Haim explained that the cost includes the artist's fee, transportation of people and materials to the site, paints, scaffolding, insurance, and CityArts' administrative costs in organizing and completing the project. A social worker/

coordinator is brought in to help with the organizing of neighborhood support and participation.

Ben-Haim continued, "We will visit the site at different stages during the process, but basically, the artist directs things at the site. Usually there are about twenty volunteers working, although in the South Bronx we had about forty-five teenagers, not all at one time, who painted on some of the murals."

A mural demands special supplies to help ensure the project's durability. Ben-Haim said, "We've worked out our paint requirements very well, and we have a paint specialist at Pearl Paint who is quite helpful." Ask for Joseph Rahner. Pearl Paint's number is 212-431-7932, or 800-221-6845. Pearl has a catalog and ships materials anywhere. "We've found a clear sealer which protects against graffiti. It can actually be washed to remove dirt and graffiti and keeps a mural clean."

Ben-Haim estimates that the life expectancy for the average mural is 15 to 20 years. It depends somewhat on where the mural is—whether it is in a protected spot or is exposed to lots of sun, precipitation, and wind. Of course, some murals are painted to be temporary, as at a building site, where plywood panels protect the public during construction. These murals are often paid for by the builder, to generate good feelings about the new building.

Artists should keep an eye out for new building sites, especially in neighborhoods where a good appearance is not only of aesthetic but also financial importance. Near Rockefeller Center, a bank undergoing renovations hired an artist to do outdoor temporary murals in the same Art Deco style as the permanent buildings at Rockefeller Center. Another dazzling abstract mural was temporarily erected inside a building while its lobby was being renovated. That artist was from Spain and directed the construction of the mural from abroad, done to his specifications by a graphics company here. CityArts oversaw the creation of two murals at Times Square during a time of construction.

A mural can be accomplished in a relatively short time, but can also take several months. Ben-Haim said, "That depends on several factors, including weather. And the decision-making process. While most of our projects out-of-doors are painted between April and November, we've had artists who painted until January. Ideally, in six weeks you could have a beautiful mural. But in six months, the artist has really become part of the community, and they're with him. He practically changes their lives and many artists have told me the community changed their lives."

What about changes in scale?

"It's a transition. Going from sketch-size to wall-size can be a surprising experience. Some things don't work large but are beautiful small-scale. Sometimes a composition disintegrates. Or one side suddenly doesn't relate to the other. Working on murals first as an assistant can give you significant insight.

"Also, keeping some design flexibility is important. If you start transferring your mural to the wall and find it isn't working, what then? You should stop and contemplate what design changes you can make to bring it back together. Collecting postcards of murals and studying how they work could be helpful. Look at the dynamics. Where do you look first? Where is your eye led? What leads it? There's nothing like learning from the old masters."

Now let's hear from some of the artists on these projects. Rose Viggiano, a teacher at the School of Visual Arts, works with SVA's Liberty Partnership organization with youth who are considered to be at risk. She has done murals with this group before, and she likens the partnership to an urban Outward Bound program.

"We had funding for a Liberty Partnership project and I approached CityArts. Our philosophies about communities were close and I wanted to make a connection, through murals, with a neighborhood."

Viggiano has temperate words for artists who are considering a mural. "First of all, it will take longer than it looks like and it is physically demanding. You'll need lots of help, in both the physical painting and in areas where artistic sensitivity is needed." Though she did not have a full-time assistant, she had "several art students from my classes at SVA. I usually try to have one good illustrator and one good colorist."

In working with a neighborhood, "It's very important to go in with a theme—it can be flexible, but should provide a framework. It will help you to have a definite direction to work in.

"It can be stressful to have kids on scaffolding. First, you have to make it clear that this is serious work. I only allowed kids over sixteen on the scaffolding and they used a buddy system where they were paired up to look out for each other."

Viggiano learned a lot "about group dynamics. And how important it is to accurately get the feeling of the neighborhood. This is actually a community asking you to give them their ultimate aesthetic."

Bill Moakler has done two mural projects for CityArts. One was funded by the state Criminal Justice Services office. The other, in Times Square, was for the new 42nd Street Development Project.

I asked him whether he had to make progress reports. "I'd just call or go into CityArts to let them know how things were going. I also kept a diary. I had the kids sign into a log on the South Bronx mural—that was actually part of the project. They were bowled over when we put their names on the mural postcard as assistants.

"At Forty-Second Street, I worked with kids and young adults from Covenant House," a facility for runaway children, "who might be there for only a couple of weeks before they'd be moved elsewhere. I find I still get a lot out of reading those diaries. And I took photographs. I'm using the diaries and photos now, in my own work."

Moakler shared anecdotes about working with the kids. "The teens wouldn't work when their friends were around, but then later they'd come back to paint. In Times Square, you'd sometimes get teenagers with *their* kids and the whole family would work."

What about neighborhoods? "You're going into a community which might not care about art. That's part of the idea: changing their mind. Later, I took some of my kids to museums. It was totally new to them."

Besides the satisfaction of working with the community, Moakler feels there is professional value to a mural project. "I think it's always worthwhile to work large and work outside. It's a completely different experience from the studio."

Pamela Shoemaker won a competition sponsored jointly by CityArts and the Jackson Heights Community Development Corporation for her mural *Tango* in 1987. Her experience is unique in that her design went from the competition to completion on the exterior wall of a supermarket without any adjustments or changes.

A total of six people worked on Shoemaker's mural. "I was supposed to have a team of kids from CVC [Civilian Volunteer Corps], but we had some delays and the kids were back in school by the time I started. I had an intern from Barnard College and one guy came by and volunteered. My husband was a great help, too. I was lucky and had good weather, so things moved rather quickly."

Her experience on progress reports was that "in dealing with the city and neighborhood bureaucracies, it is good to document everything, in order to have money flow as you need it for the project."

Shoemaker got some publicity. "Lots, actually. At the time and even three years later, I got good newspaper coverage, with photographs. Then a textbook company bought [limited rights to] the mural image to use on three of their textbooks. *Progressive Grocer*, a trade magazine, wrote up the mural and the *New York Times* gave it a large photo spread, all across the top of one page, for an article about new murals in the city."

William Walsh's mural in the Bronx stressed the environment and combined his colorful style with the neighborhood's concerns, from local to international, relating to their surroundings.

This artist had a different experience where the weather was concerned. "Surprisingly, it was the *good* weather which caused problems—the kids didn't want to be on the site. It was too nice." He also found that the work will go "slower than you think it will, when you're working with kids. You have to schedule for when they'll be around."

The Bronx mural provided a springboard for Walsh's career. He is now working on "a synthesis between public art and fine art. Not 'fist in the air' stuff from the 1960s, but a way of looking at and commenting on society. As far as getting publicity for the work, you can't ignore a five-story mural and it's on view twenty-four hours a day. I got another mural project as a result of this one, from the Knights of Columbus—a project working with disabled older kids. And I'm going to Germany to work with young people there on a mural. They're very interested in how we are working here."

When I asked Walsh what an artist should know to begin a mural, Walsh replied, "That it's *not* an easel painting. That subtlety is lost. You need to work out a composition which fits the wall. From doing a sketch on paper to putting it on a wall requires that you think in different terms. For one thing, your perspective is going to bend if it's five floors up. And even though you're working in a community project atmosphere, the artist has to keep his vision."

The artists who work with CityArts are now thinking in terms of new materials. Watch for murals that employ neon and the collage-like mixture of mosaics and paint.

CityArts would like to hear from groups or individuals who are interested in doing mural projects. CityArts is a model organization which could work in any town, bettering the surroundings for citizens and bringing the community together. For more information, contact Tsipi Ben-Haim, CityArts, Inc., 225 Lafayette St., Suite 911, New York, NY 10012, 212-966-0377.

CHAPTER 21

Winning Public Art Commissions

Burning in Your Gut: Interview with Lisa Kaslow, Sculptor

Drew Steis

The package that came to my desk from Lisa Kaslow contained a cover letter, resumé, assorted reprints from newspapers, and twenty slides of her work. Kaslow is a sculptor who creates larger-than-life figures in stainless steel, bronze, concrete, cast fiberglass resin, and other materials. She also creates massive utilitarian gazebos, gates, pergolas, arbors, bus stops, and other outdoor structures usually incorporating seating arrangements. She hoped I would be interested.

It took me over a year to contact her for this interview.

It is a classic example of the way Lisa Kaslow markets her art. She is persistent and tries everything. She leaves nothing to chance in marketing her art. While she knows that being there at the right time with the right art wins commissions, she doesn't trust luck alone. With no agent and no gallery representation, she has created monumental works from New York to the Virgin Islands. Perhaps her most famous work is a series of seventeen larger-than-life-size sculptures of athletic figures installed at the Ammendale Technology Center in Beltsville, MD. Her secret for winning that and all commissions is simple: networking and tenacity.

She has the creative part down pat, her credentials are strong, and she has studied at some of the best institutions both here and abroad.

"I've been doing art since I can remember and probably before. By the time I was six I knew I wanted to be an artist, there really was no question," she told *Art Calendar*. Growing up in New York City she studied anatomy with her physician father, illustration with Ashley Bryant, life drawing at the Art Students League, ceramics at Greenwich House Pottery, sculpture with metalsmith Maxwell Chayat, and painting restoration and antiques with Mikel Carvin. She did a fresco and a monumental sculpture at her high school while still a student. She went to Yale in the second class to accept women and then studied Japanese at Columbia before going to Japan to study printmaking with Shoichi Ida and filmmaking with Kazuo Miagawa.

"I grew up in a milieu that was so supportive of the arts, there was nothing off-the-wall or bad about earning a living from the arts. It was no different than being a lawyer, stockbroker, or a plumber. There was no stigma attached to 'Why would you ever go into the arts?'"

Her mother was an editor with Simon & Schuster and a lifelong student of languages and culture. "Instead of going to camp in the summers, we went camping in Guatemala, Mexico, Alaska, Italy, and France. The more ruins and antiquities we could visit, the more jungles we could slough through, the more it was my mother's idea of a good time. "By the time I was twelve, I had seen all the great art firsthand: the *Pietà* by Michelangelo, the *David*, the Mayan ruins in Mexico, Diego Rivera, da Vinci's *Mona Lisa, The Last Supper.*"

In the mid-1970s during the Vietnam War, she traveled through Cambodia and Southeast Asia photographing people and places. She returned to Baltimore to earn her MFA at the Rinehart School of Sculpture but continued to study film-making. When she was unsuccessful in winning a $150,000 grant to produce her own 30-minute film script, she returned to sculpture.

"I wanted to do it, just do it, and I could do that immediately in sculpture and that was the mitigating circumstance that drove me to sculpture more than anything. I had control over it, it was accessible, financially I was capable of doing it. "If you've got something burning in your gut, you'll either find a way to get the money to do it or you'll find a route for that expression to materialize in some form that you are capable of doing."

She had sold her work privately while in high school, and she was referred to her first public commission while still in graduate school.

"The first piece I ever did commercially was for the City of Baltimore. I got a One-Percent-for-Art commission at City College High School in their gymnasium, a relief of four dancing figures called *Hi-Fly*. It was a $7,000 commission and I managed the funds, had a steel company cut the material, another company weld the clips, a third company sandblast and paint the job, and I still made money at it. When I think of it now it was a nice-size commission, it was great and it got me on track.

"The most important thing about developing a career is networking, talking to people, finding out what opportunities are out there and what is happening or making opportunities happen."

Lisa Kaslow read of an artist who had done busts of all of the mayors of New York City and donated them to the city just for the public relations value. "I said, 'Hey, I'll do the same thing.' So I went to the City of Baltimore and said I will do a bust of all the living mayors of Baltimore and all that I ask is that you pay for the casting costs because I don't have the money to pay for that out of pocket.

"I got unbelievable public relations from that. I got two one-man shows and television crews came in on a daily basis to film me doing this bust of Donald Schaefer. I developed a personal relationship with Schaefer who was then mayor and is now governor of Maryland and when I was finished he loved it. But the city would not pay for the casting."

She lets nothing go to waste. Lisa made a rubber mold of the bust, put it in storage, and went on to do a designers' showcase.

"This is what I mean about making a living as an artist. You have to do everything. You can't expect anybody to come to you. You have to network, network, network.

"Two designers in New York, one who knew my aunt, loved my work, so they set up a designers' showcase but they never told anybody who made the work. But there was an article in a local magazine about me and my work and this collector saw the article and called all the Kaslows in Baltimore looking for me. When he finally reached me on his car phone, and this was in 1979 when car phones were rare, he said, 'I'm on Interstate 95, tell me how to get to your studio.' When he got there he said 'I'll take that, and that, and I want a portrait.' Then he pulls out his wallet and it's stuffed with—not hundred-dollar bills—but thousand-dollar bills and he lays ten of them on the table."

Lisa Kaslow took the money and used part of it to cast the Schaefer bust at her own expense. She exhibited it at the Life of Baltimore Gallery, where it was purchased. It is now on permanent loan and on display at the Baltimore Convention Center.

"That is how stuff happens, there is no rhyme or reason, it just happens. But I have never had another experience like that. You want clients like that.

"I don't want to belittle my work but I like to be honest. They are not banging down the door all the time to get my things. But you talk to people, and people know other people, and this designer knows that designer, and one will tell me they are looking for something, why don't you call them up—and I do."

This networking has paid off for Lisa Kaslow.

"A designer who was handling all of the work for the Peter Island resort in the British Virgin Islands was a friend of the wife-to-be of the best man at my wedding. She suggested to the designer 'Why don't you look at Lisa's work?' I made a proposal and everybody loved it and I got the job.

"I have placed in the finals and as a semi-finalist in more competitions than I care to mention. I don't always go all the way but I know that people are seeing my work. I get wonderful letters of response. Usually there is a form letter written but on the bottom invariably there is a p.s.: 'loved your work, give it a try next time.' And that is very encouraging to me. I enter any and every competition—at least three a week. I do whatever it takes, wherever they are, I scrounge them up. I haven't hit on too many."

But when she does hit she hits big. "I had been applying to the Montgomery County Government Percent-for-Art Program and I kept getting rejected by the county government. All that time a developer had seen my work and was trying to find out where I was located. Then the guy from the Montgomery County Government who had been rejecting my work constantly, wrote a letter to the developer saying 'There is this gal Lisa Kaslow who keeps sending us stuff and we keep rejecting it but her work is really terrific so maybe you will like it.' The developer says 'Oh my God, this is the woman I've been looking for.' And he gave me a commission—that is, he didn't do me any favors, but he let me submit my work."

With her foot in the door Lisa Kaslow approached the commission from a different angle.

"I made the first cut and three of us were invited to submit models. I looked at the site and saw a nice big courtyard and thought, 'You don't need something to look at here, you need something to sit in. Why don't we make an environment to sit in?' The other artists presented models of something to look at and I created a place to meet and they approved my design." The Kaslow winning design was *Cogi-Gate*, a 12' diameter by 8' high gazebo with seating for twelve which was erected in the courtyard of Northwood Senior High School in Rockville.

Lisa Kaslow knows a living can be made in public sculpture today but says having a partner to share the financial burden of day-to-day living is important.

"The more negative the situation becomes with publicly funded art work, the more that will impact on private funding, because a lot of the private funding has taken its cue from the public funding. There still is enough momentum within the private sector to keep things going but you have to really aggressively seek it out.

"If I have any one bit of advice that I don't feel will in any way compromise my competitiveness in the marketplace, it is that the key here is making a market. Not going to the market. You are the market, you create the market. "If you have an idea, you can take it to a community and you can get the money raised one way or another. If you have a dream and it is burning a hole in your gut, it can happen. You just have to visualize it happening. If you don't have the funds, you can make the funds come together. As difficult as it is to tap in to those who chronically have been tapped into, there are others. The contributions don't have to be as monumental, you can get a groundswell of contributions. There are so many ways to get things happening. If you want to do a project, you can involve some of your suppliers in that process to keep the costs down.

"There are so many ways to creatively be creative. If you've got to do it you are going to find a way to do it. It is hard and I do complain about it, because there are so many competing for such a small pie, but that is what separates those who are tenacious from those who are not. And that doesn't have one bit of impact on whether or not you have talent. The tenacious and talented are going to get the job. The tenacious alone might get the job. The talented who are not tenacious are not going to get the job. That's what it takes, pounding the pavement."

She sees a new trend in art marketing emerging. "It used to be that nobody would go to a discount house unless they were poor but now everybody goes whether it is Ikea, Wal-Mart, Kmart, Price Club. You are going to the closest source of distribution from the manufacturer as possible. In fact, the manufacturers are all doing trade shows. They are going out and selling directly off their trade show floors. This is the trend in marketing right now, and galleries are stuck in one place and they are not roving. You have got to get out there and sell yourself directly to people. The most effective way of doing that is direct, hands-on presentation.

"For example, the listings [for Art Consultants] you had in the *Art Calendar Annual,* I sent a tickler package to every one. Then I prequalified by asking them to send a resumé about themselves back to me. I got a response from everybody I contacted, every single one. Now some weren't interested in my work for a variety of reasons—size or they didn't handle that kind of thing—but everybody responded. And they are all out there working for me on one level or another.

"Basically you keep directly marketing to your market. If your market is art consultants, because art consultants are handling a lot of the jobs, then you directly market to as many consultants as possible. If architects are the people that are the decision-makers, then you market to as many of them as possible. If developers are the ones, then you market to them.

"What you need to determine—and what I have been working out because it is a long process that takes hours and hours and hours—is a pinpoint focusing to develop your niche, your marketplace. Instead of shooting a wide spray of shotgun pellets out there, you are more rifling in directly to that market. There are enough organizations out there that have determined which architects and which art consultants are handling public art—all that information is there. You just have to use it. Those are the people that are more likely to work with an artist, you just have to go after them, keep after them."

How I Won a $20,000 Commission
Stanley Sporny

The brochure arrived in the mail. "Call for entries: A $20,000 Federal Art-in-Architecture Grant competition for the new annex of the Veterans Administration Hospital in Huntington, West Virginia."

The brochure went on to explain the application procedure, which was rather simple and straightforward. All they wanted first were slides and a resumé—project proposals were optional. If the panel of museum curators and other honchos selected your work as one of the three finalists, then a proposal for the project *would* be expected. A $500 stipend would be awarded to each finalist to research and execute a maquette, model, drawing, or painting, to scale. The V.A. Hospital would keep all models.

The search was concentrated in, but not limited to, the three states of Kentucky, Ohio, and West Virginia, since the hospital serves that area. Several hundred artists responded.

I imagined that at least some of the selection committee would be rather conservative, so sending them slides of my then-recent and raunchy Mardi Gras series "Ritual Ruckus" was definitely out. I also had to consider the site, a V.A. hospital. This was something my landscape paintings could answer. I had a good track record for all my landscape work. So I sent several slides that I calculated would have a bearing on the project I had in mind.

A concept had been rattling around in my head for a long time, and it was custom-made for this particular proposition. I had completed a small painting in 1977, an intimate view of a tiny rivulet—the uppermost headwaters of the Missouri-Mississippi—and the fluidity of the paint emphasized very well the liquid flow of the composition. Since then, I had been anticipating a "message from within" to begin a big series of paintings based on the headwaters and main streams of the United States. One of the things holding me back was initial research, which would require costly travel to collect visual data and work on-site. If I were to win this grant, I could launch the series of paintings I had hoped to realize for so long.

A few months after submitting my slides, resumé, and a brief outline of my concept/proposal, the notification came. I was one of the finalists.

We three were invited to view the new $11 million annex then in progress, and the chair of the selection committee, an administrative officer at the hospital, would brief us as to what was expected.

Two of us showed up. I brought my video camera, filmed the premises, and let the camera run through the entire briefing. The service history of the hospital was reviewed, as well as the architectural plans and site functions, charts and all. The artist's theme and form was left wide open, except for one condition: war scenes, or glorification of war, would not be acceptable.

The Proposal

I later took notes from my video, and hammered out a proposal that got my concept across very strongly, yet answered questions and suggestions which came up at the briefing. My proposal, which I copyrighted, was entitled "Art in Architecture Proposal for the Clinical Addition to the Huntington Veterans Administration Medical Center." The first part encompassed the introduction and the concept/proposal. The second part covered the value, workmanship, and materials used for the actual paintings. Part three discussed maintenance, placement, installation, and some options I was making available to them. Part four announced my desire to deliver the elective presentation in person to the committee; it included a schematic drawing of where the paintings would be placed on the designated walls, and what the proportions would be.

I began my introduction with the statement that "the subject of water as the main theme of my project would embody several issues. . . . The wellspring plucks the heartstrings and speaks to a basic need and understanding common to us all. The purity of water can symbolize the cleansing and renewal of the soul and can also symbolize the life-giving thread which stitches our nation into whole fabric."

I proposed a total of twelve paintings (six diptychs) for each of the six floors in the new addition that were accessible to the public. There were to be four paintings (two diptychs) from locations in each of the three states served by the hospital: Kentucky, Ohio, and West Virginia.

Under the heading "The Actual Paintings," I answered a very specific question posed by the committee: "What is the value we are getting for the money?" I wrote, "There is the intrinsic value which is measurable only from the innermost feelings of the individual viewing the paintings," and went on to say that even though the monetary value was $20,000, this would only actually pay for the six larger paintings at my wholesale price. The other six would be a gift to the veterans because I felt very strongly about accomplishing my goals for the concept. I finished by writing, "There is value set against the passage of time, which would put the intrinsic and monetary value beyond price."

Speaking of value, an interesting feature about this Federal Art-in-Architecture project is that the paintings belong to the American people and will eventually revert to the Smithsonian's National Museum of American Art. This project therefore has personal long-term investment value for me.

My proposal addressed the integrity of the workmanship due to meticulous archival care, materials I planned to use (the best available), and maintenance: I would return to clean and varnish the paintings one year from the date of installation.

Meticulous proofreading, tweaking the drawings, and careful selection of good paper for photocopied and sleekly bound essay packets finished the task. One copy was sent to each of the twelve committee members to review before the presentation meeting.

Research

The $500 stipend we were given for research was used, in my case, mostly for travel and visual documentation. Boating on the Ohio River and its nearby tributaries in an ancient runabout with a cantankerous and moody engine made for quite a few mishaps and terrifyingly close calls with coal barges. (They look so jolly from a distance!) A Mr. Trout (his real name) rescued us once when the engine conked out downriver, saying, "Yep, them barges run over folks and drownd 'em quite reg'lar." I decided to give my captain and the boat a rest after the #2 spark plug blew out with a loud "Biff!", skipped across the shallows, and sank in a tiny cloud of steam.

Finding the sources of the tributaries that feed into the Ohio around Huntington was just as harrowing. Locating Bobs Fork, the headwaters of the Guyandotte River, on Guyandotte Mountain could have been a disaster too, and nearly was. I got caught in a violent thunderstorm at the summit, and felt like Martin Luther must have felt when he swore, *Ach! Mein Gott! I'll become a priest!"* The video camera shorted out, and when I stopped to examine it I noticed a nearly completed hornet's nest just a step below. The occupants were pretty mad because the rain had ruined their arduous efforts. I backed away slowly just in case they decided to blame it on me.

By the time I stumbled back down into the holler, soaked and shivering, Bobs Fork was happily babbling over its bed, and all was sweetness and light.

And there I found the perfect location. Water flowed through a cleft in the bedrock. Dappled sunlight glinted warmly on moist, mossy surfaces. The camera worked.

Drying out while driving home, I reflected on past events. The gunfire and the occasional dead youth in "Crack Alley" behind our O Street studio in Washington, D.C. The entire Dumbara Valley, which I could see from my studio in Sri Lanka, going up in the smoke of genocide. The jostling of frenzied Mardi Gras revelers in New Orleans. And the wild events of the last few days. Brilliant realization: The life of an artist is not for the feeble.

I had used video before with my CRM Amiga computer for the "Ritual Ruckus" series. Digitizing the buffoonery of Mardi Gras from a stop-action VCR and manipulating the imagery with a paint program prepared me for the complex waterscape project I had in mind. The Golden Section has been an enduring device since I began to toy with it 15 years ago. Since the entire hospital has a gurney railing throughout, I had to deal with just the area above the railing.

The computer helped me decide on long horizontal paintings—actually a double overlapped Golden Section—and the small painting in each diptych would be a square with dimensions equal to the height of the long horizontal one. The measurements are 30½"x80" and 30½" square, with the space of a Golden Section between them (49") to occupy a total of 13'3½" running wall space.

The Presentation

I built two models of the hospital walls to scale, hand-colored a few printouts of my composites from the computer, and showed how my work would look installed. In addition, I had collected quite a few survey maps, and I also made a large-scale map of the tri-state area, labeled with the tributaries and sources I planned to include in the six diptychs. I rounded out the site-specific visuals with floor plans. And, assuming that some of the committee members would forget to bring the proposals I had sent to them earlier, I had thirteen more made, which included a fresh copy for me.

I also brought an actual artwork. I had just completed a commissioned work of the New River in West Virginia. This painting dovetailed with the theme I was going to suggest to the committee, and was also the precise size of the larger of the paired paintings I was proposing.

So I felt fully ready.

The Day arrived. I dressed in my sincere suit with tie and Dad's bequeathed wingtips. After setting up my wares, I entertained questions. Sure enough, all had left my printed proposal behind. It soon became apparent that nearly everyone present hadn't the foggiest idea about art. Mercifully, they did not profess otherwise, but were in fact sincerely interested and quick to respond to what I was proposing. The allotted time went very quickly. There was only one disaster: The borrowed painting slipped and nearly brained someone, but it was caught in time.

Since the art advisor, a museum director, could not attend the meeting, I had to deliver my pitch again later. However, it was easier this time because this was someone who understood art and comprehended perfectly my art and my concept. Two people from the V.A. were there too, and they were quite knowledgeable as well. The museum director said the large painting helped a lot, and I was glad I had again temporarily wheedled it from the owners. He thanked me for the presentation, said it was "outstanding," and I let him know that I would not hold a decision against me against him.

The Wait

After a few months, I telephoned the V.A. offices to inquire about progress. The man in charge told me quite directly that the submissions were so good, they were having trouble deciding.

Finally, I got the letter of acceptance.

We then had to negotiate the contract. The officer-in-charge of contracting at the V.A. Hospital said something wonderful at our first meeting: "A fully negotiated contract is a partnership." With that as our guiding principle, the standard twenty-eight-page federal contract was a breeze. A lot of the content was claptrap this or that congressman or senator had stuck in. The real meat was what I specifically would do and when. They included large portions of my proposal, rewritten in federalese.

All of this went to Washington to a battery of bureaucrats to pore over. They sent it back approved, with little time wasted. Only a couple of points were a bit sticky. One was my insistence on retaining the copyrights. They countered by writing in that I may not make *exact* copies of the paintings. That being impossible, I agreed. Also, I did not like being responsible for special lighting. We finally agreed that I would buy the lights, if deemed necessary by their art advisor (the museum director) and their electricians would install them.

More than a year passed from the time I became a finalist to the arrival of my first check in the mail. The $20,000 was divided into three installment payments, which I convinced them is the standard practice for commissioned work. I had to send them an invoice listing initial expenses, and bill them for $6,666.66.

Our graduate school had a few release time offerings to enable faculty to do research. Consequently, I am relieved of teaching one class this semester, so I have been able to stay close to the completion date. But the V.A. Hospital contract officers would rather see a job well done than something less than excellent in the earlier time frame. At this writing, the project should be installed by or before September 1995—a total of 2 years and 3 months from finalist to finish.

Spec Work?

Donna Marxer

Creating work on spec for an art competition? You may want to think twice. Several months ago I got an announcement for a terrific-sounding competition. A very reliable nonprofit arts organization, Creative Time Inc., joined with the powerful Metropolitan Transit Authority, offering a prize for a billboard designed to persuade the public to leave their cars at home and use public transportation. The winner would receive $1,000 and twenty billboard-sized reproductions of the work placed throughout the New York metropolitan area plus a mailing of 10,000 postcards depicting the winning artwork.

Since the subject was an environmental one and I had been working on a series of landscape paintings with this theme, I got excited. This was right up my alley. I didn't really expect to win, as the odds are high in a contest of this kind—but I really wanted to enter it because I felt it was a good cause.

When I got the guidelines, I read that slides of existing work would not do. Entrants had to make a scale model of the two-dimensional piece which was an odd size—12"x26"x^1/$_2$", to be precise. It meant painting a custom piece. Still, there was no entry fee, which might have stopped me; so I got to work and hand-delivered my entry to the MTA.

A few weeks later I got the not-unexpected letter of rejection, which raved about the overwhelming number of works entered. When I went to pick up my entry, I saw at least 100 other rejected pieces, and I was stunned by the quality of not only the design solutions offered, but the immense amount of technical skill that had gone into practically every piece. Wow, I thought, no wonder I didn't win. The winner must be really fantastic.

When I received one of the 10,000 postcards of the winning piece I started getting angry. Not only was it sophomoric by my standards, but it managed to deliver an insult to the very public it was meant to woo. The card depicted a photograph of a doll dressed as a clown with lots of accompanying text, sort of *a la* Jenny Holzer but in italics, calling this public "Bozos" for driving instead of using public transportation.

Again, I hadn't expected to win. But I objected on behalf of myself and the perhaps thousands of entrants who put their blood, sweat, and tears into their entries. Seeing what the chosen piece was, 1980s-style in-your-face, none of these works had a snowball's chance.

I wrote to Creative Time, suggesting that their choice was demeaning to its audience. The tone of my letter was by no means angry, and I gave them a positive suggestion: that in the future, when they sponsored this kind of competition, they should host an exhibition of all the entries—or as many as space permitted—so the public could see the variety of solutions and the imagination of the entrants. That approach would foster public and artist goodwill rather than make *everyone* angry.

I received no reply.

I started thinking about how many contests we artists enter on spec—where, even though no fee is charged, something more valuable is given: our time, our energy, and most importantly our greatest asset, our creativity. This kind of effort means more than money going out for, say, sending existing slides. It means risking more.

I called the Graphic Artists Guild for an opinion. This worthy organization has been advising artists in the design field for years and began publishing guidelines in 1982. Although they do not tell artists what they must or mustn't do, they do inform artists of the risks involved with speculative work. The G.A.G. also suggests that entrants find out who the judges are. I now blush to think that I neglected to do this when I entered my competition, but what the heck, Creative Time is so respected.

Will I ever do it again? Sure. But next time, I'll think twice. I'll remember, too, that what competition sponsors need from us, even more than quality work, is our numbers. The number of entries helps them get their NEA, state, and private grants—so they make their competitions look attractive. And maybe the lack of an entry fee isn't so pro-artist after all—the NEA and state agencies almost never fund an arts organization that charges fees to the artist.

Many Percent-for-Art programs offer honoraria to finalists. We need more of this kind of fairness. A public exhibition costs little to organizations like Creative Time with lots of public spaces at their beck and call and a track record for landing large grants. Let's let the arts organizations know that artists should be treated fairly. Let's get them to think twice, too.

As predicted, there has been a public outcry from citizens who don't like being compared to clowns.

Also, it seems that someone goofed at the MTA, big legal staff notwithstanding. The well-known clown, referred to in the text, is copyrighted. The copyright owner has sued for infringement. Although the name "Bozo" is in generic usage, the resemblance in the image is close to that of the original Bozo. The case is pending.

In the meantime, all the billboards have been removed from the city. So there are no winners.

Moving Toward the Light: Video Review
Carolyn Blakeslee

The video *Moving Toward the Light: The Making of a Public Work of Art* tracks the production of artwork by Barbara Brozik for a MARTA (Metropolitan Atlanta Rapid Transit Authority) station through conception, design, planning, tracking, production, installation, and the station's use.

The film opens in a gallery, which is in the front part of Brozik's and her husband's home. Several people were very busy, touching up the final details of an exhibit and getting ready to make this video.

Interviewed about her background, Brozik explained that prior to the MARTA commission she normally worked with framed paper constructions which she sold through architectural and interior design firms. It was a challenge for her to think in terms of 3-foot-square enamel panels rather than torn 6-inch-square pieces of paper.

The film cuts to her studio, dominated by a huge model of the station perhaps 20 feet long and wide, and a foot or two high, built from the architects' blueprints. The station is complex, with many ells and wings and angles. She had the model built to give her an idea of her "work in color flowing through the station," with her designs already in place throughout the model.

Now for the execution of the designs. The film shows how she started with 6-inch squares of paper, making several designs and painting over them with watercolor in increasing dilutions. The pigments gathered into shadow areas and gave texture. Then she tore the paper and glued the pieces to a backing to make a relief upon a 1-foot square panel. Several of these constructed panels, preliminary designs, are shown.

The film goes on to show how she made a Polaroid of each panel, had several copies of each made at the local copy center, and laid out the grids/designs. She kept track of all these designs and grids carefully in a master document. Each constructed panel was then photographed in black-and-white and greatly enlarged into 3-foot-square silkscreen transparent positives.

On to the plant, where the final panels were made. Three-foot steel sheet panels were dipped into acid bath to be receptive to the sprayed-on porcelain enamel, which is the same pulverized mixture of glass, clay, and water that is applied to stoves and refrigerators. It is easy to apply (sprayed on), impervious, long-lasting, and easy to clean up.

Each silkscreen was painted with some photographic emulsion, the photographic positive was attached to it, and the screen was put into a room "with an ancient arc light" for 15 minutes to expose it. Then several panels were screened from each design.

After the screening of the designs onto the panels, the panels had to be fired. They were hung from a conveyor belt—the panels moved around into and through the furnace, like a surrealistic drycleaner's shop.

Brozik spoke of the Greek influence on her work—she was deeply impressed by the clear air, the lightness, transparency, wateriness, and mystical qualities of the Greek islands when she visited. She intended her panels to have the effect of water and other elements of nature.

The film cuts to the installation on-site. Workers and scaffolding, crummy weather. The artwork turns out to be pretty much the skin—bright white except for Brozik's panels—of the station, as the construction was close to being finished.

Next were comments from MARTA riders. Generally they all felt that the artwork was an addition to the station. We found it endearing that the producers left in some of the funnier comments: One kid said he could have done it, and a jive fellow said that if he had the artist's name and number he'd commission her to do the same stuff on the walls of his apartment.

Try to ignore the music in this film. A combination of Island, New Age, and 1960s sounds, the music is fine when it serves as a background to speech, but when it has been dubbed in to serve as transitional or feature sound the small band is out of tune and out of sync.

Other than the music, *Moving Toward the Light* is a very fine film of value to any artist contemplating applying for a public art commission, especially if the intended medium is fired enamel. The film is full of step-by-step information on how this particular project was accomplished. Even if fired enamel is not of interest to the viewer, the film presents a wonderful perspective on thinking and accomplishing on a large scale. Management and tracking of the project are presented well too.

Made in 1987, the film was funded by the Fulton County Arts Council, the City of Atlanta Bureau of Cultural Affairs, and the Southeastern Media Fellowship Program. It is a Center for Contemporary Media production. The final moral of this film is, if you've been commissioned to make some public art, why not make a documentary of it? It's a useful promotional device for you and for the city's art program, as well as an educational tool which could be aired around the world.

Moving Toward the Light: The Making of a Public Work of Art, VHS, 30 minutes, is available for purchase or rental from New Day Films, 121 W. 27th St., Suite 902, New York, NY 10001, 212-645-8210.

CHAPTER 22

Your Proposal

Competing for Commissions and Grants:
Increasing Your Chances of Being Funded
Caroll Michels

Recently, I was one of eight jurors who met to select a public art project. The proposal I liked best was imaginative and sensitive to the surrounding environment. It was playful and expressed an intelligent sense of scale. In addition, the project would have been relatively easy to install, it was maintenance-free, and it would have been able to withstand inclement weather for many years.

However, the project did not win because the artist antagonized the jury by the condescending way in which she completed the competition application. Leaving most of the questions unanswered, in the space allocated for a project description she wrote in barely legible handwriting one sentence implying that a project description was unnecessary, and that the jurors must be stupid if they didn't understand the concept of the proposal by looking at the accompanying drawings.

Although most of the jurors agreed that her project was the best, they also concurred, based on the attitude expressed in her application, that the artist would probably be difficult to work with. Whether this would have been true is speculative, but the fact of the matter is that artist did not receive the public art commission because of the way in which she completed the application.

Grant and competition applications vary in length and complexity. Some applications are very simple and only require basic vital statistics such as an artist's name, address, phone number, and a set of labeled slides. Other applications are more elaborate and require extensive and detailed information.

Regardless of whether you are applying for a public art commission or a grant from a private foundation, applications and proposals must be given tender loving care. Following are some guidelines to help you increase your chances of submitting a successful application:

- Put yourself in the shoes of a juror. Basically, you would want to read applications that are legible, clear, and come quickly to the point. You do not want to have to reread sentences for the purpose of achieving clarity.
- All photographic material should be of top quality: clear and crisp, with good lighting and tone. Photographs or slides should seduce the jurors. If jurors are confused and can't see what is going on, they will not take the time to locate your application for written clarification.
- Submit photographs/slides of your most recent work. Although there are a few exceptions, most funding agencies do not want to see a retrospective of the last 10 years of work. Jurors want a strong, clear indication of your current interests and direction.
- Select photographs or slides of the best of your recent work. You decide what is best. If you are indecisive about what to submit, consult with a friend whose taste you respect.
- Even if the sponsoring organization does not require photographic materials to be labeled, label each and every slide or photograph with the following information: your name, the title, medium, dimensions, and date of the work, and include an arrow indicating the top of the slide/photograph. This information can make the difference between your work being rejected or entering the next stage of judging.
- Complete all of the questions. If any questions do not apply to your circumstance or situation, write in "N/A" or "Not Applicable." These phrases indicate to the jury that you neither overlooked a question nor were too lazy to respond.
- Avoid a negative tone, implying that you have a chip on your shoulder, and the world owes you a grant.
- Do not talk over the heads of readers. Avoid art-world jargon and over-intellectualized dogma.
- If you are asked to provide a budget with itemized expenses, be practical and realistic. Although you should not pad the budget with questionable expenditures, do not be shy about allocating money for yourself: compensation for the time you will spend on the project. This should be included under the heading "Artist's Fee."
- Don't undervalue or underestimate your time by including a low artist fee. In many of the grant and commission applications that I have

reviewed, artists only requested funds for project materials and limited overhead expenses. Compensation for their time and studio expenses were not included. Applications that do not include artist fees or list low artist fees and below-average overhead costs can indicate to a jury that you do not believe in your own worth (so why should they give you money?), and/or that you are not knowledgeable about project costs and therefore might not be able to complete the proposed project with the amount of funds requested.

Before completing a grant application, learn as much as possible about the funding organization, and carefully read the instructions and eligibility requirements. Some funding organizations award open-ended fellowships that do not dictate how the money must be used. Other organizations are very specific. For example, the Pollack-Krasner Foundation (725 Park Ave., New York, NY 10021) does not accept applications from commercial artists, photographers, video artists, filmmakers, craft artists, or any artist whose work falls primarily into these categories. In addition, Pollack-Krasner will not make grants to pay for past debts, legal fees, the purchase of real estate, moves to other cities, or the costs of installations, commissions, or projects ordered by others, and "with very few exceptions, the foundation will not fund travel expenses."

Although most funding agencies are amenable to giving artists grants to "further their profession or career," the definition of what constitutes professional or career assistance is rather limited. For example, the definition does not usually include marketing and public relations. Marketing and public relations tools are of primary importance to artists who either want to enter the marketplace or maintain momentum in the marketplace. But for the most part funding agencies have yet to realize that grants that are specifically earmarked to help defray the cost of public relations and marketing expenses could be instrumental in helping artists become more self-sufficient. Unfortunately, the mere mention of any sort of self-promotion expenditure in a grant application is the "kiss of death," and if you state that you wish to use part or all of a grant for the purpose of self-promotion, it is highly likely that your application will be rejected.

To a certain extent marketing and public relations expenses can be buried within the budget category "Project Documentation," which allows for the cost of slides, photographs, a photographer's fee, and various types of printed materials.

Good resources for locating grants for artists include: *Money for Visual Artists* ($12.95), *Money for Film and Video Artists* ($12.95), and *Money for Performing Artists* ($12.95). All three publications are available from Allworth Press, 10 E. 23rd St., #400, New York, NY 10010. In addition, *Money to Work: Money for International Exchange in the Arts* is available from the American Council for the Arts, 1 East 53rd St., New York, NY 10022.

PART 7

Still More Exhibition Sites to Consider (or Beware Of)

Flying Free #2, 1995, hand-dyed and painted cotton fabric,
machine pieced and quilted, Caryl Bryer Fallert, Oswego, Illinois

CHAPTER 23

Non-Gallery Exhibition Sites

How I Produce My Annual Show
Barbara Dougherty

I used to go hiking with my best friend's mother. If she got too tired, we would return by hitching a ride. My friend's mother would flag down a car by literally making a menace of herself on the road.

I learned a valuable lesson from her. I use this approach in art marketing. I put myself in the middle of the road and flag down my buyers.

Last year, at my annual art show, on March 3rd, sales of original paintings totaled $16,000. I also sold numerous reproductions and books of my work for another $5,000. The show was one day only of just my work and 800 people attended.

I did all the work to organize the show myself. The tasks were, in addition to making the paintings and prints, invitation by direct mail, securing a location, and organizing a crew to help at the event.

I exhibit at many locally organized art shows. At these shows I am advertising my work and building a mailing list. I work hard at conversation with the public during these local exhibits because this effort is the most effective advertising I can do for my annual show.

When someone at one of these exhibits expresses an interest in my annual show, I provide a form for them to return by mail; if they make this effort they can join my mailing list. Otherwise I don't sign people up on the list at the local show unless they purchase a piece. Anybody can build a list full of names—the list that works, however, is a list made up of purchasers. If a person will take the time to fill out a form and mail it to you, that person is more likely to become a purchaser.

Sometimes a person insists on returning the form at the exhibition rather than mailing it to me. When that happens I try to engage them in conversation.

Afterwards I place a rank on the form from "1" to "5." A person rated "5" is in my estimation more likely to be a purchaser than a person ranked "1." This ranking helps me make decisions about the amount of time and effort to invest in mailings to a particular person.

At one time locally organized shows were too expensive for me to display at, so I built a mailing list by having art shows in the homes of my friends and patrons. Very early in my career I tried to establish a relationship with each buyer so they felt there would be not only a present but also a future opportunity to purchase my work.

I do a mailing to my entire list before my annual show. My show is in March and my mailing goes out the second week of January. Even though my mailing list has 1,000 people on it, I hand-address the envelopes and I write personal letters to everyone. I even write personal letters to art editors of the local publications as a press release. An easier technique would be to use computerized labels and duplicate letters, but I want more attention given to this mailing than people give to junk mail. Last year the *Los Angeles Times* did a feature story on my work before the show in response to a personal letter I send the art critic.

I always use first class postage and I avoid all the symbols that people recognize as "direct-mail promotion" except for a stamp that says "address correction requested." The address-correction stamp and first class postage guarantees that the post office will return incorrectly addressed mail. This allows me to keep my list current. Second and third class postage permits do not guarantee the return to sender in the event of a wrong address. The difference in price between first and third class postage is balanced by having a list with a higher percentage of deliverable mail.

My mailing consists of a handwritten letter, a picture postcard of my work, and a simple return postcard. The return postcard, when it is mailed back by February 15th, will entitle the patron and a guest to an invitation to the show and a discount on items offered for sale. Having a return deadline makes for a higher response. This year I am also including a pocket calendar in the mailing with the date of the show printed prominently.

Each time I do a mailing, I go back through the mailing list and code the responses:

"1" means a person who came to a show and purchased.

"2" is for a person who came and did not purchase.

"3" is a person who said they would come but didn't.

"4" is for a person who said they would not come but wanted to stay on the list.

"5" is a wrong address.

"6" is for no response.

When a person's coded card has three "6's" I send them a special card that entitles them to a $50 discount on their next purchase of an original painting if they return the enclosed card. If they don't return the card I drop their name from the list. Also, when I write the personal letters, looking at the coded names helps in composing an appropriate letter.

The invitations go out to those who request them by return mail 4 weeks after the original mailing, and then I personally call everyone to whom I have sent an invitation. I feel awkward sometimes making these phone calls but if the calls are not made the percentage of people who say they'll come but don't is too large.

I hold this annual show in the classiest hotel in the area and I describe the event as casual. I think the public likes a reason to go to nice places and yet they do not want to be intimidated. My arrangements with the hotel have not been difficult. I went to the catering manager and asked what was the slowest time of the year for the hotel. I told him I wanted to hold a yearly art event during that time and I explained that the show would be advertised mostly by the process of direct mail. When I was told the room charge I requested that it be waived. I agreed to pay for their catering and promised to do everything I could to bring in a quality clientele. It was agreed that I would pay the hotel for wine and punch and cheese and crackers and that the hotel would provide the space for free. I learned subsequently that the same four adjoining banquet halls rent for $15,000 a night. I have held this show 5 years and every year we have the same conversation over the room charge and every year I remind the hotel of how many people I bring into the hotel for the event. And every year I get the hall free.

I always have the wine served in a wine fountain and I have a pianist playing at my show. I do this to create ambiance. I do not use electronic music or microphones because the idea is to create atmosphere, not interference. When the piano player takes a break during the show I feel like someone has stopped the action.

The crew that helps me with this event are all friends who volunteer their time. It takes about eight people. I have one friend who is the manager. She makes sure everything is taken care of and on the day of the show she does all the interaction with the hotel staff. We try to keep the hotel staff out of the room during the show.

I need to know who comes to the show, but people are impatient with complicated entry procedures. Most people do not sign guest books with complete information and legible writing. Instead of a guest book, I have entry cards that are used for selecting the winner of a free print. A crew member, instead of the guest, fills out the card so it is complete and legible. The greatest frustration is when this is not done and I have no way of knowing who came.

I have a separate area in which prints are sold but I usually don't spend time in this area. I always have another person who is in charge of print sales. I have a sales booth in the main room created by three tables arranged in a "U." There are chairs placed for people to sit there as well as around the room. Special purchase cards are filled out and the pieces are wrapped at the booth and I provide a person who carries work to the car for the customer. I do not prevent people from taking work when it is sold—after all, the items are for sale, not for exhibition. I have noticed that this practice creates a trend for people to come to the show early in the day.

Some of the crew are hosts/hostesses, and part of their work is to keep me from being monopolized by one or two people for too long. They lead other customers over to me or lead me to others when they see someone cornering me.

I have always prepared thirty new original paintings for this show, and by the time I arrive at the show I feel like I am already a success because I have once again created a reason to do the best work I can do. Having an attitude that I have already made my own success puts my customers at ease.

My job at the show is to share as much as I can about how I feel about the new paintings and to share my personal experience of being an artist. I don't limit myself to stories of adventures in finding or painting the images. I include sharing the technical successes and failures of the individual pieces. For instance, I might tell how a particular sky in one of my paintings came nowhere near the intensity I wanted to express. I try to be revealing and to help a person see and understand my work.

Currently my show is a one-day event. In the future, as I have begun to advertise this show on local television, I might add a patrons' preview the night before.

I do not charge an admission fee, for I don't want a person to feel that he has already spent money before considering an art purchase.

The total cost of the show last year including the mailing was around $2,000. Food and drink was $1,100; transportation was $150; thank-you dinner for volunteers was $250; catalog and other printing was $100; approximately $500 for mailing. If I had the same sales in a gallery it might have cost me $10,000 in commissions alone.

When I talk to people about this show, I make it a point to tell them that the show is more of a celebration than an exhibition. I tell friends to come whom I know do not intend to purchase, because the success of the event is dependent on the atmosphere, and the more people enjoying themselves the better.

Yet I am fully confident that my show will not degenerate into just a party without sales because of the depth of preparation, the solid mailing list, and the formality of the location.

I look forward to my annual show as the highlight of my year as an artist. I plan within the next few years to sell every single one of my thirty paintings at my annual show, which will allow me to continue to find new and varied scenes to paint.

Go Where the Money Is
Debora Meltz

When the infamous Willie Sutton was asked why he robbed banks, he replied, "Because that's where the money is." If you want to sell your artwork, you too will have to go where the money is. And that money is not always browsing the galleries in whatever passes for SoHo in your area.

Artwork needn't be shown only in galleries or gallery-like settings, such as lobbies or libraries. After all, most art people buy ends up in homes or offices, in eclectic settings alongside books, computers, pots and pans, and stereo equipment. So why must it be exhibited only in places constructed solely for the display of art?

Many discretionary acquisitions are impulse purchases, so it makes sense to put your work where people are likely to have the impulse to purchase it. This may mean abandoning the mindset that art is somehow sacred and not a commodity to be marketed. Artists need to take advantage of as many possibilities for exhibiting their work as they can find—or create.

The following are some examples of unconventional locations for showing art. Such situations are obviously not for everyone, but if you think your work would do well with this type of exposure, you might want to give something similar a try.

Retailers are always looking for "tie-ins," for something attention-getting that will make people want to go into that particular store. With this in mind, an acquaintance of mine approached the owner of an upscale liquor store in his town with the proposal that he exhibit his paintings of bottles and glasses during Wine Awareness Month. The owner agreed and the artist arranged his work in the store windows and hung a few pieces on the walls. He put a card with the title and price next to each painting and left a stack of brochures by the cash register. The store owner was willing to accept payment for any paintings sold and to hold the checks for the artist. This is important since such purchases are likely to be made on impulse, and once the customer leaves the store the impulse goes with him. In this case, the artist included the sales tax in the purchase price and had the checks made out directly to him. The store owner took no commission—he figured he got a free display out of the deal.

Another artist I know paints dancers. She hung several pictures in her daughter's dancing school. While none of the exhibited pieces sold, she did sell a number of sketches to the mothers whose budding Pavlovas had pliéd beneath her paintings.

A fine jewelry shop near me displays exquisite miniature landscapes in the cases with the merchandise. The owner told me that they sold so well she no longer took them on consignment, but purchased them outright.

Another jewelry store that specializes in handmade silver also sells fine crafts and small sculpture. When the store was renovated, the owner left two large walls as a gallery area where paintings and other wall works are displayed. She told me that the art and crafts sold very well to the same customers who purchased jewelry.

A watercolorist who does large floral paintings displays one in each window of a local florist's shop at all times. Hardly a month goes by that she doesn't sell something.

A few years ago I worked with a model who owned an extensive collection of flamboyant vintage clothing in which she posed. When a friend of mine opened a boutique, I hung some pastel sketches of that model. They all sold.

My most unusual exhibition experience was at a health club where I had a membership for a few painful years. The gym was a vast mirrored room with 13-foot ceilings. The mirrors were only 8 feet high, leaving a wide band of blank wall around the entire room. One day, as I was huffing away on a machine designed by a descendant of Torquemada, the owner of the gym strolled over and informed me that he had seen some of my stuff (yes, that's precisely the word he used) at a friend's house and why didn't I bring some of it in and hang it above the mirrors. At the time I was doing pastels of figures of rather imposing proportions and he thought they might inspire the members. After my work had been hanging a while, I got a call from a man who wanted to purchase a particular piece. His wife had admired it and he had jokingly told her that he would get her the picture when she got to look like the figure in it. Her birthday was coming up, and although she didn't yet look like my drawing, he wanted to buy it for her.

Interior decorators can be excellent sources of sales. If the decorator has a showroom, she may be willing to hang your work on consignment or even purchase it outright. If there is no showroom, the decorator may want to show clients a portfolio of photographs of your artwork. Originals can be brought to interested clients later on. You will need to have 8"x10" color photographs (not slides) of your work along with a well-designed resumé and other pertinent information in a neat, attractive folio. Prints can be made from your transparencies, and most graphic arts supply stores or catalogs sell good-looking, durable presentation portfolios that can be customized for your own individual look. A number of artists I know have sold very well through decorators.

Frame shops frequently display the work of artists whose work they frame. In fact, many galleries help cover their expenses by framing. One thing to watch out for if you exhibit in a frame shop is that you do not pay a commission on any framing done for you by that shop. A number of my friends realized, too late, that after they had paid for their work to be framed, the gallery in the same store took its commission on the framed price.

Home furnishings stores will sometimes take work on consignment, or even buy it outright. When a friend of mine sold furniture at a large department store, he arranged for the buyer to look at the work of several of his friends. A number of pieces were purchased from various artists. A California artist told me that she displayed work at a Home Depot and sold every piece she exhibited!

Bookstores can offer good opportunities for selling photographs or artwork. With a little imagination, it is easy to tie into whatever the subject-of-the-month happens to be. Bookstores are excellent places for selling prints and drawings. Somehow, books and prints just seem to go together.

I know this suggestion will bring a shudder to many of you, but restaurants can be great places to show art. A lot depends upon how you, the artist, display the work. If at all possible, show pieces that are of a similar theme and/or are all in one medium. Have them all framed the same way, preferably in simple frames. This provides some continuity in an otherwise visually disrupted setting and it also makes it easier for viewers to get to know your work.

A little gourmet lunch shop on the main street in my town shows the work of local artists. Several fine pieces have sold from this modest location. The owner of the shop also offers the wares of local potters and basket weavers; she tells me that crafts that can be filled with food are big sellers at holiday times.

Get to know the type of clientele an eatery attracts before you consider putting work in it. Often the appearance of an establishment belies the nature, and finances, of its patrons. If you feel you might be able to sell your work at a particular place, but it has absolutely awful stuff already on the walls, ask the owner if it would be possible to remove the existing decoration for a short trial period while your art is being displayed. I have seen restaurant interiors transformed by artwork.

Many restaurant owners are happy to hang art. It saves them the trouble and expense of buying it themselves. A friend of mine has, for years, hung her work in a restaurant near her home. She sells consistently, both to regular patrons and to the occasional visitor. She hangs a small, printed card next to each picture, on which is printed her name, the title, medium, and price of the piece. She also includes sales tax in the selling price. When a piece is sold, the customer makes the check out directly to the artist. The owner then calls her to pick up her check. She pays the owner a 20 percent commission; to simplify bookkeeping, she pays her commissions quarterly. At the end of the year she sends the restaurant a statement of the amount of commission she has paid, keeping a copy for herself for tax purposes.

When dealing with restaurants, taverns, and other eateries, be aware of the quality of the air. Cigarette smoke and greasy cooking fumes can damage your work.

Opportunities for displaying and selling your work are everywhere. But you will have to seek them out or create them. Look around wherever you go for unused walls, tops of display cabinets, or any other usable space. Most retailers do not think of art when they plan their displays. You will have to approach the store owner with a definite proposal.

Look for locations that attract people who would naturally be interested in your subject matter. A wildlife artist in my county sells prints and drawings at local pet stores, as does another who paints pets and farm animals. The latter has sold some large paintings of horses and other livestock at feed and grain stores! Many people who keep horses or raise prize cattle have more than a little discretionary income. Don't underestimate the clientele of a given establishment. After all, a thoroughbred eats oats just as any other horse does.

If you do arrange to sell your work in an alternative setting, be sure to keep in mind that sales tax must be collected and paid by either the artist or the establishment. Records of sales and commissions must be kept and income reported.

Insurance on the work must be carried by either the artist or the establishment. If your work is not very expensive, the store's insurance policy might cover it. If not, you might work out a deal with the owner to add a rider to the store's policy for which you might have to pay. Your own homeowner's policy might cover your artwork, but don't assume that it does—most insurance companies are reluctant to insure art. You will need to have a record of recent sales in order to establish prices. Even then, your insurance policy might not cover your artwork if it is outside your home. There are companies that specialize in insuring art (see the *Art Calendar Annual*), but they tend to have high premiums; on the other hand, these policies are generally designed for artwork on display in locations other than one's studio. Finally, you can elect to "self-insure." This simply means that if a work is stolen or damaged, you bear the expense.

Keep in mind that most stores have seasonal merchandise, so if your work is of flowers or landscapes, you might want to display it in the spring or summer. If you do snow scenes . . . well, you can figure it out. A bit of trial and error marketing research might be necessary to determine what sells and when.

If you live near a resort area, remember that tourists (even sophisticated ones) love scenes that remind them of the places in which they have vacationed. And if you don't do "local color," remember that people also love to say, "Oh, this? We picked it up from a wonderfully promising artist when we were at the Cape this summer. Someday she will be famous, and this painting will be worth a fortune!" And it might very well be true.

CHAPTER 24

Cooperative Galleries

The Benefits of Membership in an Artist-Owned (Cooperative) Gallery

Rima Schulkind

Before discussing the specific benefits of membership in an artist-owned gallery, I would like to mention two general considerations. First, a nationwide survey of professional artists a few years ago revealed that less than 5 percent had any kind of gallery representation. Even if they were wrong by a factor of 100, that would still mean that fewer than 10 percent of artists in America who consider themselves to be professionals had a place to hang their work. Two, whatever personal reasons artists have for making art, communication in some form is invariably one of them. For a visual artist, communication simply means having the work seen.

Many commercial galleries look for artists solely on the basis of a museum stamp of approval or curator recommendation, often refusing to look at the work or even the slides of an artist without such credentials, the possession of which usually means instant acceptance. Another restriction is that many commercial galleries promote a certain "style" or "look," a limitation repugnant to many serious artists. Thus, in an area where the number of artists far outnumber the available gallery walls, the art scene is largely a closed shop except for cooperatives.

In addition to providing the opportunity to show one's work, cooperative gallery membership offers the artist total artistic control over work shown and created. In a commercial gallery, artists exercise little or no control over how or how much of their work is hung or how often it is featured. Further, the security of the certainty of having a place to show is an impetus toward growth. The artist who belongs to a co-op has the luxury of experimenting with new ideas and materials without fear of rejection or commercially determined disapproval.

Another benefit is the continuous interaction with other artists, who can provide technical and aesthetic feedback, as well as the milieu in which to socialize with one's peers. Most artists work alone both by choice and of necessity. In a cooperative, member artists need not experience the isolation that many artists suffer.

While I have addressed the intangible, although very real, advantages of co-op membership there is, of course, the dollars-and-cents aspect to be considered. The commercial art world rests squarely on the backs of artists—obviously without the art produced it could not exist. But except for the very top galleries and their stars, the artist is frequently expected to bear much of the cost of mailings, publicity, openings, catalogues, re-framing to gallery-recommended frames, etc. This is in legitimate, traditional, commercial galleries, where the costs can end up being as high as in cooperatives. Further, remuneration for work sold can be very problematic—despite contracts and promises, payment can be delayed or withheld. I have just received the last payment for a work sold 3 years ago to a private Indianapolis gallery, 30 percent of the total having gone to the collection agency I had to resort to, an experience far from unusual among artists. At least in cooperatives, the cost is up-front and payment is swift.

I belong to two artist-owned galleries, Touchstone in Washington, D.C., and Pleiades in New York City. For the 10 years I have belonged to Touchstone, my sales have equaled or exceeded my gallery expenses except for the past year. Touchstone's sales in 1992 equaled more than double the amount of the members' expenses, and in 1993 sales were even higher. My recent show at Pleiades resulted in a sale and a commission that exceeded my expenses.

A cooperative gallery is not the same thing as a "vanity gallery." The cooperatives with which I am familiar, both in Washington and New York, have rigorous jurying standards. No matter how much a gallery may need a full roster of members to pay gallery expenses, I have repeatedly witnessed rejection of applicants (I would estimate about 90 percent) because their work did not meet the member artists' aesthetic standards. "Vanity galleries," on the other hand, are usually privately owned, and charge one and all for wall space with little or no standards of excellence in evidence. There the artist is truly exploited, for "jurying" fees, hanging fees, agents' fees, all go to enriching the owner and giving the artist at best group shows of unrelated and uneven work. Also, each member has a say in the policies and practices of the gallery. Members know where the money goes—it isn't simply handed over to someone else.

In short, many artists prefer to be affiliated with a cooperative. The aesthetic control, comradeship, and opportunity to present our work in the manner we deem most appropriate are well worth the costs to us. After all, the members of the cooperative are joint owners of a gallery, and our dues represent the cost of doing business.

CHAPTER 25

Vanity Galleries
and Rental Spaces

Vanities: Caveat Exhibitor

Debora Meltz

Located in the art capital of the world, NYC, Gallerie Moi is actively seeking artists to exhibit in its SoHo space. Send slides, resumé, $20 review fee, SASE to Gallerie Moi, 9876 Winter St., New York, NY.

Established, artist-run, cooperative gallery seeking new members. Great NYC location in the heart of SoHo. Send slides, resumé, SASE, to VousART, 6789 Mopp St., New York, NY.

We've all seen ads like the above in the back of art magazines. They sound good—here's a chance to have your work reviewed by a New York gallery and perhaps even get a show. What've you got to lose?

Money. Possibly a substantial sum.

A prospectus I recently received from an artists' cooperative gallery lists its membership requirements as a $300 initiation fee, $900 annual dues, a 40 percent commission on work sold, gallery sitting, attending meetings, and working on committees. This entitles a member to the following: a two-person show once every 2 years, group shows July through August, use of bin facilities, continuous showing in the alternative gallery, and promo materials kept on file.

The bottom line? For $2,100 over 2 years you get one two-person show, have your stuff on file and in a bin, get a group show in the slowest time of the year, and hang work in an area that isn't part of the main gallery.

Don't be misled by the fact that cooperative galleries have jurying processes—this is because membership must be limited. Bear in mind that if every participant is promised a one- or two-person show every 2 years, the number of artists on the membership roster cannot exceed the available time slots for shows.

Membership fees can range from a few hundred dollars a year to over $4,000. One gallery charges a $500 initiation fee and monthly dues of $300. That adds up to $4,100 for the first year and $3,600 thereafter. And the gallery takes a 30 percent commission on sales. (Such a deal!)

At a "vanity" gallery, you pay to show. And you may pay a lot for very limited exposure. Before dealing with such galleries you should know exactly what you'll be getting, and not getting, for your money.

Many cooperative and vanity galleries make a point of noting that they are nonprofit. This is irrelevant. While it may seem as though nonprofit status would be advantageous to the artist, in fact it merely simplifies the operations of the gallery with respect to taxes.

I contacted a few vanity galleries to ascertain precisely what I could expect for my money. Some galleries will place a listing in your local gallery guide, but if you wish to have an ad, anywhere, you must pay for it yourself. A listing is not an ad—it is a perfunctory announcement of your show among many others, just like a movie listing. Some galleries will distribute a press release—if you give them one. Some require you to do *all* the publicity work. Some galleries will provide the wine and cheese at your opening. The printing and mailing of the invitations are usually paid for by the artist.

Traditional commercial galleries make their money from commissions received from sales of artwork. That commission is the incentive for the gallery to actively promote and market your work. If, however, your fees and dues are covering the overhead, there is no reason for the gallery to expend time, money, or effort pushing your work.

Most successful galleries do not depend on walk-in trade for their sales. The staff beats the bushes to promote its artists. They approach corporations, museum curators, architectural and interior designers, and private collectors. These galleries have substantial mailing lists of people who buy art, not just artists and their friends and families. A gallery should earn its commission.

For the most part, artists' cooperatives and artist-owned galleries are not moneymaking schemes. On the contrary, they are sincere attempts by well-meaning and serious artists to find alternative venues for exhibiting their work.

The members themselves do the work which would otherwise be done by a gallery staff.

But the cold fact of the matter is, the art world rarely takes these galleries seriously. Many critics will not review shows at such galleries. I have been told by art advisors and consultants that they do not think much of these galleries because they know the artists are basically renting space to display their work. It might be unfair, but artists who show in these spaces are considered naive. People in the very difficult business of selling art look for a certain level of knowledge and sophistication in the artists they work with.

Around 10 years ago, an acquaintance of mine belonged to one of these galleries for 2 years. Her investment was about $2,400. In those 2 years, she sold two pictures for $75 each. After the 20 percent commission she received $120. She did have her one-person show—and she paid for the invitations and mailing and she did most of the publicity work herself. She later commented wryly that there were only friends, family, and other artists at the opening. Nothing sold. Subsequently, she was advised not to list this show on her resumé, as it would only detract from her other genuine credentials.

Then there are the galleries that simply rent wall space to anyone who can afford it. These enterprises rarely even have real screening processes—if you can pay, you're in. Some charge per square foot and hang work from floor to ceiling in what they call "salon" fashion. This usually results in an overwhelming jumble in which some works become all but invisible.

A mailing I received a few months ago offered 10 linear feet at $800 for four weeks. The prospectus stipulated that work may *not* be double-hung. Another space offered 12 linear feet for $950. If you wished to double-hang within that space, an *additional* $600 was required. These places boast that they take no commission!

Vanities rarely do any serious publicity. I use the term "serious" because there are publications that specifically serve these galleries. You may be told that an article about you or your show will be placed in *ArtBabblePress*. What you may not know is that *ArtBabblePress* caters almost exclusively to the vanities (with a museum thrown in or an art celebrity name-dropped to lend it credibility). If you sign on for a show or rent wall space, *ArtBabblePress* will then try to sell you advertising space.

I'm not saying that no one ever sells from vanity galleries. I am saying, however, that few recoup their expenses. If your work is salable, it can be handled by galleries, interior designers, consultants, dealers, or others who will either buy the work outright or take it on consignment. There is a market somewhere for almost everything. If you are having difficulty selling your work, you may need to reevaluate your market and/or your promotional methods.

Marketing and promotion can be just about the most daunting, intimidating, and unpleasant aspects of being an artist. They are necessary, however, and as one comes to terms with the business of art they become less onerous.

If you are fortunate enough to have the funds to exhibit in a vanity gallery, that money might be better spent on aggressively promoting your work yourself. It will require extra effort, but you are more likely to get your money's worth.

One final note. Vanity galleries should not be confused with artists' organizations, associations, councils, leagues, or other membership groups whose members pay a small fee, usually $20-50 per year. These organizations offer a substantial additional base of support from non-artist members and community and grant moneys. Often these organizations do not limit participation in their exhibitions to their membership, although usually only members may keep slides and promotional materials on file. Frequently their exhibition spaces are donated or volunteer-run. These organizations can provide an excellent alternative to the gallery scene.

CHAPTER 26

Avoiding Sharks

Protecting Yourself from the Takers

Drew Steis

The art marketing world can be divided into three parts: the creators who make the art, the helpers who assist the artists in selling what has been created, and the takers who try to get as much as they can from the creators and give nothing or as little as possible in return.

Today we are going to talk about the takers.

The takers are the rip-off operators, the vanity strokers, and the scam makers who—even as you read this—are scheming up new, slicker, and even more effective ways of taking your money and your art from you.

The best way to protect yourself from the takers is to use common sense. Remember the "sucker is born every minute" rule. If it sounds too good to be true, take another long, hard look at what is being offered.

There are all kinds of takers. There are consultants, representatives, and agents who promise, for a fee, to sell your art. There are publishers who, for a fee, will reproduce your art in a book. There are galleries that, for a fee, will either give you a show or try to sell your art. There are competitions that, for a fee, will judge whether or not your art is worth showing to others. There are vanity galleries that, for a fee, will let you try to sell your own and others' art from their space. And, there are private, corporate, and "museum" collections that, for a fee, will look at your art for possible acquisition.

At the same time there are the helpers in all of the above categories who are sincere, honest, and working for artists for fair compensation. That's the problem: How can you tell the takers from the helpers?

Clues

1. One way to tell the takers from the helpers is to look at when fees or commissions are due. The takers almost always promise representation,

shows, services, publicity, and/or sales for money paid first and up-front—usually substantial amounts of money. Sometimes they deliver, sometimes they don't. This is a gray area; occasionally, artists are happy with what they have paid for—but most times they are not, and they are too ashamed of having been taken to protest it.

2. Another clue: The slick takers plan their deadlines and sales pitches so you have little time to make up your mind. You get the unsolicited prospectus and you have only a few days to send in your "reservations" and fees.

3. The language and format used in their ads and prospectuses can also be a tip-off:

   • The word "prestigious" is stereotypically a part of questionable competitions. A judgment like that should be left to critics and participants, not the sponsors before the event has even taken place.

   • An invitation to exhibit in "SoHo" or "the heart of SoHo" usually turns out to be a solicitation from a vanity gallery.

   • ALL CAPITAL LETTERS in magazine classified ads are awfully hypey. Designed to get the attention of as many artists as possible, these ads might be intended to solicit as many entries as possible with the entry fees benefiting the sponsors.

   • Ditto for improbably large prize amounts like "Up to $55,000 in prizes!" and for generous use of exclamation points.

   • If the prospectus says "Invitation Only" and you receive it via bulk mail, you are probably being misled. The technology associated with direct mail is very sophisticated, and those flyers can be personalized as fast as they can be printed. There's nothing wrong with someone telling you that "You are invited to enter . . ." but to tell you that you have already been accepted when in fact you have not yet been accepted may be fraud.

   • If the prospectus goes on and on about "new, emerging artists," or underrepresented artists, then consider the possibility that the artist's inexperience and hunger for recognition is being preyed upon.

4. Beware of so-called museums, institutes, foundations, collections, and galleries that may be so in name only. Reputable museums and

institutions do not solicit artists' portfolios: they are already inundated with submissions. Impressive, expensive, or beautiful stationery does not make a taker any less of a taker. If the institution has an impressive name or a drawing of columned facades on the letterhead but you just can't quite place the institution's name, get on the phone. Call the Better Business Bureau, Chamber of Commerce, and gallery dealer's association in the sponsor's area to find out whether the entity is in business and, if so, how long it has been in operation. Many so-called museums and institutions have turned out to be rented storefronts, mail drops, or even apartments. If your research reveals a rat, it can't hurt to call the state's attorney general as well as alert the post office to the possibility of mail fraud.

Examples

Everyone has his or her own story about the takers. We all have heard about the vanity book publisher in Chicago who collected $1.7 million from 3,000 artists promising each one of them one page of reproductions of their work and one page of biographical information. That book would have been a minimum of 6,000 pages long if it had ever been published. But it was not—and artists lost their money, slides, transparencies, and other materials. By the time artists got suspicious, it was too late. That publisher was enjoined from publishing any more sourcebooks in Illinois, but in the meantime he has had at least one other book published by a major New York publishing house.

Galleries have closed with artists' work lost behind locked doors or tied up in costly court battles. When dealing with agents or galleries always have a contract that indicates that your work is on consignment but still owned by you.

Art representatives, agents, and advisors have disappeared with works either sold or in hand, and the artist never sees the work again *or* any money.

It is not unheard of for the artist to receive less than his share of what a work actually sold for. To safeguard yourself against this practice of underreporting sale prices, and to build your own mailing list, always request the names and addresses of those who have purchased your art from your representatives.

A so-called foundation in New York City announced the expansion of its permanent art collection and issued a call for the works of new, emerging artists but requested a $29 processing fee. The foundation didn't exist as a nonprofit foundation. An individual, not a foundation, lived at the address listed. But according to the Postal Service, if this "group" purchased just one work they circumvented mail fraud laws.

A prestigious-sounding "institution" issued an invitation-only call for entries with a $25 entry fee; this fee was the only charge outlined in the call for entries. Nearly all entrants had two pieces accepted—and all were then hit with a $49 per piece processing fee on top of freight charges. The "institution" was only 6 months old, though they spoke of their event as if it had taken place for many years. The listed address was just a mail drop.

A museum in a foreign country may not be what we in the United States would consider a museum. One group in France calling itself a museum is actually a private home. Though the house is technically a museum because of its historic interest and its place on the nation's historic registry, according to the French Embassy this museum's shows are held in the dining room. Some prospectuses only quote one-way shipping charges, leaving the artist to decide whether to pay extra or abandon the art in Europe after the show is over. The same competition accepted an artist who had written for information but sent no slides.

Vanity galleries typically are enthusiastic as they offer a show to an artist, for the fees to the artist begin to accumulate and can exceed $5,000 when everything is added up. There may be a membership fee, a per-month or per-exhibit fee, maybe hourly fees for phone work or some other kind of additional retainer. Add on an exorbitant insurance fee, publicity and reception fees, the shipping, and the framing. Adding insult to fiscal injury the gallery will take up to an additional 50 percent commission if anything sells, and if it discounts the price, guess who loses his share of the sale price? Avoid renting wall space in galleries; typically their shows are "salon-hung" with dozens of paintings squeezed into every space from floor to ceiling.

If You're Not Sure

To protect yourself from the takers, ask yourself the following questions:
- Do I, or does anyone else I trust, know of this organization or individual?
- Do they list a street address, a telephone number, and operating hours?
- Are the dates and location of the show given?

- Is this an annual event and/or does this organization have a known track record of producing successful shows?
- Have they told me all the fees up-front? If the acceptance letter socks you with additional fees that were not outlined in the initial entry materials, then you have every right to complain to the proper authorities.
- Are the fees worth to me what they say they will provide?
- Do I or anybody else know the jurors, curators, space, etc.?
- Will they give me references?
- Do I want my work associated with this group?
- Do the shipping charges cover round-trip or one-way?
- Is there a reasonable chance I will get my work back?
- Is there a better way to spend this money to promote my art and my career?
- Will I be proud to have this connection appear on my resumé?

If You're Still Not Sure

If all of the above questions are answered to your satisfaction, here are a few more warning signs that should make you think twice about becoming involved.

- The entry fee seems unusually high to you.
- The prize moneys are directly linked to the entry fees received.
- The museum, foundation, and/or collection charges an entry or processing fee for looking at slides.
- The gallery charges an exhibition fee plus a sales commission.
- The vanity book will be seen only by the artists who buy space.
- Your state arts council has never heard of the organization, gallery, show, individual, or group.
- The solicitation or call for entry appeals to your ego or vanity more than your talent.

There is hope. We may not know the enemy but we know how the taker works so we can plan a defense. That defense is common sense. Don't be rushed into making a decision or sending money, slides, or art before you have weighed all the angles.

Pay with a credit card when possible to give yourself the option of canceling the charge if you are not satisfied or services are not provided.

Never sign a contract or agreement without having some counsel, preferably legal, also review the wording.

If you still have doubts or unresolved questions, don't get involved no matter how great the opportunity seems. Art marketing is like waiting for a bus. If you miss one opportunity, another will be along soon.

Art Calendar would never stand in the way of an artist profitably and successfully marketing his or her art. But we hate to see the takers continuing to make a handsome living from artists while giving little in return.

PART 8

Practical and Emotional Matters

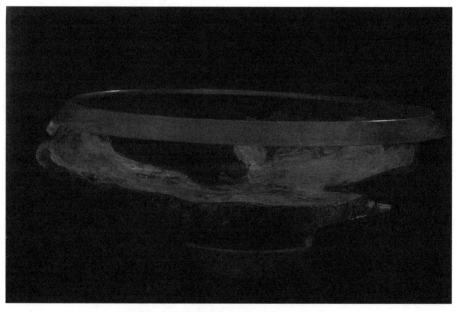

Salad Bowl, 1994, turned weeping willow and walnut,
6"x15"x15", Joe Dickey, Annapolis, Maryland

CHAPTER 27

Pricing

Pricing: A Different Notion
Barbara Dougherty

The pricing of artwork is not comparable to the pricing of any other commodity except gold. Gold is priced to what the market will bear. Art, like gold, tends to increase in price when there is a great demand. Also, like gold, the price of production (gold, mining—art, materials, and time) only minimally influences the pricing.

Then how should an artist price? I read an article recently that recommended pricing artwork by a standard derived by the number of sales one has consummated, or the number of collectors one has. The assumption behind this standard is that an artist must at all times be involved actively in the art marketplace for their art to gain recognized value. I object to this standard. I feel an artist must be involved in a serious and committed fashion to the creative task of making art and that alone is enough of a standard over time to raise value.

For instance, an artist named Edward Hagerdorn lived in California in the 1900s. Most of his work was done in the 1920s and 1930s. His work was exhibited in the Oakland Art Museum in the 1930s, and during the exhibit he was told to remove the pieces that were of unclothed females—nudes. This offended him so much that he refused to show his work publicly or make sales from that time onward. To the Bay Area artists, like Diebenkorn, he was a guru. Now his estate has been sold to a San Francisco gallery. It has overwhelming value and art significance—should it have less value because it was never really shown or marketed in his lifetime?

What of the truly dedicated artists in the colleges and universities? Does their work have less value or more because of a limited involvement in art marketing?

The value of art and its significance is in direct proportion to the serious nature of the artist's commitment to spend time—and more time. The more time an artist spends on art in a lifetime, and the more that artist's work takes on a genuine look of its own, then the more it has value. This is different than a standard of time linked to the hours it takes to do an individual piece.

Therefore when you are suddenly confronted with a marketing situation that requires attaching a price to a work of art, don't think of the piece—its materials and time—think of your life in art, your life in art in the past and projected into the future. What is your lifetime goal? What would you like your artwork to sell for when you reach an older age?

For the purpose of gathering information, I look through magazines and art catalogues. These, plus the magazines that report on art auction prices, keep me informed as to trends in the art marketplace. In the auction records, I routinely find very good living artists (of course not the art stars like de Kooning or Hockney, etc.) whose pieces are selling in a price range of $6,000 to $10,000.

I have sold paintings and art for 20 years at least. My pricing goal is to be selling art work at $6,000 to $10,000 by the time I am 55.

Whatever your price goal, after it is set, then you must visualize a pricing plan. This plan is a detailed accounting of the changes you will make and the accomplishments you plan and how those affect your pricing structure. My lifetime pricing plan was first formulated in the late 1970s after a conversation with a more experienced artist.

In 1977 I had moved to California from western New York and had decided to be a full-time painter rather than a ceramist. I joined an outdoor art show in Santa Barbara and began selling my watercolors for around $100 each. For the show, at that time it was a high price. Gradually I began to move my prices upward as events and decisions on my work allowed me to explain these price jumps to the interested and purchasing public.

For instance, I studied with a well-known California artist and his teaching had a major impact on my work. I hung at my display a statement from him as to the seriousness of work. The public liked the statement, and those that had bought my work in the past were willing to buy other pieces at higher prices.

When I had signed contracts to have my work reproduced, I placed that information at my display. Again the public nodded affirmatively to my price raising. The presentation of credentials means a lot to the public. Of course, if you don't need a sale you can price your artwork at any level you like. However, the impact of this "no need to sell" attitude on the art marketplace is that there is an eroding of buyer confidence. It makes potential collectors of art less and less willing to make purchases because there are indiscernible standards.

In other words, the public reacts to certain price jumps with understanding—as the two I just mentioned—and some with skepticism. To restate: I have found that if I accompany a price increase with the explanation that I used expensive materials, I find the public reacts with uncertainty. I also feel this skepticism when I justify a higher price because a piece took more time than another. Thus my pricing plan began to evolve using explanations I knew were accepted with confidence by the public. One such standard is the size of the work.

By 1983 I was selling my then-normal painting—an 11"x14" watercolor—for $300 to $600. I began to increase the size of my work and adjust the prices. Then I made 16"x20" watercolors and charged $600 to $800. Then I went into 24"x36" watercolors for $800 to $1,000. Next I went to 30"x40" watercolors for $1,000 to $1,500. Finally in 1990 I jumped to 40"x60" watercolors for $1,500 to $2,000.

Another justification for raising prices: My activities were different. I produced a book of my work. I did this and sold the project to a publishing company. It was exciting going into B. Dalton and other bookstores and seeing my book. With the success of this project, I raised the price of the paintings that had been published in the book by $500. The paintings I do now, I do with an eye to including them in my next book; therefore the prices of these works also have the elevated pricing structure. The past collectors of my work nod their heads in pleasure and are willing to purchase other works at the higher price.

The next increases in my prices will be accompanied with the emergence of new work in oils as well as the continued publication of books of my work. The point is that these are adjustments that are not based on principles we in the art world necessarily recognize; they are adjustments that the general public will find believable. "Believable" is the key word here. Public confidence—demand and commitment—are the tenets of this idea. In my mind's eye, I see a graph of the prices of my artwork over my lifetime. Along that graph, as there are changes, there are noted events. If I can do this I can mimic the graph that accompanies the marketing of gold.

As I write this I wonder who among the readers will be dismayed that I price "too low" or "too high." There are those who believe I should get whatever I can, those who would compare this standard to prices by artists who don't care to make sales, and those who have been lucky in singular instances. I welcome these reactions and others. I love new ideas and someone maybe has a better concept than the one I have formulated here.

Pricing is a critical issue for artists. Each time we show our work it is at the core of our dilemma. We must keep looking at this issue, evaluating our decisions and our standards.

Sell Your Art Now
Alan Bamberger

More than 45 million people visited American museums last year. Only a small fraction of those millions of people own original art. About 45 million *would* own it, however, if they could afford to buy it.

In the meantime, countless works of art sit unsold in artists' studios and storage facilities across the country, in large part because they are priced beyond the reach of art lovers of average means.

How many high-priced pieces of art do you have stored away? How does that compare with the number you have hanging in public or private collections? People have to see your art in order to know that you exist. No matter how good you are, if nobody knows you exist, nobody can consider buying your art. Conversely, the more people who know you exist, the more people who can consider you when adding art to their collections. If the bulk of your work is hidden from view, you've got to start getting it out there right now and that means one thing—pricing it to sell.

Do whatever is necessary to attract buyers, especially those of you with little or no track record of sales. For example, set yourself a reasonable hourly wage for creating art. Make it similar to what skilled workers in other fields, with experience comparable to yours, charge for their services. If you have trouble coming up with a dollar figure, use what you get paid at your regular job as a baseline and make that your approximate salary or fee structure for creating art.

Multiply the hours you take to complete any work of art by your hourly rate, add the cost of materials, factor in any commission if applicable, and make that your selling price. If your current pieces take too long to produce and price affordably, figure out how to make something less time-consuming. Make it smaller, lighter, simpler, whatever you have to do to make it affordable. You can still make the more complex pieces, but have a lower priced selection available for buyers on a budget.

For example, if you can create a competent pencil sketch or drawing or small watercolor or oil sketch in 30 minutes and sell it for $10 or $15 or $25, do it. It's OK to give someone a good deal. You can view this as giving away your art too cheaply, or you can view yourself as being capable of producing these and thousands of additional pieces that are just as good and even better during the course of your career. Don't clog your studio with yesterday's art just because "no one is willing to pay me what I really deserve."

Avoid the tendency to take selling your art for reasonable prices personally. Far too many artists make this fatal error and go for years or even decades selling next to nothing. Think of selling your art as a business, your fellow artists as your competition—and do what all successful businesses do. Give customers a product that's as good as or better than what the competition offers and provide that product at a lower price—not just a little bit lower, but a lot lower. No matter what you're selling, this system works!

Even if you have to begin by selling your current backlog of art at a loss, cost-wise or time-wise, consider it. Your art is your business card, your billboard, your brochure, your advertisement, your number-one marketing and promotional tool. Every piece you sell is out there working on your behalf 24 hours a day, 365 days a year. If it's good enough, it will pay for itself over and over again by attracting new buyers to your studio. On the other hand, it does absolutely nothing by sitting unsold on a shelf or in a stack somewhere gathering dust. And it doesn't do much more languishing at art exhibits priced out of reach of 99.9 percent of potential buyers. These strategies make you no money and they only hamper whatever efforts you make to gain recognition.

Be generous and give your customers a break. They like your art and want to own it, as long as they can do so without seriously depleting their life savings. Save the higher prices for when you become established—after a continuing regular demand develops for your art. Remember that once your career gets rolling, you can give yourself a raise anytime you feel like it.

Confuse affordable selling prices with ego, or how good buyers will think your art is, or how much money you think buyers might make reselling your art in the future, and you only torture yourself. The more breaks you give now, the more you'll get back later and the better a reputation you'll gain for being flexible, for satisfying your collectors' needs and for keeping them happy. Art buyers everywhere will have multiple opportunities to experience your art and decide for themselves whether or not they want to own it. In the meantime, you maximize your chances to sell regularly and, most importantly, you brighten people's lives and beautify their environments with your art.

CHAPTER 28

The Art of Selling

Selling Without Selling
Barbara Dougherty

A typical day at the Santa Barbara Sunday Art Show: the crowd was sparse and many of the artists spent the day complaining about the lack of sales, not only for this day but for this recession year. I had no complaints, though—I sold one 40"x60" watercolor for $2,000 and another watercolor 24"x36" for $500. These are my average weekly sales.

While technique, medium, subject, and color are all important, all too often artists neglect the presentation of their work. For display I use an overhead canopy and expensive frames. The frames are all the same—this gives unity to the display and the effect of a gallery. Loading, unloading, preparation, and setup are harder because of the frames, but they pay off, as I can sell my paintings at higher prices.

Artwork that is displayed well is easier to sell. However, artwork that is not well-displayed can also be sold. My friend exhibits oil paintings. He is a very talented painter, but he doesn't have the energy to care about his presentation. He does not frame his work. His display presentation is poor. His stands are falling apart. He doesn't make sales for himself. Nonetheless, yesterday in my display I sold five of his paintings at an average price of $150.

When I sell, I don't use a "sales pitch." I know that people who come to art shows and visit galleries like art. When prospective buyers come into a display, they do not want to be made to feel uncomfortable. They don't want you to look at them. They don't want to have to answer questions like: "Can I help you?" They want to see the art. They want you to tell them something they don't know about the art in front of them.

In my display, when a person stands before a piece more than momentarily I make my approach. I usually start with something simple, like "This is a watercolor. I am the artist." I always wear a name tag. After my opening, I listen intently for a clue about who they are. Then I look strictly at the art. I tell them something about the piece in front of us and I don't say the same thing to everyone. I might say that this is a painting of a strawberry patch in the early morning. I tell them I like the light during that time of day. I challenge myself to be sincere, to find something new and personal in each piece. This means that I, too, must look carefully at the work. This is a necessity if I want others to view the work.

While we are all looking at the piece, I say something about my feelings and my intentions in the painting. If I can't think of anything else, I reveal something technical about the work. I might say that this is a hard piece to talk about, or that I am not sure how I feel about the execution. I know that if a person has a chance to look carefully at art then he will want to own it because art is in itself enticing. I think of myself as a person with the inside story about the piece. It is also important to think about what I say before I say it. When I am asked a question, I give the most emotionally honest response I can.

I call this "selling without selling." I use tools but no pressure. My "sales" literature is about my annual show which they may attend by invitation. I also have a book that I self-published, about my paintings on display. My business card is a high-gloss color postcard of one of my paintings. The postcard works to bring me more calls than any other business card I have ever used. When I give the card to a potential patron I feel they both like and keep the card for the future.

Yesterday's sales of my works are good examples of how selling without selling works. Both were difficult sales.

My customers for the large painting were a mother and her daughter. The daughter had an energetic 4-year-old son. Small children can keep parents from spending money just by demanding attention. I handle this by relating directly to the children: I ask the child's name, make a comment about something the child would care about, like animals, thus helping to ease the child's need to compete for attention.

They were viewing my painting *Last Light*. This painting was done in the open air of a lagoon lined with eucalyptus trees in Santa Barbara. I like to paint the California waterways and eucalyptus trees that are part of our vanishing agricultural landscape.

The mother and daughter had color swatches to help them find a painting that would match their new furniture. I know that many other artists are offended by customers who want to "match" furniture but I am not. I appreciate the need to "be the artist of your own environment," to make your home or office a personal statement of your own likes and dislikes.

I encouraged them to hold up their color swatches. When color doesn't match I am the first to say so. Many of my paintings have sold despite the colors not matching furniture. I find that by confronting the question, it does not become an insurmountable issue. They will buy the work anyway if they like it. The colors were thought by both of them to be matching, and by this time everyone in the display area was looking at the piece.

I have to say my heart sank when the mother announced she didn't like the rendering of the sandbar that divided the lagoon from the ocean waters in the painting. I really wanted to make that sale. Then she asked if I could take the sandbar out of the painting. A friend of mine says "difficult situations in business can make a person feel like they are in a swamp, fearing alligators." I felt instantly like the swamp was real and the alligators were at hand. I thought of telling her that watercolors cannot be easily altered, but I decided to be honest. I replied, "No, I can't, because I like the piece the way it is." At this point I was sure there was no possibility of a sale.

I suppose I might have said something else—inside I was feeling offended. But they didn't walk away. They just kept looking at the piece. However, it was too much for me to stay there and I couldn't really just leave, so I asked them if they wouldn't mind watching my exhibit while I went to the restroom. To my surprise they said they could wait. When I returned they had decided to buy the piece. It was going into the daughter's house and she rather liked the sandbar. I know it was rather bold to walk away from my exhibit and leave them in charge, but it was the only way I had of asking them to stand in my shoes for a moment.

The second sale was to a middle-aged woman who seemed to just like my work. I told her I liked to paint large pieces because it was easier for me to paint a "mood." I explained that I feel that original paintings have a great impact on rooms and she should only buy one if she was confident that she liked it. She said she had never bought an original painting and had only a small apartment. She singled out one of the smaller pieces but hesitated, and I thought it was because she was trying to be confident of her feelings. Then she asked me if I would take $50 less for the painting.

I never give a fast answer when I am asked to negotiate price. Silence and thought make the situation easier. Her question meant that she liked the piece but for some reason did not want to pay the asking price. Possibly she didn't have the money. In these cases, I try to focus on the fact that the person likes my work and wants to own it. I don't get offended by this because the price I put on my work is an arbitrary price. It is the price at which I think I can sell work. Nobody can ever pay me what my work is worth. My work is my life and my life is priceless.

Finally I replied that the best I could do was to absorb the sales tax on the purchase price. I like to propose this because it is an easy compromise. The long wait for my reply usually ends the desire to negotiate. It seems to say that even though we are at an outdoor marketplace, this artist does not bargain. She purchased the work and I paid the taxes.

Selling without selling takes concentration and attention. Every artist has to confront selling, has to become a salesperson, whether it's to a dealer, a customer, or an art agent. We are always in one way or another acting as our own agent. We have to talk about art to sell art. Marcel Duchamp and the Dada artists felt that their work had no social or political meaning; you may feel that way. Or you may feel that you don't like to make pretty pictures or sculptures—that your art isn't meant to decorate or be used.

Whatever the intent, whatever the feeling, my experience is that sharing your attitudes about your art, and being accessible to those who may buy your art, is the best way to sell art.

CHAPTER 29

The Art and
Attitude of Display

Presenting Quilts
As Works of Art

Lynn Young

Though this article talks only about fiber art, it presents an attitude
of concern that should be observed by all artists. Ms. Young demonstrates a professional and caring mindset which is expressed through
her methods of display, shipping, storage, and communicating with
her dealers and purchasers about handling her artwork.

Just as the packaging is as important as the contents of the package in Japanese
culture, the presentation of a quilt is very important to the viewer's perceived
value of a quilt. A careful presentation of a quilt as a work of art can do much to
impress potential collectors. Somehow it's hard to picture a quilt that is folded
and lying on a shelf or a quilt that arrives in a box from the grocery store as
worth a hefty price.

Presentation needs to be considered in all aspects of showing a quilt. The
way a quilt is handled and shipped by the artist can say a lot to a museum or
gallery, just as the way a gallery displays a quilt sends messages about the value
of a quilt to potential buyers.

The optimal gallery display method: hung on a wall, the same way the
work would be viewed in the collector's home or office. The quilt needs ample
space around it for clear viewing away from other works which might block the
view or distract from the quilt. Galleries for paintings follow this format, but
unfortunately many spaces that display quilts have an abundance of other works.
They display in a manner more in keeping with a retail outlet for decorative
items. While space for quilts can be a real problem, they should never look like a
backdrop for ceramics, baskets, or jewelry. The other items will sell well and the

quilt will not get any attention. As an artist approaching a gallery, the display method should be discussed and agreed upon.

Many galleries maintain more works than they can display. To correctly store quilts, they should be carefully rolled onto padded rods and covered with a dust protector such as a length of muslin. The quilt can be labeled with a tag with all the pertinent information, including a photo of the quilt, so a collector can tell if he would like to see it.

Rolling is necessary because many art quilts are damaged by folding and stacking. Studio art quiltmakers frequently go to great efforts technically to assure that a quilt will be smooth and will hang straight. Fold creases or wrinkles are a lot of trouble to get out once they form. A folded quilt also looks more like a piece of bedding than a piece of art.

Collectors can easily follow the same storage methods for their quilts. Racks holding rolled quilts can be mounted to walls in protected closets for easy storage and access when a quilt is not on display.

It is part of an artist's job to specify the display method when arrangements are made with a gallery, and to assist collectors to properly display and store their quilts. A gallery should assure the proper handling of a quilt, but many galleries are not aware of how to do so. The artist should review these matters with any venues that show their quilts.

Shipping quilts to shows or galleries also raises the issue of professionalism. To be treated like professionals, we need to present ourselves and our quilts professionally. If you fold your quilts and ship them in a box, chances are they will remain folded and eventually will be returned to you folded and shoved into a box. Even if you carefully fold your quilt with padding in the folds, it will probably come back to you folded without the padding.

One way to eliminate this problem is to ship your quilts rolled on a rod and inside a special mailing tube. To roll your quilt, prepare a rod by padding it and covering it with muslin. Lay the quilt flat on a table with the back facing you. Place the padded rod on one end and roll. The quilt will be rolled with the front side out, which will prevent wrinkles. Wrap the rolled quilt in a protective layer of washed muslin, then a double layer of plastic to protect it from water damage and dampness. Label your quilt with unpacking and hanging instructions. If your quilt is to be stored, instruct the receiver to remove the plastic during storage. Furnish packing instructions and note your preferred method of return shipping and your shipping address. When shipping a rolled quilt, check with your shipper to see if instructions are necessary to protect the quilt in transit, as tubes are often handled differently than boxes. If your tube is oversized, consult transit firms or fine art shippers—call your local museum for references.

When your quilt arrives in its tube with complete instructions, the receivers will know an important piece of art has arrived, and they will know exactly how to handle it. Experienced artists will tell you that it might cost more to present your quilts this way, but just as professional photography shows off your quilts to best advantage, so too should the presentation and shipping be professional.

One manufacturer of mailing tubes is Yazoo Mills. They range in size from 2"-8" in diameter and 12"-60" in length. Custom lengths can be cut. Contact Tubes In Time, Yazoo Mills, P.O. Box 369, New Oxford, PA 17350, 717-624-8993, fax 717-624-4420.

Professional Preciousness

Peggy Hadden

Recently I had a conversation with an artist who is also an independent curator. She has always made a large number of studio visits; like me, she enjoys seeing how other artists go about presenting their work. She was marveling over a recent studio visit.

"He treated his work so well," she exclaimed. "Like it was gold—the way he touched and carried it, how he displayed each piece. It was like watching something increase in value before my very eyes!"

For some of you, this article will not be astonishing news. For others, it may be about some ephemeral stuff to which you've never given much thought.

They say the best way to sell a house is to bake bread as prospective buyers pass through the rooms. The wonderful aroma will create an atmosphere that helps enhance the home being offered for sale, creating in the buyer's mind an image of living in that house and having wonderful home-baked bread. Does it heighten the chance of a sale? You bet it does!

In writing this article, I was led again and again to my dictionary to research words like mystique, aura, intuition, spiritual, and magical. A person or an organization about to buy a work of art is not buying merely the supplies we have put into it. They perceive in the work some special feeling caught by the artist with which they identify. One of the fallacies of the IRS laws for donating artworks to museums is that the artist donating his own work may take credit for only those supplies he used to make the piece, while an art collector who donates the same painting can receive credit for the full market value of the work at the time it is being contributed. (This is another reason to trade art-works with other artists—you then become a "collector" and may be able to claim the full market credit otherwise denied you. Consult your CPA for details.) But the real value of the work lies somewhere in between the cost of supplies and the market value, in some mysterious place that has been convincingly and movingly achieved by the artist. Otherwise, all paintings would be equal—and we know this is not so.

Certainly, a successful painting would succeed whether it were shown in an alley or in an elegant museum. However, the viewer's ability to successfully enjoy the painting would be much diminished in the alley. The premise for this article is that you owe it to your work to give it the best possible conditions under which it may be seen.

As artists, we know the nuts and bolts of what goes into our work and what holds it together. Perhaps we are less mystified about our creations than we want our buyers to be.

As any of you who have recently framed anything will attest, when work has been framed, it takes on a slightly different personality. (Likewise when pho-tographed and in slides—but that's another article.) I'm the first to champion showing work that is unframed as well as framed, but bear with me. A well-framed piece is "dressed up"—it has an alert, front-and-center air about it. It is always a surprise to me when I see my work after it has been framed. As if before it was clean—but now the laundry has put some starch into it.

It is important, too, to treat your work lovingly. Another friend of mine was recently asked to bring his work in to show his "day job" boss, who had heard that this employee was also a painter. Slides had been brought to him and the prospect of a sale seemed imminent. The day of the appointment, my friend hurriedly put several small works into a shopping bag and took them to his employer. He later told me the boss didn't seem particularly impressed when he looked at the work. Maybe the timing wasn't good. But it also might have been because the works weren't wrapped in any protective packaging or because the shopping bag was from a discount store. And where had it been shown? These factors cast an atmosphere around your work that may devalue it.

Why do you think diamond dealers always show their wares in velvet cases or on a piece of satin, often in surroundings where they first invite the viewer to sit down? What is there about removing the beloved item from a glass case that encourages us to believe it is very precious? Some of it is the anticipation. Mounting anticipation, carefully orchestrated by the seller. Do not discount the element of creating an aura about your work. Plainly and simply, we are talking here about the value that you instill in your art. We all admire artists who can sell their work for higher prices and it's time to talk about the elements that give that work its increased value. Part of it is the way you treat it and present it.

Our salon show, about which I have spoken several times in the past, is a great opportunity to watch artists arriving with their work and to see how they handle it. Some of it looks as if it could traverse the Himalayas, it's so well-packed. Other artists run in with their pieces uncovered and flying uncertainly behind them. If they show their work to prospective buyers in this way, I can understand why they may be perceived as less than serious about art. It would be hard to keep a straight face when told that the work was priced at several hundred (or several thousand) dollars.

I recently visited an art storage warehouse to see if they had special viewing areas for works stored there. Say a painter has some work stored, and suddenly a prospective buyer expresses interest in the piece; to avoid transporting the work from storage just to show it, the warehouse provides an area where the art can be shown. The day I visited, a Brancusi was about to be shown. The room I saw was painted gallery-white and had lighting as fine as any gallery's. It was also quiet, away from the typical cacophony of moving and warehouse noise. This space had obviously been well-planned to ensure that work would be shown at its best when collectors visited.

This is not to say that the content of the work will be improved. Furthermore, there are certainly times when ideal conditions don't exist. I recall Dorothy Miller, who was curator of painting and sculpture for many years at MoMA, telling me about her first visit to see the then-unknown Frank Stella. His works were so large that he had to carry them out into the hallway and move them back in again after showing them. She recalled this visit fondly and Mr.

Stella's creative genius was soon recognized, making such awkward maneuverings unnecessary.

Back to my curator friend's recent studio visit. She was impressed by the way the work was shown—with professional hanging equipment on the wall, as opposed to one lone nail, which usually causes a work to shift about. She was also impressed by the way the work was put away after the showing. "Not just tossed, or stashed hurriedly with a minimum of care," she told me. Furthermore, she continued, his work was finished and complete from the backside, too.

For some reason, many artists have the mistaken impression that work can be raggedly stapled to a stretcher on the back or allowed to flap loosely in a haphazard way. Obviously this is part of the "La Boheme" idea of the artist seen as the devil-may-care attic dweller, which is a hundred years old and now decidedly out-of-date. Artists who see themselves as professional and ask prices to match, deliver artwork that is finished and beautifully crafted front AND back. Certainly, their attention goes to the front of a canvas, as it should; but professional attention doesn't stop there. Your attention to all the details tells your prospective buyers that your respect for the condition of the piece deserves to be matched by theirs.

Again, the ball is in your court. If you can convey by your actions that you value the artwork which you so painstakingly made, your viewers will probably get the message. Then it is probably time to raise your prices.

CHAPTER 30

Handling and Shipping Art

Basic Art Handling: Video Review
Carolyn Blakeslee

Although the opening scene of *Basic Art Handling* is as much a cutesy media assault as an attention-getter, it works. Within the space of about a minute, an arrogant Gallery Lady and her two assistants manage to turn a show installation into a slapstick disaster. The fiasco starts with an argument over how to handle a large painting (Don't pick it up by the wire, the wire might break! Don't pick it up by the frame, it might break loose! Don't pick it up by the cross brace, you'll pucker the canvas with your fingers!). The ensuing anxiety and confusion results in pierced and broken canvases, a fallen sculpture, and toppled people who spill coffee and drop Magic Markers onto the surfaces of paintings. Although these three characters won't win Oscars, they do serve to portray a few installation disasters that are all too common.

This wake-up call of an introduction leads into a serious, well-thought-out, and thorough video on handling art.

Steve Dunlop, of the Gallery Association of New York State, poses some very good questions about how to handle art to C. R. Jones, conservator for the New York State Historical Association and the Farmers Museum.

Throughout the film, Mr. Jones gives excellent directions on handling, moving, and storing crafts, relics and *objets d'art,* furniture, heavy objects, large objects, rough and/or fragile objects, works on paper, paintings both glazed and unglazed, textiles, books, and metal objects. He also goes into what to do if a piece is dropped and/or damaged.

Once the specifics of art handling are given in this film, they are easily assimilated and remembered—they are common sense.

Mr. Jones' directions begin with attitude and approach. If one treats an artwork as if it were "absolutely irreplaceable," then one will communicate that to other people who are around it. On the other hand, if one makes a value judgment that the piece is somehow inferior, then that attitude might be passed along to others, resulting in a subconscious accident proneness.

The art handler is advised to wear an apron or some other kind of smooth protective clothing to cover belts, buttons, and other clothing details that could scratch the materials being handled; similarly, he is advised to remove jewelry. Pockets should be emptied of all contents, which could fall out and strike the work.

No food, drinks, smoking materials, or ink pens should be allowed in the area at all. Besides being quite capable of damaging artworks being handled, these materials also serve as distractions. To further avoid distractions, art handlers are instructed not even to talk to anyone, unless it is about the art-handling task at hand.

Generally, washable non-slip white cotton gloves are called for, to prevent skin oils and salts from activating with a surface—unless, of course, the piece is extremely rough, like an unglazed ceramic piece with myriad projectiles that would pick up the fibers of a cloth glove.

One must consider both the structure of a piece and the materials of which it is made. Stone might crumble; glass and ceramics are fragile; wood pieces might have checks and cracks. After the materials have been considered, handle the piece from its strongest points—i.e., a heavy sculpture should generally be picked up from its bottom. Never pick up a piece by its handle—frequently an object's handle is a weak point, as it has been attached. Similarly, rest an object on its most stable part. Don't automatically place an object right-side-up: for example, a vase might be narrower at its base than at its brim, and would be more likely to be knocked over if it were placed right-side-up before its final exhibit placement.

Textiles should be stored rolled, not folded. The film shows how to roll textiles so that they are safe and yet occupy a minimum of space. If textiles absolutely must be folded, the video shows how to pad the folds with wads of acid-free paper to prevent creases and fiber damage.

The film gives an introduction to archival storage of paintings and works on paper, and explains how even acid-free materials can be contaminated merely by contacting an artwork. Some works may be stored flat, others must be stored vertically, and whens and how-to's are explained. Glazed paintings should be stored vertically in racks, with rigid leaves in between each piece. Screw eyes and wire and other hanging devices should be removed prior to storage. The condition of an artwork must be taken into consideration; an unframed oil painting in good condition should be handled and stored one way, while a painting with cracking or flaking should be handled another way, and probably should be stored horizontally until a conservator can work on it. Works sporting fancy frames should be handled in a special way, too. Using the heavy objects rule, paintings should be picked up from the bottom edge and supported on the sides. To facilitate lifting in this manner, the paintings should be stacked on padded wood blocks. Using this method of raising paintings off the floor also prevents damage to them in case of flooding.

Practical and easily accomplishable directions are demonstrated throughout the film. The questions are good; they are posed simply and at good times in the film, and they serve to break up the pure stream of information given.

One of the best questions answered is what to do if an artwork is dropped and/or damaged. Half of the question was answered at the very beginning: carefully record the condition of the artwork before even touching it. The rest of the answer is to carefully record and report the damage, too.

A videotape like this is difficult to review without making it sound like a "book report"—you know, the story is given away rather than critically reviewed. So, while we have given you much of the film's information here, the nature of this film is that it really should be seen, as the demonstrations are invaluable. *Basic Art Handling* is a must for gallery owners, art consultants, art center directors, artists, collectors, and all others who are installing and/or storing artworks.

While the *Basic Art Handling* film may be rented by anyone, other films are available only to Gallery Association members. The Association has an associate membership category for those interested in their film program only. *Basic Art Handling*, VHS and ³/₄" U-matic, 26 minutes, is available for rent or purchase from Gallery Association of New York State, Box 345, Hamilton, NY 13346-0345, 315-824-2510.

How to Build a Shipping Crate
Raymond Markarian

Museums and individual artists alike have unnecessarily made shipping a nightmare. I've seen museum crating, and the lack of damage they encounter is due to their use of art shippers, not the careful packing they use. I've uncrated a few national juried exhibitions and artist crating runs the gamut all the way to bizarre. The various packing materials I've seen artists use are bed sheets, toilet paper, towels, newspaper (sometimes wadded up, sometimes not), excelsior—a great wood shaving fire hazard—and styrofoam peanuts, an environmental and packing menace. One loony photographer mummified his framed piece with masking tape. I thought it was a conceptual piece until I saw the slide of the entry and discovered you were supposed to see the photo. I've received wooden crates that were nailed shut, screwed together with screws with square holes instead of slotted or Phillips-head, and had crates with hasps that were tied down with heavy gauge electrical wire. I remember one lumber crate that weighed in at 250 pounds, and the painting inside weighed less than 30. And, cardboard boxes are no good for shipping art. They lose their strength if they get damp, are punctured easily, and don't seal properly after they have been cut open.

I build my crates like a photographer's camera case. They have a lightweight sturdy outside, with a foam cavity that corresponds to the size of the art. The foam I'm referring to is cushion or mattress foam, not styrofoam. If the crate is struck hard or fractured, the foam holds the painting away from all sides of the crate. If the crate is dropped, the foam acts as a shock-absorber and prevents the painting from smashing against the inside walls. This type of shipping crate can also be used for sculpture.

Fiber art or unframed paper works can be gently rolled up and shipped in a plastic drain pipe. Drain pipe is lightweight, very strong, comes in a variety of sizes, and the price is right. You can find it at your favorite lumber yard in basic black, snow white, or occasionally sea green. Caps for the pipe are also available.

Let's run through the steps to build a shipping crate for a 24"x30" painting that is 2" deep. To determine the size of any shipping crate, you add the magic number 5½" to the height and length for a painting. A crate for sculpture gets this magic measurement added to the height, length, and depth. So, the size of your shipping crate for the 24"x30" painting is 29½"x35½" (more on depth later). Go to your handy lumber yard and get a sheet of ¼" shop ply (occasionally, ⅜" plywood will be cheaper). Ask them to cut two pieces 29½"x35½". You will also need:

- a box of medium-sized ring nails or screw nails
- a package of ¾" Phillips-head pan screws

- a bottle of white glue or wood glue
- two 8-foot-long one-by-three boards.

Next stop: your local upholstery shop for a 5'5" length of ½" thick sheet foam (usually 58" wide). You also need some 2" foam which you will cut into 2"x2" strips (about 10') that will ring the inside of the crate. Ask if they have any scrap, which should be about 50¢ per pound.

When you get home, cut the 1"x3" boards into lengths to fit the sides of the crate. Nail the plywood to the 1"x3" boards with the ring nails—these nails won't work loose. If you blunt the points of the nails with your hammer, then the nails will not split the wood. Work some glue into the joints where the ends of the boards meet. Drive in a nail to hold these joints together while the glue sets. The glue is going to secure the corners better than any nail or screw.

You now have the shell that forms the base of your shipping crate. At this point, cut the 2" foam into strips and glue them to the sides of the crate inside. Next, cut the sheet foam and glue it to the top and bottom insides of the crate to line it. Once the glue is dry, you have a shipping crate that has packing material that always stays with the crate and won't get torn, lost, or discarded.

Use the pan head screws to secure the lid to the base. These screws, usually used with sheet metal, are ideal in this instance because they won't tear up the lid when being repeatedly screwed in and out.

You now have a shipping crate for under $20 that will last for years, protecting your painting faithfully. You also have some leftover materials to create another crate.

CHAPTER 31

Rejection

Rejection vs. Acceptance: The Numbers Game

Carolyn Blakeslee

Rejection is hard to take, but in the arts it's simply the way it goes. However, once you become aware of what I call the Numbers Game, it's impossible to take rejection personally any more. And it becomes easy to formulate a good reliable plan.

We read about the Numbers Game in the literary world. How many publishers—fifty?—rejected Jack London before someone finally took him on? That's a lot of rejections. It doesn't occur to most people that fifty rejections might actually be the norm for every acceptance, and that persistence and continuing to play the Numbers Game is what pays off.

The same phenomenon is true in the art world. For every 100 promo packets you send out, you'll get three to five concrete expressions of interest. By "concrete" I don't mean compliments, nibbles, or even attendees to your next show. I mean solid offers of opportunities from curated group shows to solo exhibitions to culminated sales.

If you don't already do it, start collecting art magazines. Clip ads from galleries with whom you would like to work. The ads might feature work similar to yours or a gallery located in a good demographic area for you. Hopefully you've been keeping track of dealers whom you know to be reputable, attending their galleries regularly to keep in touch, and you have a list of a few nonprofit spaces where you would like to show.

Those are the people and places to whom you should send your promo packets. Whether you use slides or a catalogue (or both), send your packets with a personalized cover letter, and be sure you spell the recipient's name correctly and get his title right.

Most importantly, be prepared for the Numbers Game. For every 100 promo packets you send, you'll get several nice letters, a few nondeliverables, and some who won't respond at all. Most of the responses you get will be "thanks but no thanks." You'll get ten to fifteen nibbles—people who will want to come to your studio, people who will ask you for more information, and people who will say "not right now" but will ask you to keep in touch. These ten to fifteen nibbles are your hot prospects. Out of these ten to fifteen tentative responses, 20-50 percent will yield shows and/or sales for you.

Thus it becomes possible to plan.

What do you want? What will you be prepared to respond to?

If you send out 1,000 catalogues to a carefully targeted list of architects, interior designers, art consultants, and others with the intention of soliciting commission work, you'll get 970 rejections. But will you be prepared to respond to nibbles, nit-picking, and twenty to thirty commissions?

Would you be more comfortable having one or two solo shows a year? If so, maybe fifty slide packets are all you need to have circulating during the year. You'll get forty-eight rejections. But send one slide packet each week to hand-picked recipients and you will achieve your goal.

Each artist's percentage of response—rejections vs. concrete opportunities and sales—will vary. But with careful tracking you will soon know your own Numbers Game. Not only will you be able to make the art your heart is whispering to you to make, you will literally be able to count on your results.

Embracing Rejection
Lisa Almeda

This article is about how rejections can fit into the process of art-making in a constructive way. It is based on my personal experience, dealing with a spate of rejections. These rejections followed close on the heels of a fairly successful year for me in terms of sales, my inclusion in a museum show, and a show at my gallery.

As a result of the self-examination forced on me by my sudden difficulties, I found a completely new direction in my work. In retrospect, I think my success, minor as it was, caused my work to become complacent and dull. The series of paintings I am now working on are my most personal ever, and I think my most authentic. I can tell they're the real thing because I don't care whether anyone else likes them.

Every artist faces rejections, some of us more often than others. Painful as it can be, rejection is not just an obstacle to endure or overcome. It is an important part of the creative process that can be used to the artist's advantage. Rejection *can* be a positive experience, if the artist chooses to make it one. Acceptance is good for the ego and the resumé, but rejection is an occasion for self-examination—a crucial step in every artist's development.

The next time you face rejection, try these constructive responses.

Define Success for Yourself

Give yourself realistic goals for success. If you are just beginning your career, build a local reputation first. Start with local shows, build a devoted group of followers, and gradually work toward larger goals. If you begin competing at a national level without first building a local foundation, then you might be setting yourself up for unnecessary discouragement and disappointment.

Set Goals for Yourself

Just like any other businessperson, the artist should set both short- and long-term goals. Keep a notebook for this purpose and periodically review it. You may even want to keep track of slide submissions and slide entries in this same notebook.

As you review your notes, you will quickly see whether you are making progress or going off track. If you are consistently failing to achieve your goals, either your goals or your methods need modification.

What Does Rejection Mean?

Rejection after rejection does not necessarily mean the quality of your work is to blame. But when rejection never ends, it means *something*.

Examine every detail of your submissions. Are your slides absolutely perfect? Always view them projected before sending them out—most faults will simply not show up on a light box.

Are you submitting to the right places? If you can, find out what kind of work was accepted when yours was not. Perhaps you are a realist, and the award winners were all abstract painters. Finding the right market, whether in the gallery or competition arena, is imperative. You just aren't going to succeed if your work is wrong for the market you're going for.

Another question to ask yourself is whether you are ready for this level of competition. If you are regularly showing locally but can't break into the national scene, then you might not yet be ready for the bigger leagues.

Look at the Work

This is the most basic, and the most painful, part of your inquiry. Could the problem be with the work itself? If you are a professional artist, you need to face this question. Are your technical skills and polish everything they should be? Do you have your own style and vision, or are you trying to paint whatever is in this month's art magazines? Have you built a body of work that is consistent, unique, and reflects your concerns as an artist?

If the problem is with your work, you must recognize that. Then you must do whatever it takes to make the improvements that will help you succeed.

Keep Working

If you give up, your work will never be rejected again. But if you do give up, you will never succeed. If you have examined every facet of your work and its presentation, and you are satisfied that you are doing your best in every respect, keep on working, keep on submitting. True confidence in your work and your abilities can't be faked. It will come across when you present your work to others, and it can only help you.

Of all the qualities an artist must possess, pure stubborn tenacity is the most important. If you feel that art is what you are meant to do—if making art makes you feel alive—then forget what the rest of the world thinks and just do it.

Rejection: Interview with Robert Johnson, Curator

Beky Carter

Robert Johnson, a native of Jersey City, New Jersey, has been the curator of contemporary art, Old Masters, Indian miniatures, and Japanese prints at the Fine Arts Museums of San Francisco, Achenbach Foundation for Graphic Arts since 1975 and a lecturer in art history at the San Francisco Art Institute since 1980. He has given numerous lectures on the graphic arts through the years and has curated major exhibitions at the Legion of Honor, among other museums.

The Fine Arts Museums are the city museums of San Francisco. As the curator of the Achenbach Foundation, I am a public servant. Any particular artist deserves to have his or her day in court in terms of showing work to me, and, you might say, to have that work accepted or rejected. If I made myself available for studio visits I would spend my whole career doing that and if you have a one-on-one studio visit with an artist you can't breeze in there for three minutes.

How does an artist get access to someone like me? One of the ways I've been able to solve this is by having what I call Artists Days. Viewing slides just doesn't make it for me. Taking a large oil on paper or a pastel and having me or anyone else judge whether that's something worthy of exhibition through a reproduction that's 1"x1" is ridiculous. A slide review to my mind, from 20 years' experience, is a semi-worthless type of situation. Unless I am familiar with an artist's work, when they send me slides I simply don't have a point of reference. I instituted Artists Days as soon as I came to San Francisco. I hold it the last Thursday of every month, by appointment only. (The appointments are made by calling the museum at 415-750-3679 after 9 A.M. on the first business day of every month, with the exception of December and August.) Once those appointments fill, that's it until the next month.

Many of these artists have never met me before. And I've never met them. So it's kind of a mutually difficult situation. It's the old line, "Hope for the best but expect the worst." Somebody once said that artists have got to be the best egotists. It doesn't mean they have to be egomaniacs, but they have to believe in themselves. And nobody, neither myself nor any other curator or collector, should be able to put more than a nick in the bottom of their boat. A little leak here and there you can patch up. But nobody should sink your boat with an opinion, even if it's cruel or devastating or even negatively insightful. Still, it should not shake one's ultimate belief in oneself.

Most artists are very happy that they have the chance to have the interaction with me, but it's also a little scary for them. The artist should know that it's scary for me too. It's not like I have a bunch of slides which if I don't like I can throw across my desk. I've got another human being there. I always go into every single artist's meeting believing in the integrity and the originality of that individual—that they aren't painting little green apples on the tabletop because they think this is the way to make a great living. And that they are doing it in a premeditative way. I see the artists making their work with a sincerity. Some of it can be quite dreadful. Being a bad singer, sculptor, or actor or actress has nothing to do with the sincerity of the effort. Creativity is not an objective science; it's subjective. So, when artists bring works to me, I try to treat them with respect.

Artists don't quite seem to know what they are there for. It's funny. Are they there for some positive feedback to go back and work on the ideas that I give them? Do they expect me to buy one of their works? Do they expect me to take one of the works as a gift, if offered? Do they think if I really like the works that I will give them a show? I'm sure they have all those things floating through their heads. The bad side is that they may think I'm snotty, difficult, or perhaps very critical. They may be afraid that after looking at their paintings, I'll say something like, "Maybe you should think about changing careers."

There really is no absolute truth in art. There is only the individual truth of what an artist does. For example, in a show I once participated in as a juror, the vast majority of the artists who submitted were rejected. In turn, of the artists that were included, there were four cash awards. So the artists who were in the show were "rejected" also by not winning one of the cash awards.

How I feel about this is that if you're selected, you should be relatively happy, and go back to work feeling like you got a little feather in your cap. But realize that it is a subjective feather. If, however, you are rejected, it's just one person's opinion, or maybe three people's opinions. In that particular case the dynamics of those three people could have been that if only one of those people had been the juror, you might have been selected. Who knows exactly whether you were the first artist to be scratched off the list or the last. But the most important thing, if you are rejected, is to go back to being a great egotist. To believe that your painting is still good and the jurors, from your perception, are wrong. And to go back in the studio and say, "I'm going to keep painting the way I want to keep painting," and just be resolute.

There is one area of rejection I sometimes have to deal with on these Artists Days. An artist will bring me these absolutely commercial works of art and say, "What do you think of them? Do you think I have some promise for a museum show?" They will be the most blatant kind of "please the public" thing—apples on the tabletop with a duck decoy—and I will say, "Are you fairly successful selling these works?" And the artist will say, "Oh yes. I'm selling them. I'm making limited edition offset reproductions, signed and numbered."

You can't have it both ways. If you want to be an absolutely great, roaring financial success, and you paint for the great middle-ground taste, then you're not going to be taking chances or exploring the creativity and the art you may have in you. But if you have a show of works that are really tough and challenging, and you don't sell anything, but you get a terrific review in *Artweek,* does that constitute success in your mind? Or would you prefer no reviews in the paper, and a tremendous amount of sales to people who buy things for their country homes? What is your definition of success?

In America we are so hung up on money that we confuse the terms success and excellence. People think if they are successful, by definition they are excellent. If you aim for excellence, success will very often follow. But if your basic content is simply success, excellence will get lost in the shuffle.

It's very important that artists know where they are coming from in terms of this whole question of success or excellence. If you're doing apples on table-tops, I might hate them, but a gallery downtown might be able to sell loads of them. But if you want to do a charcoal series of dead seagulls found on the beach at Stinson, I might think they're fabulous and I might get one for the collection. And yet you wouldn't be able to give them away downtown on Grant Avenue.

If an artist always strives for creative excellence—and is not trying to paint to please, but trying to paint or draw as best they can, totally oblivious to those other factors—there is a chance that artist will be misunderstood. Most great artists are misunderstood because most great artists paint beyond the level of common recognition. The thing that makes me happiest is when certain artists, in a rather lonely way, do strive for that excellence and make uncompromising work. In certain cases they get very little attention by collectors and dealers. I'm happy at times that I've been able to give these people some recognition.

Case in point is Jackie Kirk. I gave her a retrospective show, "The Face of AIDS," at the Legion of Honor because I thought that body of work was absolutely extraordinary. But she is also an artist in the Bay Area who has no gallery representation. No gallery will show her work because her stuff is tough and they can't sell it. Of course they have their rents to pay, but it's a tragedy that someone like her is good enough to get national attention and a show at the Legion of Honor, but she can't sell her pictures through any of the commercial galleries.

So I want to, in a certain sense, reinforce those artists who strive for excellence. But I am willing, in a polite way, to question those artists who say, "I sold $75,000 worth of art last year. Now that I'm making lots of money I would like your museum to put the benediction on me critically too." And I tell them that I think it's marvelous that they are so financially successful, and that as businesspeople I give them great credit. But from the creative end I cannot give them the recognition they want. It's interesting to me that people really do believe that if they are doing really, really well, why aren't museums paying attention to them too. They aren't making art; they are making a product.

The only unfortunate situation I sometimes come across is that occasionally I'll have an artist come up and see me who might be on the faculty of a local university or art school, and that person feels like a significant presence in the community. I will be polite, but I'll be honest and say that the work just doesn't fit in with what I am about. That person might take offense because they believe that somehow they should get a free pass into the collection.

If a work of art isn't good in my opinion, I won't accept it. It's as simple as that. I'll turn it down. If the artist is a good artist and wants me to accept a bad work, I'll try to deflect it off to a good one. I should say that one of the things people don't really understand about being a curator is that if there is an artist—let's say the Sam Smith of the community—and if I don't love but still respect Sam Smith's work personally, and if I have limited funds, there are so many things I need that I probably won't rush off and buy a Sam Smith. But if somebody were to fill our need for that Sam Smith through a gift, of course I'll want it for the collection—because the collection is bigger than Robert Johnson's personal taste.

I obviously have personal beliefs. I'm not going to spend 6 to 8 months working hard on a show of an artist who I know is historically important but doesn't move me. For instance, minimalist art, to my mind, is like watching grass grow. It is an important movement, and it's important that the Achenbach have Robert Rymans, Brice Mardens, Mel Bockners, and similar works in the collection. We recently acquired a significant collection of very fine minimalist works through our Crown Point Press acquisition. Further than that, I went out and bought a very good Donald Judd for the collection. But I bought it with my head, not my heart.

My role as a curator is to use both my head and my heart. When my heart can't follow, I just use my head to acquire those necessary things so that long after I'm gone, someone can teach the history of twentieth-century printmaking and drawing in the Achenbach and won't come to some giant gap and say, "Oh my God! This guy bought only the stuff he liked and left out the whole history of a certain aspect of art." It's a balance.

One of the things about my recent acquisition shows—like the one that's up now—is that if anybody thinks there is an absolute consistent viewpoint throughout that show, then I've failed. Because it isn't an exhibition of my tastes. If you go to see the Charles Sacchi collection, the big London collector, then you are looking at a man's personal taste. In my particular case, if you like minimalist art or abstraction, I've got a wall of it. If you like kind of funky representation, like Wiley, there's a wall of that. If you like poignant expressionism, there's a wall of that with a Neri and a Johnathon Barbieri.

So in a sense, I always say that there should be something to please and offend everyone in the show. Nobody is going to like the same thing. But hopefully any artists who come to see a show at the museum, if they work minimally, expressionistically, or in superrealism, they will say, "Hey, there's a chance that Johnson will like my work."

Whereas if you go to a museum and everything has the certain aesthetic party line of that institution, any artist that doesn't conform to that party line—the style-police running that institution—then the artist feels that it's a waste of time going to visit that curator or those directors because they only like a certain extremely narrow look. You have a museum like the Guggenheim, and if you aren't Jim Dine or Chuck Close or Alfred Leslie, you would be wasting your time. The Guggenheim is into Dan Flavin and Donald Judd and maybe Mark Rothko. And that museum has a certain look, with history that goes back to Kandinsky, etc. You would be wild to try to sell them a Lucian Freud of a naked woman. They wouldn't know what to do with that.

I've got to be tough just as a critic has got to be tough. While it's marvelous that some Hollywood movie made $85 million, it may be a fluffy piece of entertainment and it's not really art. It's not really being tough. It's not really being uncompromising. It's very important to know that my taste is my truth through experience. Zola said that art is reality filtered through temperament. So my view of the world artistically is filtered through my background, my history. And it is what it is, just as each artist has their reality filtered through their temperament.

One of the great things about the subjectivity of art is that it extends to the subjectivity of the curators themselves. Consequently, one of the things that is fascinating is when an artist will show their works to me, and let's say I will acquire something—either through gift or purchase—and then they will go to John Caldwell at the Modern and expect him to like it because I did. Or Jackie Bass over at Berkeley. This idea that somehow art is such that if one person likes it there should be universal acceptance just isn't true. The fact is that unlike many things in life that are absolute—thumbs up or thumbs down—in the case of art it all depends. There are many famous novels that were turned down by twenty different publishers and the twenty-first publisher publishes the thing and it wins the Pulitzer Prize. Now were the twenty people who rejected the book stupid? No. Because they viewed that reality through their own temperament, they weren't able to grasp the qualities and the twenty-first person was. And it's the same with all art.

Art is a journey, not a destination. There is no artist—I don't care whether it's Picasso, Matisse, Francis Bacon—who hasn't been ridiculed or dismissed as worthless. It's the nature of the beast. In a sense, artists have it easy. Artists have total control of their sculpture, their painting, their ceramic. If the dealer doesn't want to show it, too bad, the artist is not going to change the piece. If a person doesn't want to buy it, so be it. In a way artists have tremendous control over their creative output and the artistic face they show to the world. Whereas in many other fields of endeavor, things are compromise, compromise, compromise. At least a painter can say, "If you don't like my piece, fine. Take it or leave it."

The people who have it much worse are actors and actresses. They are told that they are too fat, too thin, too old, too young and when they finally get the part and make the movie, some of the best scenes end up on the cutting-room floor. They have no control. They hardly recognize their performance when they see it on the screen. But that's what goes out to the public. When a critic says it was a bad performance, they are helpless.

The appreciation and perceptiveness of choosing art changes. I've got a feeling my taste in art will be very different 5 years from now because my mood and how I view the world will evolve. The one thing that helps me in terms of dealing with contemporary art is being on the faculty of the San Francisco Art Institute for the past 12 years and having interaction with young artists. I teach the history of printmaking in the spring semester. It's like the *Goodbye, Mr. Chips* story—they stay the same age each year and I keep getting older. But as they are the same age they have opinions in 1990 that the kids in 1978 didn't. And so I am able to pick up moods about creativity by having this interaction with these younger creative people, and I add that to my interaction with artists who are older and more experienced—more established artists—and that just gives me a broader perspective to judge from. Whereas if I sat in my office and I only interacted with upcoming artists on Artists Day and with the big established artists, my perception of quality would probably get narrower and narrower, which would be sad and not beneficial to the institution.

Artists should realize that the art they make is their truth, but to the world it will be viewed subjectively. And, in turn, curators or collectors or dealers can only be themselves. It's not a popularity contest, it's a search to make connections. A rejection is simply a missed connection. I think that's probably what I most would like to say. That the term rejection and critique are just too harsh. It's just a missed connection.

About the Authors

Lisa Almeda is an artist living in Jacksonville, Florida.

Alan Bamberger is a nationally syndicated columnist and the author of two books on collecting art affordably. He lives in San Francisco.

Carolyn Blakeslee was the founding editor of *Art Calendar* magazine. A realist oil painter, she lives on an island in the Chesapeake Bay. She is active in the pro-life movement and is also a pianist.

Beky Carter is an artist living in Marin County, California.

Michelle T. Carter is an art advisor based in Irvine, California. She offers seminars, lectures, and private consultations.

Barbara Dougherty is an accomplished agricultural watercolorist and oil painter. She also enjoys working with cameras, computers, and filmmaking equipment. She is the owner/publisher of *Art Calendar* magazine.

Peggy Hadden, a graduate of the Parsons School of Design, is a painter and mixed media artist whose home and studio are in New York City's West Village.

René Joseph is an artist who is active in the Minneapolis/St. Paul area.

Constance Hallinan Lagan is an award-winning quilt designer who lectures nationally on art and craft marketing. She lives in North Babylon, New York.

Harold Lohner is the director of the Russell Sage College Gallery at Sage Troy Campus in New York.

Raymond Markarian is a San Diego-based artist and curator.

Donna Marxer is a painter who lives in SoHo.

Debora Meltz is a painter, pastelist, and free-lance writer who divides her time between Newton, NJ and Manhattan.

Patricia Meyerowitz, a sculptor, lives in Easton, Pennsylvania.

Caroll Michels, a career coach for artists, is the author of *How to Survive and Prosper As an Artist.* She lives in Manhattan.

Julia Muney Monroe is curator of the Indianapolis Art Center.

Roberta Morgan is an artist and critic living in Laurel, Maryland.

Sharon Reeber is an artist living in Weston, Missouri.

Rima Schulkind, a painter, lives in Washington, D.C.

Stanley Sporny teaches art at Marshall University, Huntington, West Virginia.

Drew Steis was the publisher of *Art Calendar* magazine. He worked for UPI for 18 years and was Washington, D.C. bureau chief for the *Boston Herald Traveler.* He also was a consultant to the National Endowment for the Arts and is now *Art Calendar*'s editor-at-large.

Milon Townsend, a glass sculptor, lives in Hilton, New York.

Lynn Lewis Young is a quilt artist living in Houston, Texas.

About the Artists

Jan Camp is a photographer/filmmaker living in Berkeley, California. The founder of Iris Arts and Education Group, Inc., she has shown at the Southeast Museum of Photography in Daytona Beach, the Museum of Contemporary Art in Baltimore, and other spaces.

Joe Dickey is a wood turner living in Annapolis, Maryland. His work was included in the International Turned Object Show, which toured the nation for three years, the invitational show The Turners Challenge, and other imported exhibitions.

Barb Dougherty is owner and publisher of *Art Calendar.* She has pursued a successful career in visual arts for more than 25 years. Her experiences in art marketing range from owning and managing a California gallery to years spent "on the circuit" as a professional potter and then painter.

Elvi Jo Dougherty, an artist who works in a variety of media including oil paints, clay, charcoal, and paper mache, now lives in Upper Fairmount, Maryland. She attends the University of Maryland Eastern Shore. Other schooling includes: University of California at Santa Barbara, College of Creative Studies; Parson's School of Design; and the California School of Arts & Crafts.

Caryl Bryer Fallert is a textile artist living in Oswego, Illinois. Her two- and three-dimensional quilts, distinguished by their brilliant colors and illusions of movement and light, have been exhibited nationwide as well as in Europe, Japan, Singapore, Australia, and New Zealand.

Will Hildebrandt, an artist in LeGrand, Iowa, has taught art at the high school and college level. His paintings and pastels have been shown at the Carnegie Museum of Art, the Polk County Heritage Gallery, and other nationally known spaces.

Norman J. Mercer, a sculptor utilizing acrylics and polymers, lives in East Hampton, New York. After a distinguished 40-year career in international design and trading, he was educated at the Parsons School of Design and became a sculptor. He is represented by the Benton Gallery in Southampton.